Composing for Japanese Instruments

Eastman Studies in Music

Ralph P. Locke, Senior Editor
Eastman School of Music

Additional Titles in Music since 1950 and World Music Traditions

Concert Music, Rock, and Jazz since 1945: Essays and Analytical Studies
Edited by Elizabeth West Marvin and Richard Hermann

Elliott Carter: Collected Essays and Lectures, 1937–1995
Edited by Jonathan W. Bernard

French Music, Culture, and National Identity, 1870–1939
Edited by Barbara L. Kelly

The Gamelan Digul and the Prison Camp Musician Who Built It: An Australian Link with the Indonesian Revolution (includes CD)
Margaret J. Kartomi

"The Music of American Folk Song" and Selected Other Writings on American Folk Music
Ruth Crawford Seeger, edited by Larry Polansky and Judith Tick

The Music of Luigi Dallapiccola
Raymond Fearn

The Music of the Moravian Church in America
Edited by Nola Reed Knouse

Musical Creativity in Twentieth-Century China: Abing, His Music, and Its Changing Meanings (includes CD)
Jonathan P. J. Stock

Musical Encounters at the 1889 Paris World's Fair
Annegret Fauser

The Pleasure of Modernist Music: Listening, Meaning, Intention, Ideology
Edited by Arved Ashby

Portrait of Percy Grainger
Malcolm Gillies and David Pear

Representing Non-Western Music in Nineteenth-Century Britain
Bennett Zon

Ruth Crawford Seeger's Worlds: Innovation and Tradition in Twentieth-Century American Music
Edited by Ray Allen and Ellie M. Hisama

The Sea on Fire: Jean Barraqué
Paul Griffiths

The Substance of Things Heard: Writings about Music
Paul Griffiths

A complete list of titles in the Eastman Studies in Music Series, in order of publication, may be found at the end of this book.

Composing for Japanese Instruments

Minoru Miki
Translated by Marty Regan
Edited by Philip Flavin

UNIVERSITY OF ROCHESTER PRESS

Copyright © 2008 Minoru Miki
Translation copyright Marty Regan

All Rights Reserved. Except as permitted under current legislation, no part of this work may be photocopied, stored in a retrieval system, published, performed in public, adapted, broadcast, transmitted, recorded, or reproduced in any form or by any means, without the prior permission of the copyright owner.

Original edition published in Japanese in 1996 by Ongaku No Tomo Sha, Tokyo.

First published 2008
Reprinted in paperback and transferred to digital printing 2015

University of Rochester Press
668 Mt. Hope Avenue, Rochester, NY 14620, USA
www.urpress.com
and Boydell & Brewer Limited
PO Box 9, Woodbridge, Suffolk IP12 3DF, UK
www.boydellandbrewer.com

Hardcover ISBN-13: 978-1-58046-273-0
Hardcover ISBN-10: 1-58046-273-1
Paperback ISBN-13: 978-158046-552-6
ISSN: 1071-9989

Library of Congress Cataloging-in-Publication Data
Miki, Minoru
[Nihon-gakkihou. English]
Composing for Japanese instruments / by Minoru Miki ; translated by Marty Regan ; edited by Philip Flavin.
    p. cm. — (Eastman studies in music, ISSN 1071–9989 ; v. 57)
Includes bibliographical references and index.
  ISBN-13: 978-1-58046-273-0 (hardcover : alk. paper)
1. Composition (Music) 2. Musical instruments—Japan. I. Regan, Marty. II. Title.
  MT58.M5513 2008
  784.13′0952—dc22

                                              2008007392

A catalogue record for this title is available from the British Library.

This publication is printed on acid-free paper.
Printed in the United States of America

Contents

List of Illustrations   vii

List of Audio Examples   xiii

Foreword   xix

Translator's Preface and Acknowledgments   xxiii

Introduction   1

1   Wind Instruments   6
     1–1: *Shinobue*   7
     1–2: *Ryūteki*   16
     1–3: *Nōkan*   24
     1–4: *Shakuhachi*   35
     1–5: *Hichiriki*   54
     1–6: *Shō*   63

2   String Instruments (Lutes)   71
     2–1: *Biwa*   71
     2–2: *Shamisen*   88
     2–3: Special *shamisen*   103
     2–4: *Kokyū*   116

3   String Instruments (Zithers)   125
     3–1: *Koto*   125
     3–2: Special *Kotos*   148

4   Percussion Instruments   156
     4–1: Membrane Percussion   156
     4–2: Wood and Bamboo Percussion   182
     4–3: Metal and Stone Percussion   190

Afterword	203
Appendix I: Works for Japanese Instruments by Minoru Miki	207
Appendix II: Contemporary Works for Traditional Japanese Instruments by Composers Other than Minoru Miki, 1981–2015	228
Notes	243
Glossary	249
Index	253

Illustrations

I.1	Five Japanese scales	2
1.1	Japanese transverse flutes	6
1.2	The *shinobue*	7
1.3	Different kinds of *shinobue*	8
1.4	*Shinobue* pitches	9
1.5	Basic scales and application ranges for each *shinobue*	11
1.6	An eight-length *shinobue*	13
1.7	*Shinobue* finger ornaments	15
1.8	The *ryūteki*	17
1.9	Names of holes and pitches for the *ryūteki*	17
1.10	Range and basic scale pitches for the *ryūteki*	18
1.11	Various techniques and melodic patterns	19
1.12	Three kinds of *yuru*	21
1.13	An example of use of tremolo by the *ryūteki*	22
1.14	The *nōkan*	24
1.15	*Nōkan* finger holes	25
1.16	Range and basic scales of the *nōkan* (type II)	26
1.17	A special *nōkan* technique: *Hishigi*	27
1.18	Possible *nōkan* tremolos	28
1.19	The *netori* technique for *nōkan*	31
1.20	Some *nōkan* playing techniques in classical pieces	31
1.21	*Paraphrase after Ancient Japanese Music*, second movement: *Sōmon*	34
1.22	The five-holed *shakuhachi*	35
1.23	The *shakuhachi* mouthpiece	36
1.24	Different kinds of *shakuhachi*	36
1.25	Basic pitches for the *d-kan*	37
1.26	A fingering chart for the *shakuhachi*	39
1.27	Diagram of the basic pitches and scales and usable range for each size *shakuhachi*	40
1.28	An example of the extended *kan* range	42
1.29	Unique *shakuhachi* playing techniques	44
1.30	Possibilities for tremolos on a *shakuhachi*	46
1.31	Examples of special fingering techniques	49
1.32	The *hichiriki*	55

1.33	The names of the *hichiriki* holes	55
1.34	Phrases with traditional *enbai* patterns	57
1.35	Beginning section of *Hyōjō-chōshi*	58
1.36	An excerpt from *Etenraku*	58
1.37	An example of a raised *enbai* on the *hichiriki*	58
1.38	Tremolo techniques for the *hichiriki*	60
1.39	Musical excerpts that correspond to the mnemonic *e-i-ra*	62
1.40	The *shō* from many angles	63
1.41	The *shō* seen from above	64
1.42	The 17 *shō* pipes, their names, and their fixed pitches	64
1.43	The 17 pipes of the *shō*, in order based on fingerings	65
1.44	Notes that can not be produced simultaneously due to fingering rules	65
1.45	*Aitake* chords of the *shō* (11 chords used in classic *gagaku*)	66
1.46	An example of a quick diminishing of *shō* volume	67
1.47	An example of monophonic and diaphonic performance techniques	68
1.48	An example of *te-utsuri* (fingering change), excerpt from *Etenraku*	68
1.49	Simplified *te-utsuri* notation	69
1.50	Excerpt from Minoru Miki's *Yui I*	70
2.1	*Gaku-biwa, Satsuma-biwa, Chikuzen-biwa*	72
2.2	*Satsuma-biwa* and *Chikuzen-biwa*	73
2.3	Frets of the *Satsuma-biwa* and *Chikuzen-biwa*	74
2.4	Range of each *biwa*	76
2.5	Tunings for many *biwa*	77
2.6	Intervals produced above open strings for various *gaku-biwa* tunings	79
2.7	Frequently produced pitches produced for the *Satsuma-biwa*	80
2.8	Frequently produced pitches for the *Chikuzen-biwa*	80
2.9	Sample *yuri* on *biwa*	82
2.10	*Biwa* glissando and portamento patterns (pressing technique)	82
2.11	*Biwa* glissando and portamento patterns (sliding technique)	83
2.12	Left-hand pizzicato *biwa* technique	83
2.13	Striking the body of the *biwa* technique	84
2.14	*Biwa* tremolo	84
2.15	Dynamic expression, *biwa* example	85
2.16	Ways of indicating a *biwa* arpeggio in a score	85
2.17	Various *biwa suri* techniques	86
2.18	*Kuzure* triplet rhythm pattern in the *biwa*	86
2.19	The limit of high-pitched tunings for modern *biwa*	87
2.20	The three *shamisen* classification groups: *futozao, chūzao, hosozao*	89
2.21	The groups shown with details: *hosozao, chūzao, futozao*	90
2.22	Sample ranges for the three *shamisen* groups	93

2.23	Various *shamisen* tunings	94
2.24	Adjusted tunings for *shamisen*	94
2.25	Various notes and their positions for each string	95
2.26	Glissando and portamento for *shamisen*	97
2.27	Ornamental sliding *oshide* for *shamisen*	97
2.28	*Hajiki* techniques for *shamisen*	98
2.29	An example of *uchi* for *shamisen*	98
2.30	An example of left hand portamento for *shamisen*	99
2.31	Harmonics in *shamisen*	99
2.32	Left hand pizzicato combined with an arpeggio in strict time	100
2.33	Reverse arpeggio in *shamisen* playing	100
2.34	*Kakebachi* in *shamisen* playing	101
2.35	*Soto-hazushi* in *shamisen* playing	101
2.36	*Sukui-hajiki* in *shamisen* playing	101
2.37	Excerpt for *hosozao shamisen*	102
2.38	Excerpt for *hosozao shamisen*	103
2.39	Mnemonics for the *shamisen*	104
2.40	Various notes and positions for each string of the *futozao* (*gidayū*) *shamisen*	105
2.41	Sound techniques for the *gidayū shamisen*	106
2.42	Sound techniques for the *gidayū shamisen*	109
2.43	The *Tsugaru shamisen*	110
2.44	Striking area of the *Tsugaru shamisen*	111
2.45	Dynamic markings for the *Tsugaru shamisen*	112
2.46	The *sanshin*	114
2.47	Various notes and their positions for the Ryūkyū scale for the *sanshin*	114
2.48	Characteristic *sanshin* patterns	115
2.49	The *kokyū*	117
2.50	The *kokyū* and bow	118
2.51	Tunings of the traditional *kokyū* and *chū-kokyū*	119
2.52	Classical fingering for the *kokyū*	120
2.53	Multiple stops technique for the *kokyū*	120
2.54	The *kokiotoshi* or *kokioroshi* technique for the *kokyū*	121
2.55	Techniques for the *kokyū*	123
3.1	The *gakusō*	127
3.2	The 17-string *koto*, the 21-string *koto*, the 13-string *koto*	128
3.3	Illustrations of the Ikuta plectra and the Yamada plectra	129
3.4	A 20-string (21-string) *koto* on a standard *koto* stand	130
3.5	The range of different-sized *koto*	131
3.6	Traditional *koto* tunings	133
3.7	Modes and other scales for the 13-string *koto*	134
3.8	Tunings for the 17-string *koto*	134
3.9	Tunings for the 21-string *koto*	135

3.10	*Oshide* technique	136
3.11	Some *oshibiki* techniques	137
3.12	An *ato-oshi* technique	137
3.13	The *oshi-hanashi* technique	138
3.14	The *yuri* technique	138
3.15	The *hiki-iro* technique	138
3.16	The *tsuki-iro* technique	139
3.17	The *keshizume* technique	139
3.18	The technique of muting	139
3.19	Pizzicato	140
3.20	A harmonics effect on the *koto*	140
3.21	The *voix céleste* effect	141
3.22	The *awasezume* technique	142
3.23	Various right-hand *koto* techniques	143
3.24	Examples of *sukizume*	144
3.25	The *kozume* technique	144
3.26	The *chirashizume* technique	144
3.27	The *surizume* technique	145
3.28	The *uchizume* technique	145
3.29	The *uchikaki* technique	145
3.30	Glissandi in the *koto* repertoire	146
3.31	Various *koto* playing positions	147
3.32	*Kinuta mono* rhythm in *koto*	148
3.33	Various tunings of the *gakusō*	149
3.34	*Kakite* and *kozume* on the *gakusō*	149
3.35	Patterns for 17-string bass *koto*	150
3.36	20-string (21-string) *koto* strings and tunings	153
3.37	The soprano 21-string *koto*, the 21-string *koto*, and the bass 21-string *koto*	154
3.38	Tunings for each 21-string *koto*: the soprano, 21-string, and bass *kotos*	155
4.1	The *ko-tsuzumi*	157
4.2	Ways of striking the *ko-tsuzumi*	158
4.3	Striking technique of the *ko-tsuzumi*	159
4.4	A glissando effect	160
4.5	Examples from *ko-tsuzumi* excerpts	160
4.6	The *ō-tsuzumi*	166
4.7	Striking technique of the *ō-tsuzumi*	166
4.8	Ways of striking the *ō-tsuzumi*	167
4.9	The *san-no-tsuzumi*	168
4.10	The *kakko* on a stand	168
4.11	Characteristic *kakko* playing techniques	169
4.12	The *da-daiko*	170
4.13	The *tsuri-daiko*	170

4.14	The *ō-daiko*	172
4.15	Various kinds of *ō-daiko* mallets	173
4.16	Atmospheric musical effects of the *taiko*	174
4.17	Rim technique of the *taiko*	175
4.18	The *gaku-daiko*	176
4.19	The *shime-daiko*	176
4.20	Traditional *shime-daiko* performance techniques accompanied with mnemonics	177
4.21	*Shime-daiko* dynamic expressions in the form of accents	178
4.22	Differences in pitch creating unique effects	180
4.23	*Dai-byōshi* and *okedō-daiko*	180
4.24	*Uchiwa-daiko* (fan drums)	181
4.25	The *sasara*	182
4.26	*Sasara* playing techniques	183
4.27	The *binzasara*	183
4.28	*Binzasara* playing techniques	184
4.29	The *shakubyōshi* and the *hyōshigi*	185
4.30	*Hyōshigi* used in Edo *kabuki*	186
4.31	*Mokushō*	187
4.32	A set of four *mokushō*	187
4.33	*Mokugyō*	188
4.34	A musical example using *mokushō* and *mokugyō*	188
4.35	*Yotsudake* and *kokiriko*	189
4.36	*Naruko* and *banki*	190
4.37	*Bonshō*	191
4.38	*Kin*	192
4.39	*Kin* playing techniques	192
4.40	The *shōko*	193
4.41	Various kinds of *shō*	194
4.42	*Matsumushi*	194
4.43	*Kane* (*atarigane*)	194
4.44	Left- and right-hand techniques for playing the *kane*	195
4.45	*Kane* (*atarigane*) left-hand playing techniques	196
4.46	*Awa* dance *kane* playing technique	196
4.47	The *wadora*	197
4.48	*Nyōbatsu*	197
4.49	*Chappa* (*dobyōshi*)	198
4.50	Types of *suzu*	199
4.51	An *orugoru*	200
4.52	*Sanukite*	201
4.53	Range of the *sanukite*	202

Audio Examples

Note: All audio examples are available on the book's companion website. Please see the URLs provided below each instrument class.

The *Shinobue*

http://hdl.handle.net/1802/30019

> Example 1.5: Range and basic scale of 10-, 8-, 6-, and 3-length *shinobue*
> Example 1.7: Musical excerpts (a–c)

The *Ryūteki*

http://hdl.handle.net/1802/30022

> Example 1.10: Range and basic scale of the *ryūteki*
> Example 1.11: Musical excerpts (a–d)
> Example 1.12: *Yuru* (a–c)

The *Nōkan*

http://hdl.handle.net/1802/30023

> Example 1.16: Range and basic scale of the *Nōkan* (type II)
> Example 1.17: *Hishigi*
> Example 1.19: *Netori*
> Example 1.20: Musical excerpts (b–j)
> Example 1.21: Musical excerpt, Minoru Miki's *Paraphrase after Ancient Japanese Music* (1966), second movement *Sōmon*

The *Shakuhachi*

http://hdl.handle.net/1802/30024

> Example 1.27: Range and basic scale of the *shakuhachi* (only six of the fourteen *shakuhachi* listed in the text have recorded musical examples)
>
> a   (1.1), higher octave
> f♯   (1.4)
> e   (1.6)
> d   (1.8)
> b   (2.1)
> a   (2.4), lower octave
>
> Example 1.28: Extended *kan* range
> Example 1.29: Unique playing techniques
> > *Sorane*, musical example 1.29.2 (3b in the text) is demonstrated after 1.29.1 but there is no corresponding score in the text. There are no concrete musical examples provided for 1.29.3 or 1.29.4, which would correspond to 3. *komi* and 4. *flutter-tongue* in the text.
>
> Example 1.31 (a–k)

The *Hichiriki*

http://hdl.handle.net/1802/30025

> Example 1.34: Traditional *enbai* patterns
> Example 1.35: Excerpt from *Hyōjō-chōshi*
> Example 1.36: Excerpt from *Etenraku*
> Example 1.37: Raised *enbai*
> Example 1.39: Musical excerpts that correspond to the mnemonic *e-i-ra*

The *Shō*

http://hdl.handle.net/1802/30026

> Example 1.42: Seventeen pipes of the *shō*
> Example 1.43: Seventeen pipes of the *shō*, in order based on fingerings
> Example 1.45: Eleven *aitake* chords of the *shō*
> Example 1.46: Quick diminishing of volume
> Example 1.47: Monophonic and diaphonic performance techniques
> Example 1.48: *Te-utsuri* (fingering change)
> Example 1.50: Excerpt from Minoru Miki's *Yui I*

The *Biwa*

http://hdl.handle.net/1802/30028

> Example 2.5: Tunings of various *biwa*
> Example 2.6: Intervals produced above open strings for various *biwa* tunings
> Example 2.7: Frequently produced pitches for *Satsuma-biwa*
> Example 2.8: Frequently produced pitches for *Chikuzen-biwa*
> Example 2.9: *Yuri*
> Example 2.10: Glissando and portamento patterns (pressing technique)
> Example 2.11: Glissando and portamento patterns (sliding technique)
> Example 2.12: Left-hand pizzicato
> Example 2.13 (a–e): Striking the body of the *biwa*
> Example 2.14 (a–c): Tremolo
> Example 2.15: Dynamic expression
> Example 2.16 (a–c): Arpeggio
> Example 2.17 (a–i): Various *suri* techniques
> Example 2.18: *Kuzure*
> Example 2.19: Excerpt from Minoru Miki's *Kuse*

The *Shamisen*

http://hdl.handle.net/1802/30029

> Example 2.23: *Shamisen* tunings
> Example 2.24: Adjusted tunings
> Example 2.25: Various notes and their positions for each string
> Example 2.26: Glissando and portamento
> Example 2.27: Ornamental sliding: *Oshide*
> Example 2.28: *Hajiki* techniques
> Example 2.29: *Uchi* (striking technique)
> Example 2.30: Left hand portamento
> Example 2.31: Harmonics
> Example 2.32: Arpeggio
> Example 2.33: Reverse arpeggio
> Example 2.34: *Kakebachi*
> Example 2.35: *Soto-hazushi*
> Example 2.36: *Sukui-hajiki*
> Example 2.37: Excerpt from Minoru Miki's *shamisen* work *Tan no Mai*

Special *Shamisen*

Gidayū

http://hdl.handle.net/1802/30030

> Example 2.40: Various notes and their positions for each string (*Gidayū shamisen*)
> Example 2.41 (a–f): Excerpts from the classical *Gidayū* repertoire
> Example 2.42 (a–d): Excerpts from Minoru Miki's works for *Gidayū shamisen*

Tsugaru

http://hdl.handle.net/1802/30031

> Example 2.45: Excerpts from standard *Tsugaru shamisen* repertoire

Sanshin

http://hdl.handle.net/1802/30032

> Example 2.47: Various notes and their positions for each string (*sanshin*)
> Example 2.48: Excerpts from *sanshin* repertoire

The *Kokyū*

http://hdl.handle.net/1802/30033

> Example 2.51: Tunings of various *kokyū*
> Example 2.52: Fingering employed in a classical piece
> Example 2.53: Multiple stops
> Example 2.54: *Kokiotoshi* or *kokioroshi* (sliding down)
> Example 2.55 (a–c): Excerpts from classical *kokyū* repertoire

The *Koto*

http://hdl.handle.net/1802/30034

Example 3.6: Traditional *koto* tunings
Example 3.7 (a–d): Modes and other scales
Example 3.8: 17-string *koto* tuning
Example 3.9 (a–e): 21-string *koto* tunings
Example 3.10 (a–c): *Oshide*
Example 3.11 (a–f): *Oshibiki*
Example 3.12: *Ato-oshi*
Example 3.13: *Oshihanashi*
Example 3.14: *Yuri*
Example 3.15: *Hiki-iro*
Example 3.16: *Tsuki-iro*
Example 3.17 *Keshizume*
Example 3.18: Muting
Example 3.19: Pizzicato
Example 3.20 (a–b): Harmonics
Example 3.21: *Voix céleste*
Example 3.22: *Awasezume*
Example 3.23 (a–e): Various right-hand techniques
Example 3.24: *Sukuizume*
Example 3.25: *Kozume*
Example 3.26: *Chirashizume*
Example 3.27: *Surizume*
Example 3.28: *Uchizume*
Example 3.29: *Uchibiki*
Example 3.30 (a–e): Glissando
Example 3.31: Various playing positions
Example 3.32: *Kinuta mono* rhythm

Special *Kotos*

http://hdl.handle.net/1802/30035

Example 3.33: Various *gakusō* tunings
Example 3.34: *Kakite* and *kozume*
Example 3.35 (a–c): Excerpts from Minoru Miki's works for 17-string bass *koto*
Example 3.36 (a–d): Excerpts from Minoru Miki's works for 21-string *koto*
Example 3.38: Tuning for each 21-string *koto* in Minoru Miki's *Cassiopeia 21*

Foreword

This is the first English translation of Minoru Miki's influential *Composing for Japanese Instruments*, which is now in its sixth Japanese edition, and is also published in Chinese and Korean. This translation, by composer Marty Regan, who has worked closely with Miki on recent projects, is based on the third edition, published by Ongaku no Tomo sha in Tokyo in 1998. The translation has been edited by Philip Flavin, ethnomusicologist and scholar-performer of Japanese music.

This volume includes a comprehensive list of Miki's works for Japanese instruments, the author's Afterword, a Glossary of Terms, and a track listing of the recorded examples included with the book. Because Miki draws exclusively on his own work for demonstration in both printed and recorded examples, an appendix has been added that directs readers to selected works for traditional Japanese instruments, both by Japanese composers other than Minoru Miki and by non-Japanese composers. Of the vast number of compositions using Japanese traditional instruments, only the relatively few works available either in score or on recording are included.

Minoru Miki was born in Tokushima, on Shikoku island, in 1930. His hometown area is noted for the *Awa odori* (dance), and the traditional arts were also a part of Miki family life. His great-grandfather had been a chanter in *bunraku*, one of his grandmothers was a well-known *shamisen* player, and an uncle played the *shakuhachi*. A childhood during wartime prevented him from actually participating in traditional music, however, and it was not until after World War Two ended that Miki became involved in music-making. He enjoyed singing, and joined the men's chorus in high school.

Minoru Miki's formal education in music was in the Western tradition, as "music" in Japanese schools meant Western music. In the 1950s, Miki composed for piano, wind ensemble and percussion, and orchestra. In 1955 he graduated from the Tokyo National University of the Arts (known as Geidai) in composition. He, like others who were to become some of Japan's most famous and influential composers of the last half of the twentieth century, was a student of the late Akira Ifukube. By the time he graduated he had already received a prize in composition from the NHK (Japan Broadcasting Corporation) for an orchestral piece, *Trinita Sinfonica*, performed by the NHK Symphony Orchestra in 1953.

At the end of the 1950s and the early 1960s, possibly in preparation for hosting the Olympics, there was a gradual reawakening of cultural consciousness and pride in Japan. That led to requests for Miki to write pieces for the *shakuhachi*, and he composed *Sonnet* for three *shakuhachi* in 1962. Because he had been accustomed to writing for larger groups of Western instruments, Miki at first felt uncomfortable being limited to only three, so in the same year he wrote *Kurandando*, a choral piece based on a Japanese folk song that was accompanied by a small orchestra of traditional instruments. The result of this foray into writing for Japanese traditional instruments was the establishment of the Pro Musica Nipponia (*Nihon Ongaku Shudan*) in 1964. The organization allowed Miki to work with a consistent group of virtuoso players who were committed to contemporary music for traditional instruments. In the early years the group consisted of 13 players who performed works by Miki and other composers; the number of performers gradually grew. That ensemble provided the musical examples for the CDs in this book. Among the earliest members was Keiko Nosaka with whom he collaborated in the development of the 20-string *koto*.

In his Afterword, Miki explains how he came to write this book and touches on the Pro Musica Nipponia and the opportunities it provided to perform contemporary works using traditional Japanese instruments. During his 20-year tenure as Artistic Director of the ensemble they performed more than 160 concerts around the world in efforts to internationalize traditional Japanese instruments. Miki took a hiatus from the organization in the mid-1980s. Thereafter, he began to use instruments from other Asian countries and, in 1993, formed Orchestra Asia to perform works using Japanese, Korean, and Chinese instruments, as well as those from other Asian countries.

That Miki is one of Japan's most famous and influential composers is not in doubt. He combines Western-type training as a composer with a deep interest in traditional music. His output has been prolific and ranges from film to operas to ballets, symphonies, song cycles, chamber works, choral pieces, and compositions for a variety of instruments, including the marimba, for which he collaborated with Keiko Abe. As can be seen in Appendix I, opera has been a particularly consuming creative pursuit. In 1975 he wrote his first opera and since then has written many, several with Colin Graham: chamber and choral operas, educational small operas, operettas, musical dramas, one-act, twin chamber operas, folk, and full-scale operas. His series of eight grand operas reveal the entire historical cycle of Japan; the last, *Ai-en*, completing the cycle, premiered in February 2006.

Miki's album *The Music of Minoru Miki* won the Grand Prize in Japan's 1970 National Arts Festival, and his next album, *Minoru Miki-Keiko Nosaka: Music for 20-string Koto*, won the Prize of Excellence in the 1979 National Arts Festival. His *Eurasian Trilogy* (*Jo-no-Kyoku, Ha-no-Kyoku, Kyū-no-Kyoku*) links Japanese instruments with Western orchestral instruments. The last of the three symphonies, *Kyū-no-Kyoku* (*Symphony for Two Worlds*) was commissioned by the Leipzig

Gewandhaus Orchestra for its bicentennial, and had its world premiere in 1981 conducted by Kurt Masur (the American premiere, by the New York Philharmonic under Masur, took place in 1994). In addition to his composing and ensemble direction, he has served as Director of the Japan Federation of Composers, and as professor at Geidai and visiting professor at Shikoku University.

I first met Minoru Miki when he was on a concert tour in 1974 with *koto* virtuoso Keiko Nosaka and the Pro Musica Nipponia, and I have remained interested in and supportive of his creative activity in the sphere of contemporary Japanese music for traditional instruments ever since. I am delighted to be a part of making Miki's book, *Composing for Japanese Instruments*, available to an English-reading audience and hope that composers will find it useful as they explore new and meaningful ways to create music.

Bonnie C. Wade
Berkeley, California
May 2008

Translator's Preface and Acknowledgments

In this book, rather than following the Japanese practice of placing family names first and given names second (MIKI Minoru), Japanese names are presented in the Western practice of given names first and family names second (Minoru Miki). Following the Hepburn romanization system, long vowel sounds in Japanese, as in the word (sho-u), are phonetically romanized as *shō* (Japanese mouth organ). Japanese terms are defined in the footnotes. For recurring musical terms, however, the definition will be given for the first appearance only. For subsequent recurrences, readers unfamiliar with the Japanese terms may refer to the glossary for their definitions. Pitches are designated by the Helmholtz octave designation system (middle c is referred to as c^1). With Japanese instruments that transpose up an octave, such as the *shinobue, ryūteki, nōkan*, and *shō*, or down an octave, such as the *biwa* and *shamisen*, notes are indicated at the written pitch, not sounding pitch.

    I would like to thank several people who have helped this translation come to fruition: Yoko Ide for her help with the *biwa* chapter, Yoko Kurokawa for her help with the *ryūteki, shō, nōkan,* and *kokyū* chapters, Darin Miyashiro for his help with the *hichiriki* chapter, David Wheeler and Seizan Sakata for helping me with Tozan fingerings and names of pitches in the *shakuhachi* chapter, and my advisor at the University of Hawai'i, Manoa, Dr. Donald Womack, who advised me on early drafts, and who wholeheartedly supported me throughout my doctoral studies in my work with Japanese instruments. I would also like to express my gratitude to Yoko Sato, who has supported me in countless ways from the very beginning of this project, and who, despite the miles that sometimes separated us, was always willing to help with Chinese character readings and opaque passages.

    I would also like to thank the John Young Scholarship Foundation at the University of Hawai'i, Manoa, as well as the editor, Philip Flavin, for his unforgiving eye and meticulous attention to detail as I worked through several drafts of the translation manuscript. Also, this translation would not have been possible without the generous support, encouragement, and patience of Bonnie Wade.

Finally, I would like to express sincere thanks to my teacher and mentor, Minoru Miki, for giving me the opportunity to become intimately familiar with Japanese instruments through the translation of this book, and for teaching me how to compose for Japanese instruments. His boundless knowledge, life experience, contagious energy and drive inspire me every day in my own work with Japanese instruments; our fateful meeting in April 2000 has changed the direction of my life.

I hope that this book helps to promote Japanese instruments as vital media for cross-cultural composition in the twenty-first century, giving English-speaking composers and ethnomusicologists the technical and practical resources to explore the possibilities of these wonderful instruments, leading to a body of new and innovative repertoire for traditional Japanese instruments.

Marty Regan
Tokyo, Japan
June 2008

Introduction

While the people who originally settled these islands had their own instruments, most of the instruments presently considered "Japanese" were imported from China and the Korean kingdoms during the sixth and seventh centuries CE. From the ninth century CE, these instruments were modified according to indigenous tastes. Consequently, Japanese instruments differ greatly in form and function from the present instruments in China and Korea.

Outside of *gagaku*,[1] imported to Japan nearly 2,000 years ago, there was until recently no other ensemble that incorporated various types of Japanese instruments. In 1964 we formed the Pro Musica Nipponia with the purpose of addressing this problem and, from that time on, we have created a know-how of contemporary ensemble playing for Japanese instruments. As a result, traditional Japanese instrumentalists have developed the technical capabilities to perform with Western orchestras, and there is now a large body of works written to include Japanese instruments in Western music ensembles. Henceforth, these capabilities will be invaluable when working with other Asian instrumental ensembles. This does not mean that the Japanese have become more westernized or globalized. Rather, it signifies that we have learned how to maintain our Japanese identity as we expand our traditional music vocabulary.

In explaining how to compose for Japanese instruments, I think it is necessary to first write down my understanding of their shared characteristics. Judging the quality of something, of course, depends on culturally established values. When Japanese instruments are compared to Western instruments or to other Asian instruments, some Japanese instruments seem extremely inconvenient and impractical to use. If, however, value judgment is based on the instrument's relationship to the natural environment, there are instances where Japanese instruments demonstrate great strengths. It is thus necessary to consider the most effective way to use each instrument. In politics or society, disparate elements can coexist: this should also pertain to composition and performance practice.

Scales: The Chosen Sounds

As with all music instruments, Japanese instruments have been made to produce the scales that we have chosen throughout our history as being "natural."[2]

The first scale, the *yō* scale, is the oldest Japanese scale and is still used as the primary scale for folk songs. The second scale, the *ro* scale, belongs to the scales and modes imported with *gagaku* but is, however, no longer used in this genre. It was "recreated" during the Meiji period (1868–1912) as the *yonanuki* scale,[3] and is now the representative Japanese scale through its use in the popular genre of *enka*. The scale that forms the basis of contemporary *gagaku*, the *ritsu* scale, is shown below the *ro*. During the Edo period (1603–1868), some of the pitches for the *ro* scale were lowered, which resulted in the most "Japanese" scale, the *miyako-bushi*, or *in* scale. The *Ryūkyū* scale of Okinawa appears to be derived from the *Yo* scale with some pitches raised.

Fig. I.1. Five Japanese scales (from top to bottom: *Yo, Ro, Ritsu, In, Ryūkyū*)

All of the instruments in a Western orchestra have been developed to uniformly produce equal-tempered chromatic scales. Asian instruments could take the same path, but in doing so they would lose their original characteristics. It is necessary to create contemporary music for Japanese instruments that incorporates their original characteristics. In my own work, for example, I have tried to exploit the characteristics of the pentatonic scales and have created and expanded pentatonic scales that are adapted for each instrument.

Presently, with some effort, a well-trained performer can produce nearly all of the chromatic pitches within the standard range. Producing any pitches other than the fundamental ones, however, for example, the *meri* pitches of the *shakuhachi* that lead to a loss in volume, or pitches that require moving the bridges on the *koto*, requires specific treatment. It is completely unsuitable for Japanese instruments to modulate according to Western functional harmony. Instead, the *shakuhachi* is able to produce delicate microtonal inflections. The *shamisen* and *koto*, besides their ability to produce subtle intervallic nuances, are also able to manipulate reverberating pitches and produce a combination of tone colors.

Timbre

Historically, the Japanese have cherished timbre. Even today, traditional Japanese musicians are extremely conservative. When improving Japanese instruments, there has never been an attempt to increase functionality or acquire a greater volume of sound at the expense of destroying the instrument's traditional timbre. Materials unique to Asia—bamboo, paulownia wood, mulberry wood, cat skin (which replaced python skin)—are decisive in determining the timbre of Japanese instruments. When substitute materials are used, approximating the original timbre to the greatest possible extent is always of primary importance.

Imitating the sounds of Japan's natural environment is a fundamental precept in composition and performance. The non-musical sounds produced by the instruments are also considered an integral part of the music. With the works of John Cage, this approach influenced contemporary composition on a global scale.

The Connection to Song

Nearly all instruments throughout the world were originally made to accompany voice or movement. With the exception of *gagaku* and a very limited number of genres, instrumental music did not develop in Japan. Each instrument thus developed from its relationship to and function within vocal music, which accounts for the presence of many unique, vocal-like techniques.

Mnemonics

As mentioned above, a fundamental part of music pedagogy in Japan is the use of instrument-specific mnemonics (*shōga*), the purpose of which can vary according to the instrument. The melodic lines for the instruments are realized through syllables assigned to different techniques or fingerings. The mnemonics for the *shinobue* and *koto*, for example, represent the actual melodic line, and they provide a means of understanding musical nuances. There is, however, no indication of fingerings or string numbers. Mnemonics for the *shakuhachi*, on the other hand, indicate fingerings, and *shamisen* mnemonics indicate both string number and performance technique. *Shōga* bears some resemblance with Western solfège.

The Unit of One Breath and One Strike

Under the influence of Buddhism, especially Zen Buddhism, the value of one breath and the weight of one strike—the concept of enlightenment through one tone—corresponds with the function of Japanese instruments. To produce a rich full sound on any Japanese instrument requires considerably more energy than is necessary for Western instruments. Also closely connected to Buddhist thought is the concept of free meter. The space between one note and the next is not considered a "rest," but rather an important space containing the absence of sound.

This does not mean, however, that all Japanese music is ponderous or lacking in liveliness. Popular music, for example, is characterized by lightness.

Relationship to Nature

In the East, especially in Japan, the union of human culture and nature has been held as an ideal since ancient times. In buildings made from stone, where the outside is completely separated from the inside, sounds echo for extended periods of time and rich harmonics are born. In buildings open to the outside, however, such as those found in traditional Japan, or even present-day spaces, which use materials such as *tatami* and *fusuma* that absorb the sound, one cannot hear high harmonics.[4] In traditional Japanese music, bright sounds rich in harmonics were considered undesirable. As a result, sounds containing percussive elements become important. These aesthetic preferences are considered evidence demonstrating that in Japan, there is no conception of creating an artificial soundworld in confrontation to nature.

In the ninth century, as instruments imported from abroad were modified to Japanese tastes, two distinguishing characteristics emerged. First, all low-pitched instruments disappeared as their easily produced harmonics destroy subtle pitch inflections, which may have been seen as an undesirable trait or deemed unnatural.

Second, the sustained sound of bowed instruments was disliked. Perhaps this was due to the poor acoustics of indoor spaces in Japan where the instruments did not resonate well. It may also have been a resistance to the sound of a bow scraping over a string, or that this was also perceived as being somehow unnatural.

Certainly, low-pitched, sustained tones, and heterophony are unsuitable for *wabi-sabi*[5] and the state or space that embodies *ma*.[6] I want the Japanese people to respect the existence of instruments that are suited to the Japanese natural environment. This is where we can feel supreme contentment. It is true, however, that this side of Japanese music does not reflect the lively, explosive side of our human nature. For a long time, young men have been fascinated with the noise and energy of festival *taiko*, and the endless endurance it requires. Surely, their activities are a reaction to the ponderous character of many genres of traditional Japanese music.

There are two major aspects of traditional Japanese music: the static side of our art music, and the dynamic side of our folk music. Keeping these traditions in mind, we must think about how to develop and use Japanese instruments in the future. At the same time, by working in partnership with other Asian instrumentalists in an effort to supplement and improve the shortcomings of Japanese instruments, we can create a musical world different from that of the West, and thus contribute something new to humanity.

N.B. This is not limited to Japanese instruments, but recently, the pitch of instruments has risen. Among Western instruments, $a^1 = 442$ Hertz is generally recognized as the standard, and in many cases Japanese ensembles and performers have also adopted this. *Gagaku* uses $a^1 = 430$ while there are some Asian nations that use $a^1 = 440$. With ensembles, it is best to compose a work and program a performance after determining whether or not it is possible for each instrument called for in the piece to adjust to the same tuning.

Chapter One

Wind Instruments

Representative Japanese transverse flutes include the *kagurabue*, the *komabue*, the *ryūteki*, the *nōkan*, and the *shinobue*, while representative vertical flutes include the *shakuhachi*, the *hichiriki*, and the *shō*. The *komabue*, *ryūteki*, *hichiriki*, *shō*, and *shakuhachi* came from the Asian mainland as *gagaku* instruments. The *kagurabue*, however, is said to have existed in Japan before the importation of *gagaku*, and is also known as the *yamatobue*.[1]

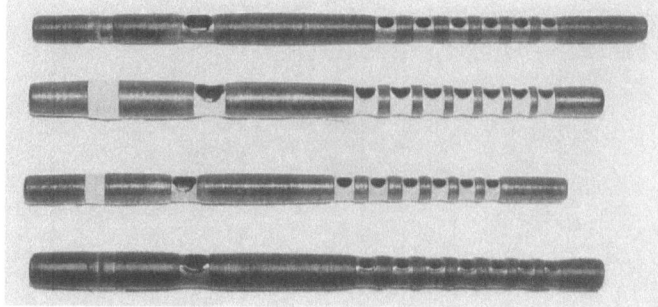

Fig. 1.1. Japanese transverse flutes (from top to bottom: *kagurabue*, *ryūteki*, *komabue*, *nōkan*)

The wind chambers of these wind instruments are all made from bamboo. When bamboo dries, however, it cracks easily. To prevent this, and to beautify the appearance, the outside surface of the instrument is wrapped in cherry bark or birch bark and then coated with lacquer. The *shinobue* and *shakuhachi*, however, maintain the appearance of natural bamboo. Except for the *nōkan*, which is unique, the wind chamber for many Japanese wind instruments is constructed from natural, unfinished bamboo. The resulting sonorities cannot be calculated, as with completely cylindrical or conical tubes it is necessary to adjust the intonation after making the instrument. The mouthpieces are simple and seldom have any mechanical features. This simplicity, however, results in timbral nuances seldom found in Western instruments. These "imperfections" are part of the instrument, creating what is considered a magical sound quality.

Each of the wind instruments has distinctive characteristics that will be discussed in this chapter. Discussions of the *tempuku* and *hitoyogiri*,[2] however (instruments rarely used in concert and close to vanishing), have been omitted.

There is an instrument often used among the Ainu people of Hokkaido called the *mukuri*. In standard Japanese, this instrument is known as the *kokin*. A type of Jaw's harp, it is made from long, thin bamboo (sometimes metal) with a deep cut in the middle of the instrument body where the lips are placed. The left edge is held with the left hand allowing the right hand to pull a string on the right edge of the instrument; the fissure vibrates, and the mouth cavity functions as a resonating chamber. As in speech, if the shape of the mouth cavity is changed while playing, the sound changes accordingly.

Occasionally, *shakuhachi* performers use an instrument called the *takebora*, which is made from one hollowed node of naturally thick bamboo. While the instrument can produce only one pitch, it is possible to cover a lower range unavailable on any of the normal *shakuhachi*, hence its usefulness.

Made famous by Japanese mountain priests, the *horagai*[3] was originally used in India as a Buddhist instrument. In classic Chinese warfare, this instrument was used on the battlefield to signal troops, and is the Eastern equivalent of the Western trumpet shell. A mouthpiece is fixed to the *horagai* and blown like a brass instrument. There are many sizes and it is possible to make a variety of sounds by using overtones. There are many *taiko* groups that now use the *horagai*; however, none of these quasi-instruments will be discussed in any depth in this book. We begin with the *shinobue*.

1–1: *Shinobue*

(1) Construction

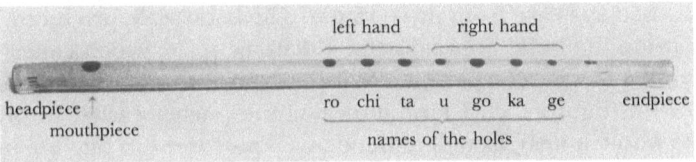

Fig. 1.2. The *Shinobue*

8 ❧ WIND INSTRUMENTS

The *shinobue* is made from *shinochiku* bamboo (*medake*).[4] The head (*utaguchi*) of the instrument, located next to the mouthpiece, and the open end of the flute, are both wrapped in birch bark. The outside surface of the *shinobue* has a smooth, skin-like texture. Used in festivals, the *hayashi* ensemble of *nagauta*,[5] the off-stage music of *kabuki*, and *sato*, or village *kagura*,[6] it has also been adopted as a concert instrument.

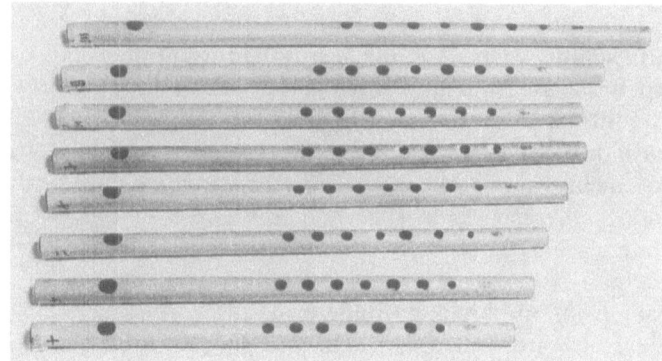

Fig. 1.3. Different kinds of *shinobue* (from top to bottom: 3, 4, 5, 6, 7, 8, 9, 10 length pipes)

The standard *shinobue* has seven holes, but six-holed *shinobue* are also used in instrumental folk music festivals. Fingerings for the seven-holed *shinobue* are shown in figure 1.4.

(2) Basic Scales, Derived Pitches, and Fingerings

By switching between flutes of different lengths, the *shinobue* player can play in many different keys. Names of various shinobue lengths such as *sanbon* (三本) and *happon* (八本)[7] are based on the fifth above the fundamental of each flute, which is the pitch produced when the four holes closest to the mouthpiece are covered.[8] Theoretically, there are twelve different sizes, but in practice, the most commonly used sizes are from three to ten. The basic scale produced by opening and closing the holes approximates a diatonic scale, which comes as a surprise given that the stereotypical melodic lines are always pentatonic. Using the *happon* (八本) (figure 1.4), I have indicated the pitches easiest to produce at *forte* (white whole notes), as well as the derived *meri* and *kari* pitches, notes produced by half-holing or adjusting the embouchure (changing the angle of the lips against the mouthpiece), and the fingering for these pitches.

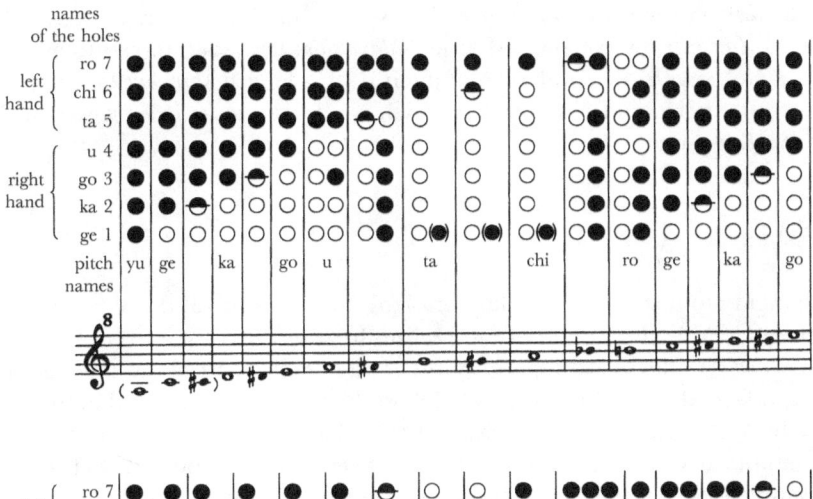

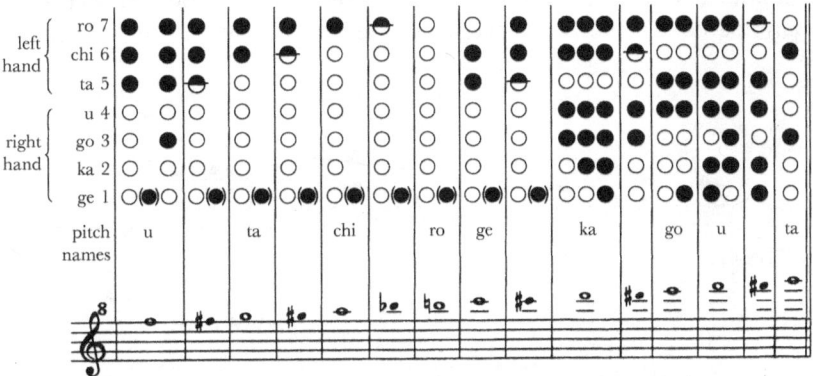

Fig. 1.4. *Shinobue* pitches

Within the fingering chart:
- ● indicates a closed hole.
- ○ indicates an open hole.
- ◐ indicates a half-holed or shaded hole.
- (●) indicates that the hole may be closed in order to stabilize the instrument.
- ○ can also be used.

Within the staff:
- o indicates fundamental pitches (does not include half-holed pitches).
- • indicates derived pitches.

The term *meri* is derived from the word *meru*, which means "to lower." A lowered minor second is called *chū-meri*, while a lowered major second is called *ō-meri*. *Kari* is derived from the verb *karu*, which means "to raise." With wind instruments, normally, the pitch can be raised only a minor second. There are very few instances where fundamental pitches can be raised a major second.

N.B. In *Kantō* (eastern region) style *shamisen*, the pitch *a* is referred to as *ippon*, while in *Kansai* (western region) style *Gidayū shamisen d* is referred to as *ippon*. On a *shinobue* with the fundamental pitch *d* (this length *shinobue* exists only in theory), the perfect fifth above is *a*, which is referred to as *ippon*, and thus follows the *Kantō* method.

(3) Range and Timbre

By changing to instruments of different lengths, the range of the *shinobue* family is extremely wide. It is necessary to realize, however, that the effective range of each *shinobue* is narrow. In figure 1.5, the most effective part of the *shinobue's* register is indicated by the bracket labeled B, while the pitches indicated in the lower range by A are weak. It is best to avoid the fundamental pitch. The range of high pitches indicated by C can only be played at *forte*, and it is impossible to play them with any degree of dynamic nuance. This range is unsuitable for melodic passages.

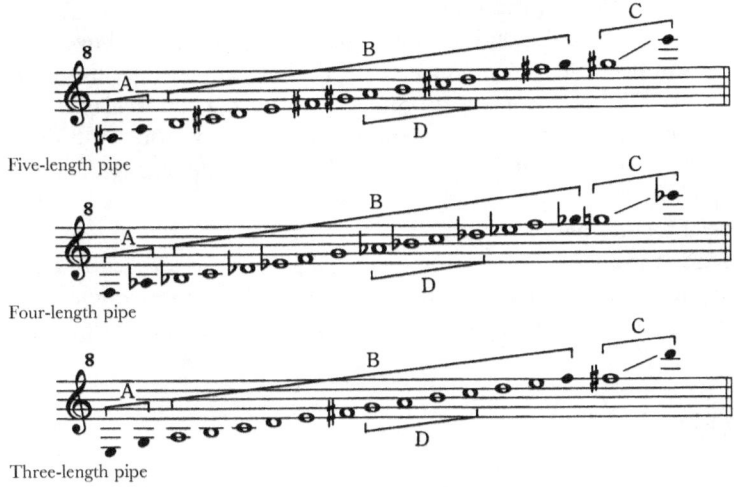

Fig. 1.5. Basic scales and application ranges for each *shinobue*

The brightest middle register of the *shinobue* is indicated by D. Again, with the theoretical *happon* (8) *shinobue*, this register would encompass the range of c^3 to f^3. In this register, an accomplished performer can play with lyricism and expressivity, and can easily execute technically demanding passages.

(4) Performance Technique

a) Breathing

Traditionally, tonguing is not used with Japanese wind instruments, and if tonguing is used in a traditional musical phrase, the resulting sound is considered incongruous. The phrase is normally given shape by pushing air from the abdomen through the mouth while using the fingers to re-attack the hole. Similar to Western flute technique, the Japanese method of producing vibrato is to move the mouth against the mouthpiece, which yields vibrations in the airflow. Like the flute, vibrato can also be produced by an undulating movement from the abdomen. Of course, in contemporary music, all techniques, including tonguing, are used.

Playing the lowest and highest registers requires more air than when playing in the middle register. Since the mouthpiece is primitive, air leaks easily; nevertheless, most people, even beginners, can produce a sound on a *shinobue*, unlike with the *shakuhachi*, which requires considerable effort and patience. The reason for this is the horizontal mouthpiece.

b) Expression through dynamics

Dynamic expression depends on the register. As mentioned above, in the high register, it is impossible to produce a *piano*, while at the other extreme, anything in the low register above a *piano* produces overtones. The *shinobue* is effective at entering *piano* and building to *forte*, and in the middle register, the *shinobue* can move freely between *piano* and *forte*. It is adept at producing *fp* throughout the entire register.

c) Special techniques

As with other wind instruments, some *shinobue* players can vocalize as they perform their instrument. As mentioned in the previous section, flutter-tonguing and most other flute and piccolo techniques can be employed in contemporary compositions.

(5) Fingering Techniques

For some reason, the normal performance practice for Japanese transverse flutes is to extend the finger joints, rather than the finger pads, over the holes, for pitch control and shading. Unlike the Western flute, the *shinobue* does not have mechanical pads, and the production of derived pitches and their accuracy is therefore more difficult. Nevertheless, once the instrument is made with the holes correctly placed, and the performer has made what adjustments desired, the *shinobue* is among the more accurate of Japanese wind instruments. In figure 1.4, the black notes indicate pitches produced by half-holing and shading; in the hands of a mediocre performer, the volume of these particular pitches will decrease. Unlike the Western flute, a *shinobue* performer cannot play with uniform volume and a constant degree of nuance throughout the register. Since there are no pads, and a performer can freely shade the holes, the *shinobue's* ability to produce subtle intervallic nuances surpasses that of the Western flute. The *shinobue* has a natural advantage in producing *portamento* and *glissando* as well.

a) Tremolos

As discussed above, it is difficult to transfer Western flute or piccolo fingering techniques to the *shinobue*. By indicating the feasibility of playing a tremolo above each of the pitches, it is possible to understand the degree of difficulty in playing a melody with intervallic accuracy. The theoretical eight-length *shinobue* is used in figure 1.6. Tremolos are possible between white notes, which are notated in the following manner: ♫ These tremolos can be played even if the tempo is faster than ♩ =138. A triangle symbol △ above a pair of black notes indicates that, while a tremolo is impossible, if the phrase is notated like ♫ and the tempo is ♩ = 100 the pitches may be slurred. Pairs of black notes marked with an X can only be played within the context of the following type of musical phrase ♫ (♩ =100). Pairs of pitches marked with a slur can be played legato in an ascending or descending melodic line. Black notes marked with an X indicate that it is impossible to alternate between the two pitches in a legato manner. There are differences between instruments and performers, and the information given here only applies to competent performers. As the quality of Japanese traditional instruments varies, it is difficult to fix a standard for performance technique. The data should be interpreted in the same way for the following explanations.

Fig. 1.6. An eight-length *shinobue*

Fig. 1.6. (continued)

b) Other Techniques

As mentioned above, Japanese winds do not use tonguing; and intervallic relationships and repeated pitches are articulated through highly nuanced ornamentation—"finger play," if you will. Classically trained performers finger their instrument by mnemonics, and when composing for them, a skeletal melody with the *shōga* syllables given above the notes is all that is necessary. Figure 1.7a is a section from the *nagauta hayashi, Kandamaru*. Ignoring the ornamentation in the score, if the mnemonics are added beneath the melody, for example "*hyarara*," the performer will insert the ornamentation without being instructed to do so. For performers unfamiliar with mnemonics, it is necessary to notate the ornaments in detail. *Shinobue* mnemonics allow for playful, nuanced fingerings.

Fig. 1.7. *Shinobue* finger ornaments. (a) Excerpt from the *nagauta hayashi Kandamaru*

In order to understand the significance of these finger ornaments and how fundamental they are to most *shinobue* techniques, I have provided "Moon over the Ruined Castle" (荒城の月) as an example. A classically trained *shinobue* performer would instinctively insert the fingered ornaments in long, broad phrases as illustrated in figure 1.7b without resorting to tonguing.

Fig. 1.7. *Shinobue* finger ornaments. (b) Excerpt from Rentarō Taki's *Moon Over the Ruined Castle*

Fig. 1.7. *Shinobue* finger ornaments. (c) Excerpt from Minoru Miki's *Danses Concértantes I "Four Seasons"*

Wind instruments in contemporary music are often required to produce multiphonics. The *shinobue*, however, being short and thin, has very few overtones and is ineffective in producing multiphonics.

When adopting contemporary Western flute techniques for Japanese tranverse flutes, I recommend consulting with the performers. The *shinobue* is a simple instrument, and the effectiveness of a particular technique is difficult to grasp unless tried.

1–2: *Ryūteki*

(1) Construction

Except for the area surrounding the mouthpiece and the finger holes, the entire surface of the *ryūteki* is wrapped with strips of cherry bark or rattan bark over which *urushi* lacquer is applied to harden the surface. The end near the mouthpiece is stopped with a piece of wood covered with red brocade, while the space between the top end and the mouthpiece is plugged with wax, behind which a lead weight has been inserted to balance both sides of the mouthpiece. The *ryūteki* was modeled after the *ōteki*, an instrument imported from T'ang dynasty China in the Nara period (710–94), and later evolved in imitation of Tibetan flutes. Traditionally, the *ryūteki* is used in the "music of the left" (*tōgaku*), *gagaku*, and *kumeuta*.

WIND INSTRUMENTS 17

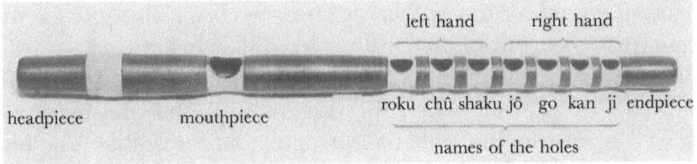

Fig. 1.8. The *Ryūteki*

There are seven finger holes, the names of which are given in figure 1.9.

(2) Basic Scales, Derived Pitches, and Fingerings

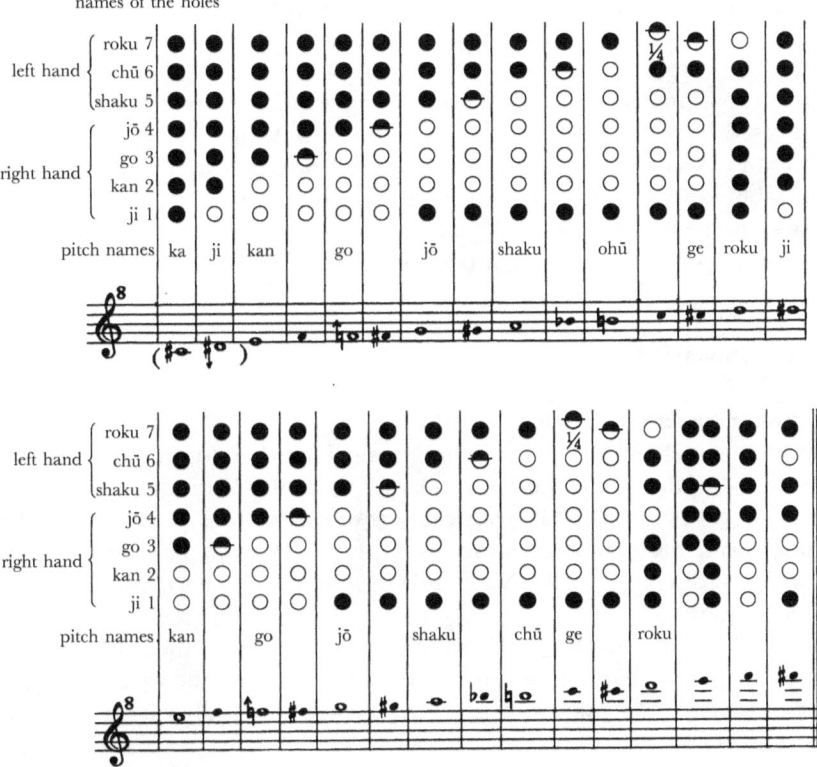

Fig. 1.9. Names of holes and pitches for the *ryūteki*

The fundamental pitch of the *ryūteki* is c^2 (or $c^{\#2}$), but if this pitch is thought of as the "tonic," the corresponding scale is irregular. Beginning with the fundamental tone (*ku*), which is produced with all holes closed, figure 1.9. shows the name assigned to each hole when the fingers are lifted one by one in turn.[9] From this we can see why the scale feels irregular and unstable. The black notes in figure 1.9 also indicate the pitches produced by half-holing or breath manipulation. The *ryūteki*, however, also uses alternate fingerings. As with other wind instruments, *ryūteki* performers constantly study and devise new fingerings.

(3) Range and Timbre

Fig. 1.10. Range and basic scale pitches for the *ryūteki*

Figure 1.10 demonstrates scale pitches using a different-sized *ryūteki* from the *ryūteki* used in figure 1.9. In the register marked A, the pitches *ku* (c^2) and *ji* ($c^{\#2}$) are weak and unstable; thus they are not normally used in performance. The usable range begins from the pitch named *kan* (e^2). Notes in the highest register, marked C, can be only played *forte* and their timbre is piercing; it is therefore preferable to use the B register.

(4) Performance Techniques

a) Breathing and the angle of the lips

Breathing technique for the *ryūteki* resembles that for the *shinobue*. The mouthpiece of the *ryūteki*, however, is larger than that of the *shinobue*, and thus requires a deeper breath. In classical *gagaku* pieces, the *ryūteki* does not use vibrato, but if the composer indicates its use for a contemporary piece, performers can, of course, make use of this technique. This also applies to tonguing techniques.

Although not a classical *ryūteki* technique used in *gagaku*, the following is possible: if the player changes the angle and widens the space between the lips and the mouthpiece, the pitch will rise; this technique is called *karu*. If the performer narrows the space between the lips and the mouthpiece, then the pitch will become lower; this technique is known as *meru*. These techniques can be graphically shown after the note with a line like •〜. In the performance of *saibara* and *rōei*[10] there are two other *meru* (pitch-lowering) techniques: *yōyū* and *iribushi*. *Yōyū* is graphically expressed as •〰︎, but is also occasionally indicated in staff notation, as in figure 1.11a.

Fig. 1.11. Various techniques and melodic patterns. (a) Excerpt from the *saibara* Sekida

The symbol for *iribushi* is •〰︎ and the staff notation for *iribushi* is shown in figure 1.11b.

Fig. 1.11. Various techniques and melodic patterns. (b) Excerpt from the *saibara* Koromogae

b) Dynamic expression

The rules for dynamics on *ryūteki* are largely the same as those of *shinobue*. *Gagaku* is devoid of any dynamic variation, and the performers always play at *mezzo forte*. In the register marked B, however, it is possible to play from *piano* to *forte*.

c) Special techniques

a) *Ateru* (to attack): the second of two repeated pitches is blown more forcefully to create an accent. The tenuto mark in figure 1.11c corresponds to this technique.

Fig. 1.11. Various techniques and melodic patterns. (c) Excerpt from *Etenraku*

Fig. 1.11. Various techniques and melodic patterns. (c) (continued)

b) *Fukikomi* (to breathe into): *Fukikomi* refers to the initial upward glide of a pitch with the use of full breath force. Similar to trombone glissandi, the technique is represented with this line [⌒•] before the note. I have written the beginning of each phrase shown in figure 1.11d with the assumption that the performer would play these notes by using fingering techniques. It is interesting, however, to employ *fukikomi* technique as well.

Fig. 1.11. Various techniques and melodic patterns. (d) Excerpt from Minoru Miki's *Iki*

c) Flutter tongue: as with other wind instruments, the *ryūteki* is capable of using flutter tongue.

(5) Various Techniques and Melodic Patterns

In figure 1.11.c I have given the opening phrase of *Etenraku* as a representative example of *gagaku* music. In this example, the transcriber indicates a crescendo and diminuendo from *mezzo forte* to *forte* and back, but *gagaku* musicians traditionally have no cognizance of dynamics. For the reader's reference, I have added the mnemonics for the *ryūteki* under each stave.

In contemporary compositions, whether for *gagaku* orchestra or in combination with other instruments, composers have taken various approaches to the *ryūteki*. Effective phrases will incorporate knowledge of the above-mentioned limitations and characteristics of the instrument. In figure 1.11d, I have shown an excerpt from a composition that I wrote in the 1960s.

As with the *shinobue* and the *nōkan*, multiphonics are not effective with the due to the size of the instrument.

(6) Fingering Techniques

Generally speaking, fingering techniques for the *ryūteki* are the same as for the *shinobue*; however, because the finger holes of the *ryūteki* are larger than those of the *shinobue*, it is easier to create semitones smaller than a minor second with a half, quarter, or even smaller partial hole openings.

a) *Ugoku*: the hole nearest the endpiece is opened by rotating the finger towards the left in a kneading motion, then immediately closing it again. This produces the effect of a glissando between the initial pitch and the adjacent higher pitch. *Ugoku* always returns to the initial pitch.

b) *Yuru*: As shown in figure 1.12, there are three kinds of *yuru*. *Yuru* lowers an initial pitch approximately a minor second, through fingering, then returns to the initial pitch. The second example employs a special fingering (see figure 1.9), and while the indicated intervallic change is imprecise, it has a distinct nuance.

Fig.1.12. Three kinds of *yuru*

c) *Tataku* (striking): the hole located immediately to the left of the rightmost closed finger is tapped rapidly. Although the pitch is lowered only momentarily, it has a remarkable embellishing effect. In figure 1.11c, the grace note on the fourth beat in the fifth measure is created by this technique. Since *tataku* is similar to the *shakuhachi* technique *yuru*, I use the same symbol ↑.

(7) Tremolo

Although the *ryūteki* does not traditionally use tremolo, in figure 1.13, I have provided an example of this technique because an objective of contemporary music is to exploit all instrumental possibilities. I indicate the degree of difficulty in the same manner as in the *shinobue* example: pairs of white notes represent possible tremolos, while pairs of black notes are difficult. I have marked those pairs of notes that can be performed at a slower tempo with a triangle, and the X indicates that the two notes are impossible to execute as a tremolo. Among the pairs of notes indicated with an "X," a slur is used to indicate those which can be executed within the context of a legato melodic line, even if it is impossible to play them as a tremolo. It is best to ask the player about the feasibility of tremolos, as, like the *shinobue*, there are differences depending on the instrument and the performer.

Fig. 1.13. An example of use of tremolo by the *ryūteki*

Fig. 1.13. (continued)

Fig. 1.13. (continued)

1–3: Nōkan

(1) Construction

The *nōkan*, originally called the *nōteki*, is a transverse flute created for use in the *hayashi* ensemble[11] of *nō* plays. Developing from the *hayashi* music of *dengaku*,[12] the *nō hayashi* was an established musical ensemble by the end of the fourteenth century. The structure of the original *dengaku* flute was altered in order to produce a stronger sound and now closely resembles the *ryūteki*. In spite of a nearly identical appearance, there are several aspects in which they differ.

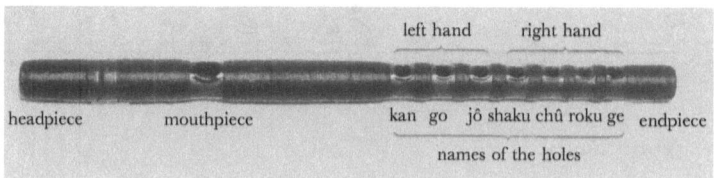

Fig. 1.14. The *Nōkan*

The *ryūteki* uses an unbroken bamboo tube for the body of the instrument, whereas the body of the *nōkan* is constructed by cutting a tube of bamboo vertically into several strips, reversing the pieces so that the skin faces inwards, and fixed inside out with *urushi* lacquer. The outside surface of the body is wrapped with birch-bark or cherry-bark string and then lacquered once again with *urushi*. The hard-surface skin of the bamboo on the inside of the air chamber creates a timbre more piercing than that of the *ryūteki*. Some *nōkan* have a round pipe (*nodo*, or "throat"), hardened with *urushi*, and attached inside the body between the mouthpiece and the first finger hole, that produces an even sharper sound. A gold piece is inserted at the upper end of the *nōkan* instead of the *ryūteki* brocade.

As with the *ryūteki*, there are seven finger holes; the order of the hole names, however, is opposite from that of the *ryūteki* (figure 1.15).

(2) Basic Scales and Fingerings

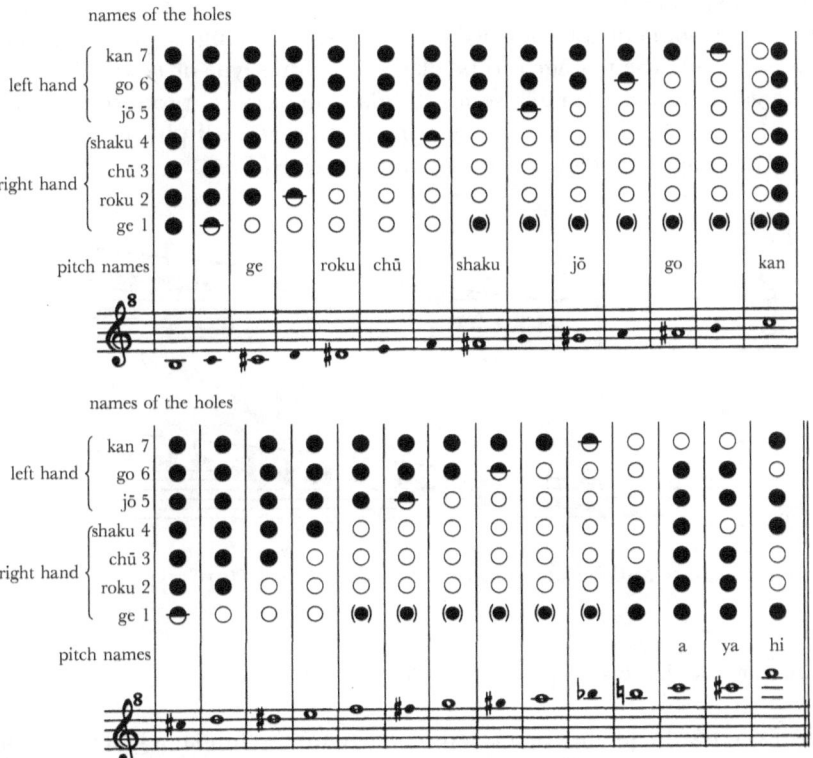

Fig. 1.15 *Nōkan* finger holes

Due to its physical structure, the pitches of the *nōkan* are extremely imprecise and vary from instrument to instrument; the fingering for one instrument will produce different pitches on another. Even within a scale produced by one instrument, there is no mathematical concordance between the fundamental (*otsu*) and the higher octave (*kō*). In my opinion, the *nōkan* was specifically created as an instrument to express human instincts and feelings in the breath blown through the flute. Given these unique qualities, it is impossible to notate its distinct scale in Western notation. Instead, a notation system specifically designed for the *nōkan* (*nōkan* mnemonics, a type of tablature) or a graphical notation may be more useful. Nonetheless, Western staff notation has been customarily employed with the understanding that it indicates only approximate pitches. Skilled *nōkan* players can match the pitches of other instruments through lip and finger manipulation. If, however, a composer wants to use the unique pitches of the *nōkan*, this should be indicated in the score. If melodic content is to be prioritized, other flutes such as the *shinobue*, rather than the *nōkan*, should be used. Figure 1.15 shows the scale, hole names, and fingerings for one *nōkan* played by a professional musician.[13]

There are many players who also use a *nōkan* pitched a minor second higher than this example. If the composer does not know the type of *nōkan* the player will use, I recommend avoiding elaborate passages. As long as the melodic movement is smooth, the passage can be played on either type of *nōkan*. Figure 1.16 illustrates the range and pitch series (fundamental scales) produced by the two types of *nōkan* through normal fingering and breath. All pitches are approximate. The examples below all employ the first type of *nōkan*.

Fig. 1.16. Range and basic scales of the *nōkan:* type I (top), type II (bottom).

(3) Range and Timbre

In figure 1.16, the pitches bracketed under A are the fundamental scale. These tones are characteristically weak in volume and have a soft timbre. The pitches under B are usually loud with a piercing sound quality, although they can be played softly. The pitches under C, the highest register, are used in the *hishigi* motive explained below. The pitch f⁴ can only be played *ff*, but c⁴ and c[#]⁴ can also be produced at *p*. The fundamental pitch, or *tsutsune* (the pitch produced with all the finger holes closed) is normally not used.

(4) Performance Techniques

a) Breathing and *enbai*

As with the *shinobue*, *ryūteki*, and other Japanese flutes, tonguing is not used in traditional *nōkan* performance. Without using the tongue, the *nōkan* player articulates a phrase by pressing breath from the diaphragm into the mouthpiece, and emphasizes the sound attack with the fingers. In modern compositions, any contemporary performance techniques can be used.

The *nōkan* also employs *meri* and *kari* (*enbai*), pitch alterations created by changing the angle of the lips against the mouthpiece. These techniques are used in *netori*, discussed below in the section entitled "Fingering Techniques."

b) Dynamics

As mentioned in Section 3 (range and timbre), the *nōkan* has different dynamic capacities depending on register. While the notes of the fundamental scale bracketed under A in figure 1.16 cannot be produced at *forte*, they nonetheless can achieve complex and delicate expression through the use of various breathing techniques in the dynamic range of *pp* to *mf*. In the B register, it is possible to perform from *mp* to *ff*.

c) Special techniques

1. ***Hishigi***: *Hishigi* was originally created for *nō* and *kabuki* as a sound pattern to accompany the appearance of ghosts and spirits as they enter the stage (figure 1.17). Generated with a particularly forceful breath, *hishigi* is an extremely high-pitched dramatic motive used for heightening the tension of a scene.

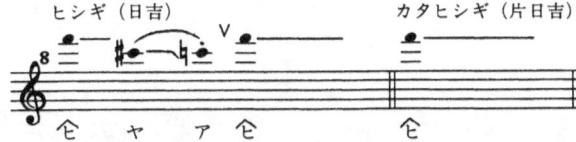

Fig. 1.17. A special *nōkan* technique: *Hishigi, Kata-hishigi*

2. ***Kata-hishigi***: *Kata-hishigi* uses only the last "*hi*" of the *hishigi* pattern shown in the above figure. Like *hishigi,* calling for a specific pitch is problematic.

3. **Flutter tongue**: This technique is only used in the performance of contemporary music.

4. *Netori:* See the section on "Fingering Techniques."

(5) Fingering Techniques

Along with its unique set of pitches, the *nōkan* can also produce complex pitch inflections through different fingering combinations. It also excels in portamento and glissando. Techniques that consist of striking the holes with the fingertips are also effective, just as with instruments such as the *ryūteki*.

a) Tremolo

Traditionally, the *nōkan* does not employ tremolo; in figure 1.18, I have shown, however, what possibilities there are. The white notes are possible, the triangles are difficult, and the X above black notes indicates that a tremolo is impossible. The patterns that can be played legato within a melody are indicated with a slur.

I would like to emphasize that the possible tremolos indicated in the figure are based on the first type of *nōkan* shown in figure 16. It is important to understand that only well-trained musicians can execute these kinds of tremolos properly.

Fig. 1.18. Possible *nōkan* tremolos

Fig. 1.18. (continued)

Fig. 1.18. (continued)

b) Various techniques and patterns

a. *Netori*: the gradual sliding of a finger while shifting the angle of the lips produces the effect of a *yuri* (vibrato). In the off-stage music of the *kabuki* theater, this technique is also used to represent a ghost or spirit, but only in the A register (figure 1.16). The composer should connect notes with a line, as shown in figure 1.19, so that the player visually understands the composer's intention. It is also possible to give detailed instructions regarding pitches, as in compositions of contemporary music. *Netori* are not found in *nō* music.

Fig. 1.19 The *netori* technique for *nōkan*

Figure 1.20 b–j, shows performance techniques used in the classical repertoire. The characters under the notes are the mnemonic syllables for the *nōkan*.

Fig. 1.20 Some *nōkan* playing techniques in classical pieces. (b) In *Chū no mai*

This figure (1.20b) of *Chū no mai* is without ornaments and has unstable intervals indicated as approximate pitches.

Fig. 1.20. Some *nōkan* playing techniques in classical pieces. (c) In *Banshikigaku–Shodan*

The fingerings for the pitches indicated by numbers enclosed in circles are different from those found in figure 1.15.

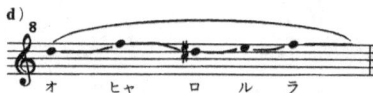

Fig. 1.20. Some *nōkan* playing techniques in classical pieces. (d)

Pitches that continually wander across the staff lines in the following manner are called *wataribyōshi*.

Fig. 1.20. Some *nōkan* playing techniques in classical pieces. (e)

Fig. 1.20. Some *nōkan* playing techniques in classical pieces. (f)

Fig. 1.20. Some *nōkan* playing techniques in classical pieces. (g)

Fig. 1.20. Some *nōkan* playing techniques in classical pieces. (h)

Fig. 1.20. Some *nōkan* playing techniques in classical pieces. (i)

Fig. 1.20. Some *nōkan* playing techniques in classical pieces. (j) In *Chū no mai*

Fig. 1.20. (continued)

This figure of *Chū no mai* uses a different instrument from the one used in figure 1.20b; the notation is also more precise.

Figure 1.21 illustrates the *nōkan* playing legato with a voice.

Because the length of the *nōkan* body and its inner diameter are too small to create overtones, the *nōkan* is unsuitable for producing multiphonics.

Fig. 1.21. An excerpt from Minoru Miki's *Paraphrase after Ancient Japanese Music*, second movement *Sōmon*

1–4: *Shakuhachi*

(1) Construction

The *shakuhachi* is the most common vertical Japanese flute. The name of this instrument is derived from its length of one *shaku* (30.3 cm) and eight *sun* (3.03 cm), for a total length of 54.5 centimeters. An ancient *shakuhachi* imported from T'ang China along with *gagaku* in the eighth century is preserved in *Shōso-in*.[14] This *shakuhachi*, however, has six holes, and its relationship with the five-holed *shakuhachi* that developed in the Middle Ages is problematic. It is said that Kakushin, a thirteenth-century Zen Buddhist priest, brought back the modern shakuhachi and its repertoire to Japan after completing his studies in China. His return marks the beginning of a style of performance known as the *Fuke shakuhachi*. The *shakuhachi* as we know it today was perfected in the seventeenth century. With the abolishment of the *Fuke* sect in 1871, the *shakuhachi* became popular among the general public and was incorporated into an ensemble with *koto* and *shamisen*. Like the *shinobue*, the *shakuhachi* is also constructed in different lengths that correspond to different keys. In addition to the classic five-holed *shakuhachi*, recently created seven- and nine-holed *shakuhachi* also exist. The seven-holed *shakuhachi* is especially well suited for contemporary music, and since classical fingerings for the five-holed *shakuhachi* can also be used by the seven-holed *shakuhachi*, many professionals use a seven-holed *shakuhachi*.

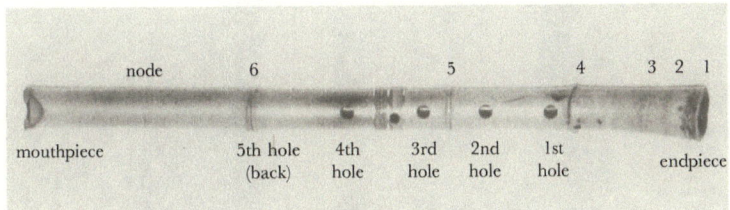

Fig. 1.22. The five-holed *shakuhachi*

The *shakuhachi* is a stalk with seven nodes taken from the root of *madake* (timber bamboo). The upper edge of the bamboo tube becomes the mouthpiece (figure 1.23) where a piece of water buffalo horn (ivory and deer horn are also used) is inserted into an area that has been cut diagonally along the seventh node.

36 • WIND INSTRUMENTS

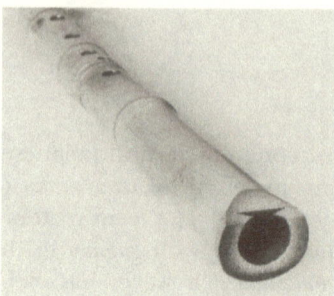

Fig. 1.23. The *shakuhachi* mouthpiece

Since these materials are difficult to obtain, artificial ebonite is often used instead. The root of the bamboo becomes the bell of the *shakuhachi*. The position of the holes in relation to the nodes is shown in the following diagram. The inside of the tube is hardened with red or black lacquer, which smoothes the timbre.

(2) Various Lengths of *Shakuhachi* and Their Corresponding Fingerings

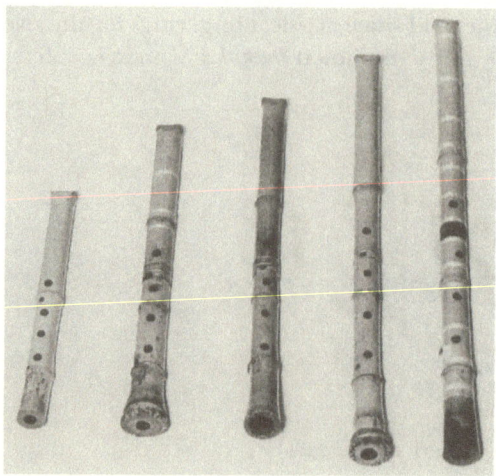

Fig. 1.24. Different kinds of *shakuhachi* (from left to right): 1.1, 1.6, 1.8, 2.1, and 2.4, all seven-holed

As mentioned above, the *shakuhachi* comes in different lengths that correspond to different keys. The name of each length is determined by the pitch produced when all of the holes are covered and the *shakuhachi* is blown normally. The standard *shakuhachi*, producing the nuclear pitch d^1, is called the *d-kan*. From this standard, each increment of one *sun* lowers the pitch by approximately a minor second, while a reduction of the same length raises the pitch a minor second. The shorter and longer tube lengths, however, have greater margins of error. For example, the *a-kan* (nuclear tone a), pitched a perfect fourth below the standard *d-kan*, is two *shaku* and four *sun*, not two *shaku* and three *sun*.

Figure 1.25 illustrates the easily produced basic pitches for the *d-kan* (indicated by the white whole notes), as well as the *meri* and *kari* pitches, which are derived by half-holing and embouchure adjustment (indicated by the black notes) with a corresponding fingering chart.

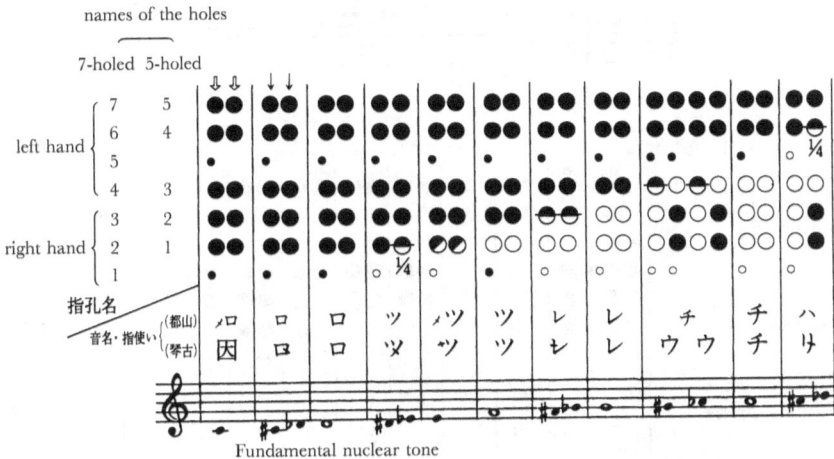

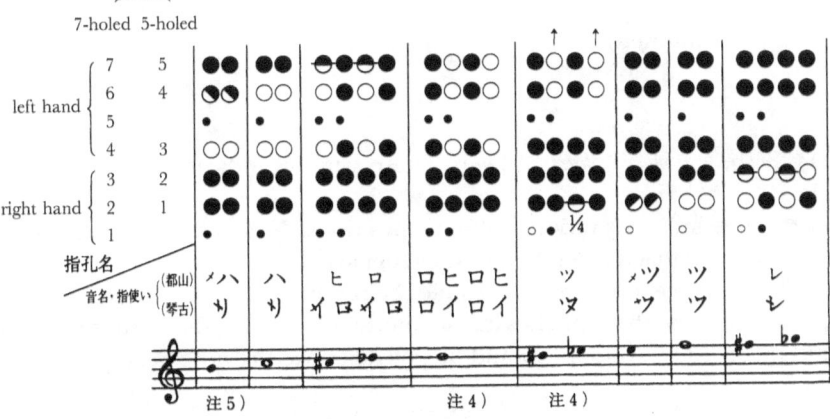

Fig. 1.25. Basic pitches for the *d-kan*

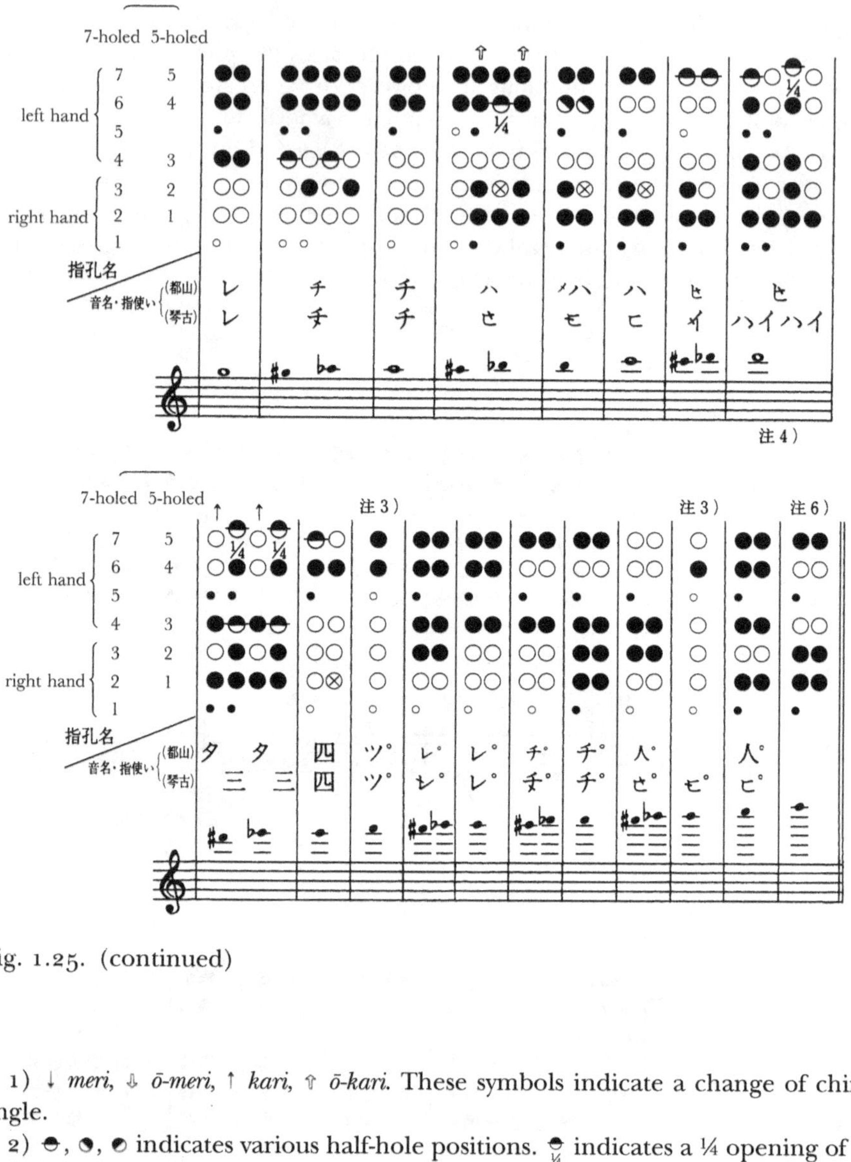

Fig. 1.25. (continued)

1) ↓ *meri*, ⇓ *ō-meri*, ↑ *kari*, ⇑ *ō-kari*. These symbols indicate a change of chin angle.

2) ◓, ◐, ◔ indicates various half-hole positions. ◯ with ¼ indicates a ¼ opening of a hole. ⊗ indicates that the hole may be open or closed.

3) These two pitches (f³ and b³) cannot be produced on a five-holed *shakuhachi*.

4) Each of these three pitches has an alternate fingering that results in a softer sound quality. The symbol ° should be placed above the note head as follows:

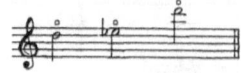

	TOZAN	KINKO
Otsu range		
c^1	Ro na dai-meri	Ro na dai-meri
$c^{\#1}$	Ro na han-on	Ro no meri
d^1	Ro	Ro
$d^{\#1}$	Tsu no han-on	Tsu no meri
e^1	Tsu no meri	Tsu no chū meri
f^1	Tsu	Tsu
$f^{\#1}$	Re no han-on	Re no chū meri
g^1	Re	Re
$g^{\#1}$	Chi no han-on	U
a^1	Chi	Chi
$a^{\#1}$	Ha no han-on	Ri no meri
b^1	Ha no meri	Ri no chū meri
c^1	Ha	Ri
$c^{\#1}$	Hi no han-on	I no meri
$c^{\#1}$ (alternative fingering)	Ro no han-on	Ro no meri
d^2 (alternative fingering)	Hi	I
Kan range		
d^2	Ro	Ro
$d^{\#2}$	Tsu no han-on	Tsu no meri
e^2	Tsu no meri	Tsu no chū-meri
f^2	Tsu	Tsu
$f^{\#2}$	Re no han-on	Re no chū-meri
g^2	Re	Re
$g^{\#2}$	Chi no han-on	Chi no meri
a^2	Chi	Chi
$a^{\#2}$	Ha no han-on	Hi no meri
$a^{\#2}$ (alternative fingering)	Chi no kari	San no u
b^2	Ha no han-on	Ho no chū-meri
c^2	Ha	Hi
$c^{\#2}$	Hi no han-on	I no chū-meri
d^3	Pi	Ha
$d^{\#3}$	Ta	San no Ha
e^3	Shi	Yon no Ha
Dai (tai)- kan range		
f^3	Tai-kan no -tsu	Dai-kan no Tsu
$f^{\#3}$	Tai-kan no Re no han-on	Dai-kan no Re no meri
g^3	Tai-kan no Re	Dai-kan no Re
$g^{\#3}$	Tai-kan no Chi no han-on	Dai-kan no Chi no meri
a^3	Tai-kan no chi	Dai-kan no Chi
$a^{\#3}$	Tai-kan no Ha no han-on	Dai-kan no Hi no meri
b^3		Dai-kan no Hi no chū-meri
c^3	Tai-kan no Ha	Dai-kan no Hi

Fig. 1.26. A fingering chart for the *shakuhachi*

40 • WIND INSTRUMENTS

5) This pitch also has an alternate fingering.

6) This pitch can only be produced up to a 1.6 *e-kan*. It is impossible to produce on *shakuhachi* shorter than 1.6.

On the chart (figure 1.26), the fingerings for the seven-holed *shakuhachi* are on the left, and those for the five-holed *shakuhachi* are on the right.

Figure 1.27 is a diagram of the basic pitches and scales and usable range for each size of *shakuhachi*.

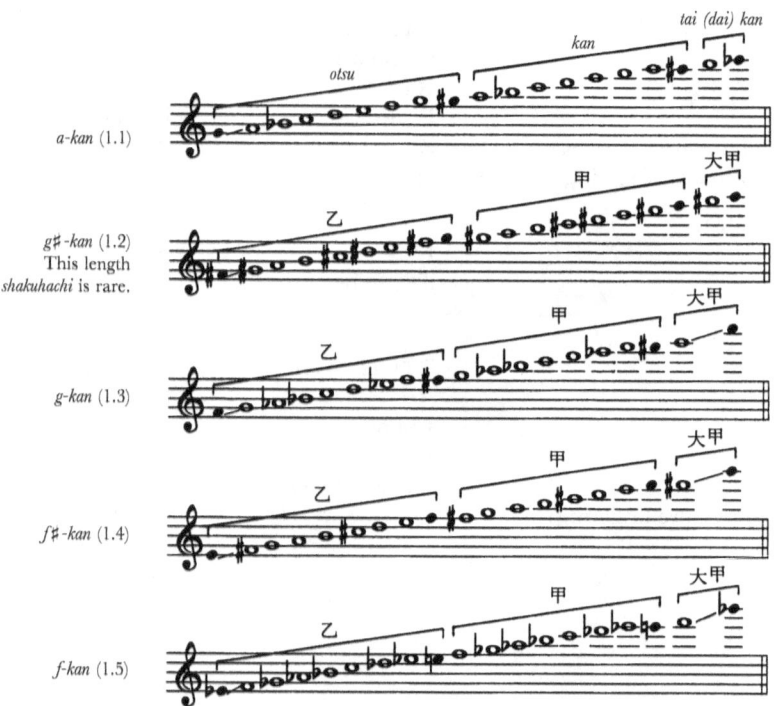

Fig. 1.27. Diagram of the basic pitches and scales and usable range for each size *shakuhachi*

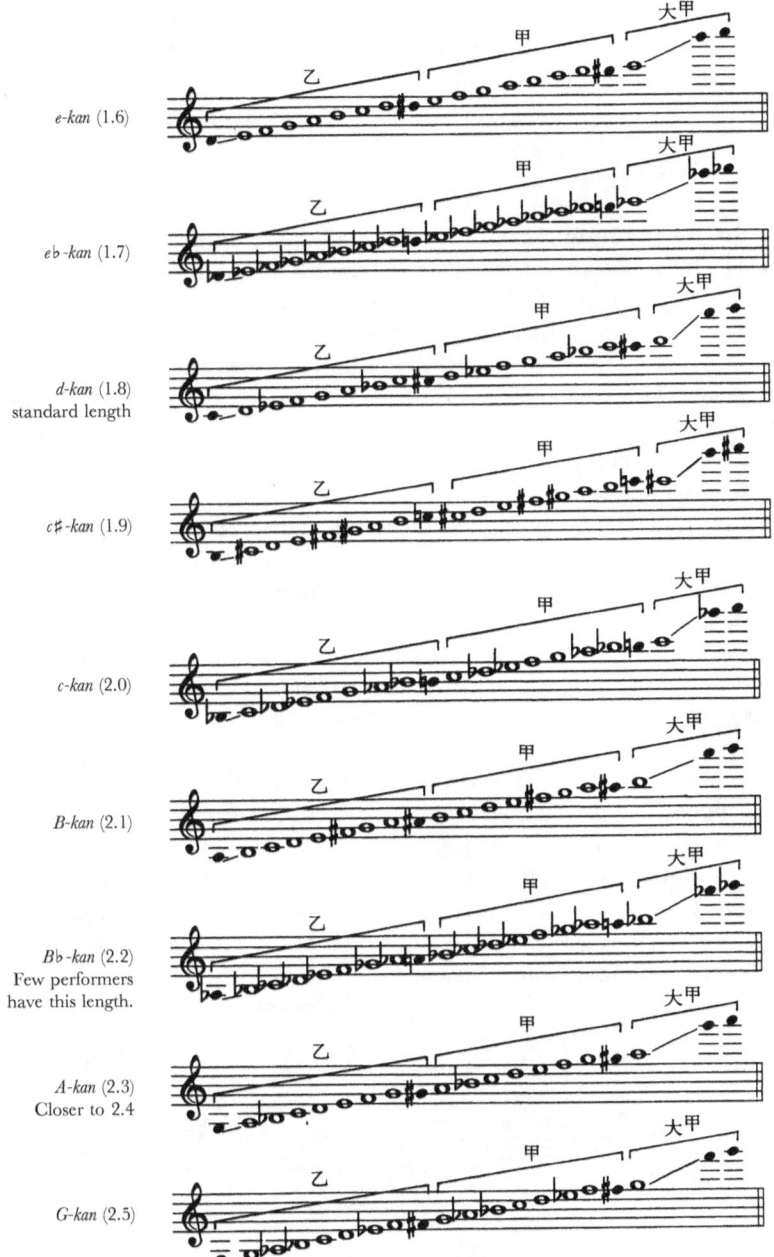

Fig. 1.27. (continued)

The *g-kan* approaches 2 *shaku* 7 *sun* in length, which makes it extraordinarily difficult to use. Few performers own a *g-kan*, and this length is rarely seen.

(3) Range and Timbre

While the range of the *shakuhachi* is limited, like the *shinobue*, exchanging one *shakuhachi* for a *shakuhachi* of a different length allows for a wider range. In figure 1.27, if a performer overblows the *otsu* range, the number of overtones increases, and when underblown, there is significant difference in the tone color. In a solo performance, or even in a small ensemble, the flexibility and range of sound color hold enormous expressive potential. It is also highly effective for several *shakuhachi* to provide a background or secondary lines within a large ensemble, but *shakuhachi* can be overpowered when grouped with instruments with larger sounds. Unlike the transverse flutes, in the hands of a well-trained performer the lowest pitch of the *shakuhachi* can be produced with sufficient volume and extremely rich expression. The extended *meri* pitch (a major second below the fundamental tone), however, is rarely used outside of traditional *shakuhachi honkyoku*.

In the *kan* range (the second overtone series), the tension in the lips increases and the sound is extremely bright and piercing. Even if the volume changes, there is very little change in tone color, and it is rarely covered by other instruments.

In the *dai-kan* (extended *kan*) range (above the third overtone series), the sound is extremely piercing to g^3, but above this, the sound is unmusical. With the shorter *shakuhachi*, it is extremely difficult to play in the *dai-kan* range. Figure 1.28 illustrates pitches that can be produced in the *dai-kan* range of the *d-kan* in order of decreasing difficulty.[15] Since it is easier to produce overtones with the longer flutes, there is greater potential in the higher range; however, there are few well-made long *shakuhachi*.

Fig. 1.28. An example of the extended *kan* range

(4) Blowing Techniques

a) Breathing

As with the transverse flutes, traditionally, the *shakuhachi* usually does not use tonguing. There are, however, many contemporary pieces that would be difficult to perform without tonguing, and well-trained performers will tongue certain passages unless specifically asked not to. Without using the tongue, when breath from the abdomen is blown through the *shakuhachi* and assisted by finger attacks, a quintessential Japanese sound is produced. Lowering the position of the chin against the mouthpiece results in the pitch dropping. A lowered minor second is called *meri*, while a lowered major second is *ō-meri*. By raising the chin, the pitch can be raised a minor second, which is known as *kari*. *Kari* is easier to play with correct intonation in the *otsu* range than in the *kan* range. Within the *otsu* range, it is easier to produce wider intervals by means of the *kari* technique on the higher pitches. *Meri-kari* technique is easier on the shorter *shakuhachi* than on the longer *shakuhachi*. With this technique, the *shakuhachi* can produce minor second or major second adjustments, and imbue a melodic line with subtle and profound shadings. As a result, the *shakuhachi* has become globally popular. As indicated in the expression, "Three years to produce vibrato by shaking your head,"[16] vibrato on the *shakuhachi* is normally produced by moving the head horizontally, vertically, and sometimes by moving the head in a circular manner. Naturally, Western wind techniques, including double and triple tonguing, can be performed on the *shakuhachi*. There are also many performers who use circular breathing.

b) Expression through dynamics

The fundamental pitches, which are produced by completely opening or covering the holes, can be produced at a rich volume, but the volume decreases for pitches produced by half-holing or the *meri-kari* technique. This, however, varies with the level of the performer. Basic pitches throughout the *otsu* and *kan* range can be produced from *pp* to *ff*; it is also possible to execute crescendo and diminuendo passages expressively. In the *dai-kan* range, however, the timbre is piercing and thin, and performers can only produce pitches at *f*. Overall, the expressive possibilities of the *shakuhachi* are phenomenal when compared to Western woodwinds.

c) Unique playing techniques (figure 1. 29)

1. ***Muraiki:*** the sound of the performer's breath is emphasized. Rather than producing a musical sound, it is a technique where the performer consciously blows violently into the mouthpiece to create a specific effect. This technique is extremely effectively for pitches in the *otsu* range. Blowing strongly into the *shakuhachi* produces overtones and the *muraiki* pitches often give the impression of being an octave higher. It is advisable to avoid tonguing. *Kazaiki* is another sound effect that contains even more breath than a *muraiki*. To indicate this, *kazaiki* should be written above the pitch.[17]

Fig. 1.29. Unique *shakuhachi* playing techniques. (1) *Muraiki*. An excerpt from the classical *shakuhachi* repertoire *Shika-no-tonne* ("Cry of the Distant Deer") and a excerpt from Minori Miki's *Kokyō*

2. ***Sorane:*** similar to *muraiki*, but used with pitches of shorter duration. Sometimes confused with *kazaiki*.
   In the score, with ♭ or ♮ it is unnecessary to write *sorane*.
3. ***Komi***: staccato produced by stopping the airflow.
4. ***Flutter-tongue*** (flutter-tonguing): a technique, originally called *tamane*, in which the uvula is fluttered as with a rolled German "r." When this technique is executed by fluttering the tongue, it is called *tabane*, and results in an increase of non-pitched sounds. It is suitable for all pitches except those in the *dai-kan* range.
5. ***Iki-yuri:*** similar to Western flute vibrato, produced by emphasizing breath from the abdomen in gentle, wave-like intervals.
6. ***Ago-yuri:*** vibrato produced by keeping the lips on the mouthpiece while moving the chin. There are three kinds of *ago-yuri*. *Yoko-yuri* is produced by moving the head horizontally, producing no change in pitch. *Tate-yuri* is produced by moving the head vertically, and creating a recognizable change in pitch. *Mawashi-yuri* is a combination of both, where the head is moved in a circle to create a vibrato effect. Usually, *mawashi-yuri* begin slowly, build in intensity to a wide vibrato, and then slowly return to a non-vibrato state. The shape of the vibrato is written as a graphic line to aid understanding. One may also write *yuri*.

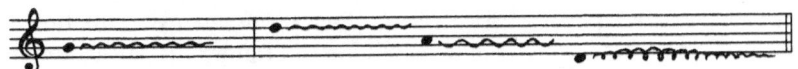

Fig. 1.29. Unique *shakuhachi* playing techniques. (5/6) *Yuri*

7. **Otoshi:** a technique that involves dropping the chin to lower the pitch at the end of sustained note. At the end of the line ↓ or ↯ may be added.

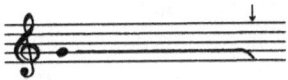

Fig. 1.29. Unique *shakuhachi* playing techniques. (7) *Otoshi*

8. **Furi-kiri:** resembles *otoshi*, except that the performer immediately returns to the original pitch before ending. The performer should understand what to do by means of the line. (↓ or ↯ may be added for further detail.)

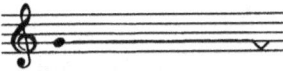

Fig. 1.29. Unique *shakuhachi* playing techniques. (8) *Furikiri*

9. **Circular breathing:** Nowadays, many performers have mastered this method of breathing. It is unnecessary, however, for the composer to indicate this in the score. While a unique performing technique, audiences are no longer impressed by performers with remarkable breathing and lung capacity.

(5) Fingering Techniques

As with other Japanese flutes, the *shakuhachi* has no pads or mechanical features, but instead demands sophisticated fingering technique. Well-trained *shakuhachi* players can accurately play scalar melodic passages on both the seven-holed *shakuhachi* and the five-holed *shakuhachi*. There are many players who can achieve an even balance of volume, but this level of precision is not found with all performers. Normally, precise intonation and an evenly balanced volume can be easily produced when playing basic scales on the various lengths of five-holed and seven-holed *shakuhachi*, but half-hole technique can render the intonation unstable and the volume weak. The *shakuhachi* is recognized as requiring the highest level of technique and expertise to control subtle intonation and nuances.

a) Tremolos

In figure 1.30, pairs of notes that can be performed as a tremolo on a *d-kan* are indicated by white note-heads. Pairs of notes that can be performed legato within the context of a melodic line are indicated by black note-heads marked with triangles. Tremolos are more difficult on *shakuhachi* that are markedly longer or shorter than the *d-kan*, and the composer should consult with the performer.

As with other wind instruments, asking a performer to play a tremolo between the notes of the overtone series in different ranges (i.e., *otsu* and *kan*) is very problematic, even if the distance between the two pitches is close.

Fig. 1.30. Possibilities for tremolos on a *shakuhachi*

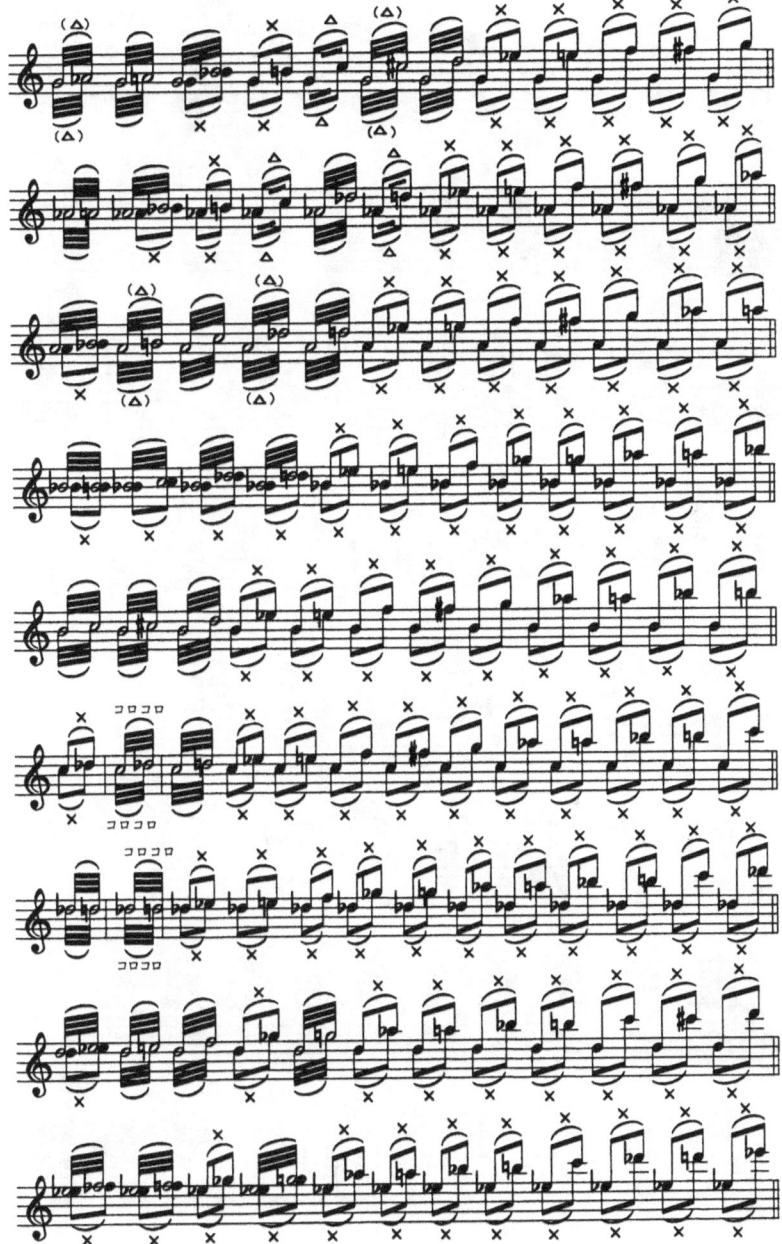

Fig. 1.30. (continued)

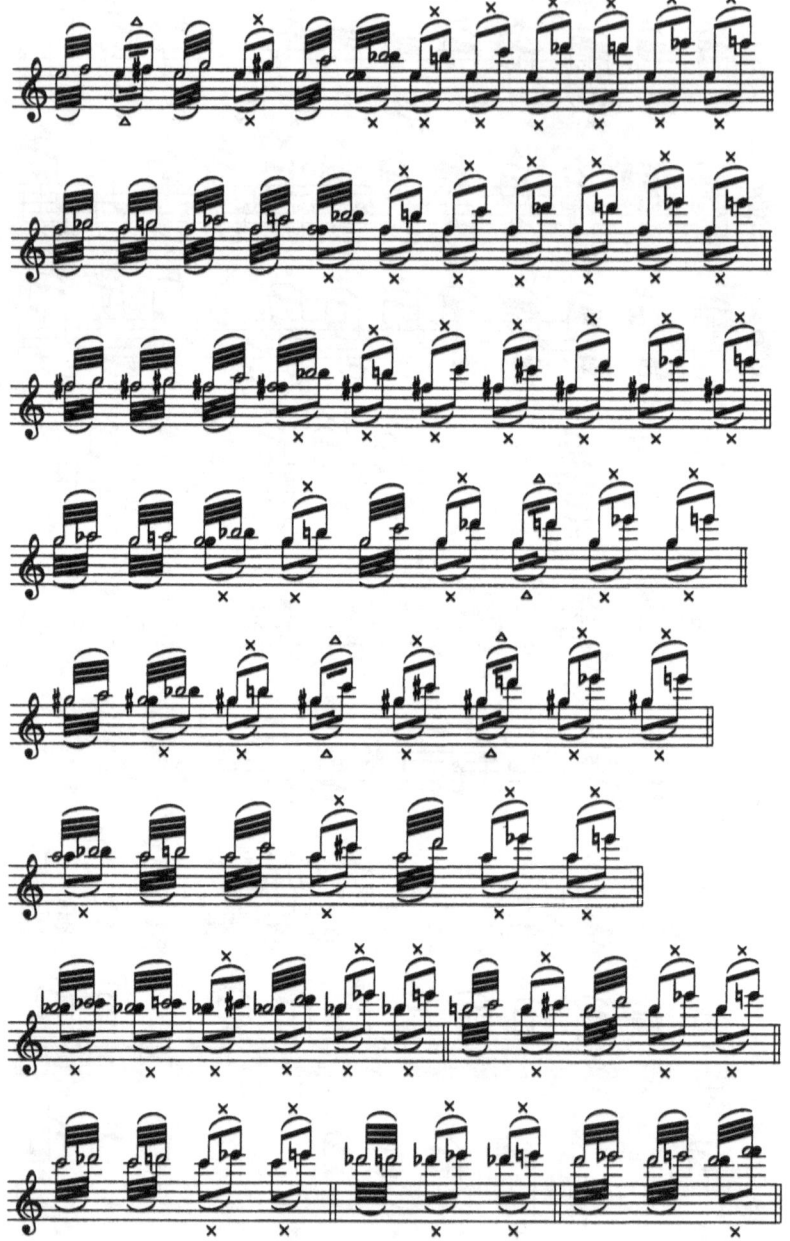

Fig. 1.30. (continued)

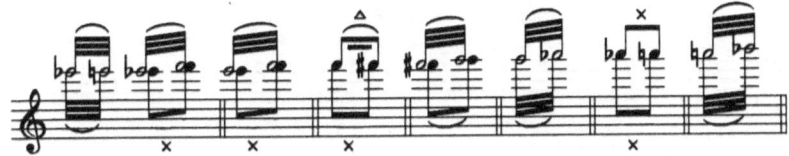

Fig. 1.30. (continued)

In figure 1.30 *d-kan* (1.8): pairs of notes with upward stems apply to seven-holed *shakuhachi*, while pairs of notes with downward stems apply to five-holed *shakuhachi*.

b) **Special fingering techniques**

1. ***Koro-koro:*** a trill with special fingering only for the two pairs of pitches indicated in figure 1.31a. The dynamic for *koro-koro* is from **pp** to **mp**. The fingering for *koro-koro* differs from that of a tremolo between the same pitches (c^2 and d^2); their timbres and frequencies slightly differ. This technique can be indicated with the symbol ⨍, but "⊐ ⊓ ⊐ ⊓" or "*korokoro*" must always be written above the notes. In the following figure, the second pitch d^2 and the fourth pitch $d^{\#2}$ pass by ever so faintly. If *korokoro* is played slowly, these two pitches are heard as c^2 and d^2, respectively.

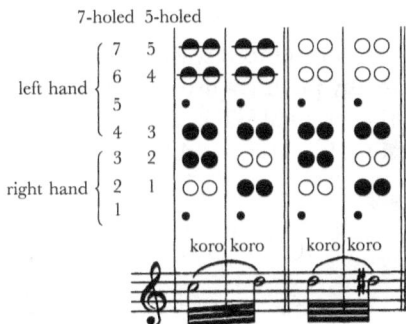

Fig. 1.31. Examples of special fingering techniques. (1) *Korokoro*

2. ***Kara-kara:*** a trill executed by rapidly tapping the first hole of a five-holed *shakuhachi* (or the second hole on a seven-holed *shakuhachi*) while performing a glissando between $b^{\flat 2}$ and $d^{\flat 2}$ (or d^2) in the *kan* range. C^2 is the loudest of the pitches, but this technique cannot be performed at ⨍⨍ on any of the pitches. The performable range for *kara-kara* is

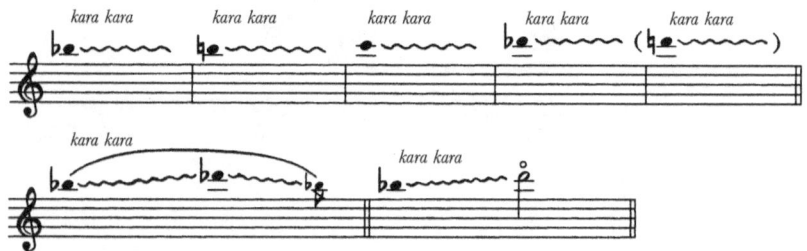

Fig. 1.31. Examples of special fingering techniques. (2) *Karakara*

3. Suri: a portamento produced by slowly covering or uncovering a hole while sliding to the next pitch. It is easier to execute when moving to a higher pitch rather than a lower one. It is often used with the pitches shown in figure 1.31.3.

Fig. 1.31. Examples of special fingering techniques. (3) *Suri*

4. Nayashi: a portamento produced with the fingers, the chin, and the lips, which may be applied to any pitch (figure 1.31.4). A sustained note is lowered, and then returned to the original pitch. Several *nayashi* gestures may be performed in rapid succession. It is also possible to raise a pitch and then return to the original pitch.

Fig. 1.31. Examples of special fingering techniques. (4) *Nayashi*

5. Take-yuri: vibrato produced by moving the instrument in a circular manner (figure 1.31.5).

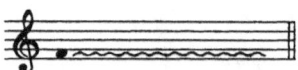

Fig. 1.31. Examples of special fingering techniques. (5) *Takeyuri*

6. **Kobushi:** a characteristic ornament in Japanese music. Well-known in folk and popular *enka* songs, this technique is also well suited for classic *honkyoku*,[18] but it is difficult to notate in Western notation. If a composer desires for a particular passage to be ornamented with *kobushi*, yet is unable to find a suitable notation, adding the indication "*kobushi*" above the appropriate place in the passage may be practical. The composer must then rely upon the performer's sensibilities, which can be problematic. It may be best for the composer to provide a detailed pattern that will serve as a model. There are many ways of playing that make partial use of *kobushi*-style ornamentation. Figure 1.31.6 illustrates a few of these.

Fig. 1.31. Examples of special fingering techniques. (6) *Kobushi*, excerpt from Minoru Miki's *Sonnet I*

7. **Yuru:** a covered hole is momentarily opened and immediately closed (figure 1.31.7). This technique is also called *ren-on* and can be applied to any of the basic pitches.

Fig. 1.31. Examples of special fingering techniques. (7) *Yuru*

8. **Utsu (Uru)**: an open hole is momentarily closed and immediately opened (figure 1.31.8). Most commonly used with the first and second holes (or the second and third on the seven-holed *shakuhachi*).

Fig. 1.31. Examples of special fingering techniques. (8) *Utsu (uru)*

9. **Techniques used in *shakuhachi honkyoku*** (figure 1.31.9)

Fig. 1.31. Examples of special fingering techniques. (9) Excerpt from the classic *honkyoku Shika-no-tonne* ("Cry of the Distant Deer")

10. **A common *honkyoku* pattern** (figure 1.31.10)

Fig. 1.31. Examples of special fingering techniques. (10) A common pattern found in *honkyoku*

11 and 12. Techniques that make use of the seven-holed *shakuhachi* (figures 1.31.11/12)

Fig. 1.31. Examples of special fingering techniques. (11) An excerpt from Minoru Miki's *Ruika*

Fig. 1.31. Examples of special fingering techniques. (12) An excerpt from Minoru Miki's *Autumn Fantasy*

13. Multiphonics: an extended technique developed in contemporary music for Western wind instruments, which soon appeared with great frequency in new compositions for the *shakuhachi*. I have indicated some of the most common multiphonics in the diagram, but the intonation is very unstable (figure 1.31.13).

Multiphonics are best used for effects. Pairs of notes indicated with a star symbol can only be produced with a seven-holed *shakuhachi*. All the other pairs of notes can also be produced on a five-holed *shakuhachi*.

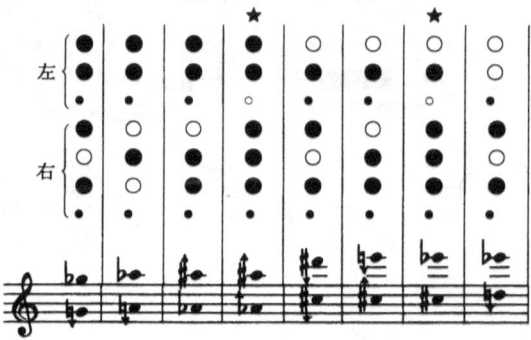

Fig. 1.31. Examples of special fingering techniques. (13) Multiphonics

As with transverse flutes, when asking a *shakuhachi* player to incorporate extended Western wind techniques, the composer should consult with the performer. Since the body and holes of the *shakuhachi* are relatively large, fingering techniques that allow the sound of the striking of the holes to be heard are effective, and can create a humorous effect.

1–5: *Hichiriki*

(1) Construction

The *hichiriki* (figure 1.32), introduced to Japan at the end of the seventh century or the beginning of the eighth century, is an instrument of the *gagaku* ensemble. Originating in Western Asia, it is part of the same family as the Chinese *kanshi* (*guanzi*, also known as *bili*) and the Korean *piri*. In the early Heian period (794–1185), the *hichiriki* used in *tōgaku*, or "music of the left," began to be used in *komagaku*,[19] or "music of the right," and the *dai-hichiriki* (large *hichiriki*) in use at that time was eliminated. The main body of the *hichiriki* is six *sun* (18.2 cm) in length. The part nearest the Chinese bamboo root reed is the head, and the part furthest from the bamboo node is the tail. It has seven holes on the front and two on the back; the area between these nine holes is wrapped with birch or cherry or wisteria bark, and is coated with lacquer.

WIND INSTRUMENTS 55

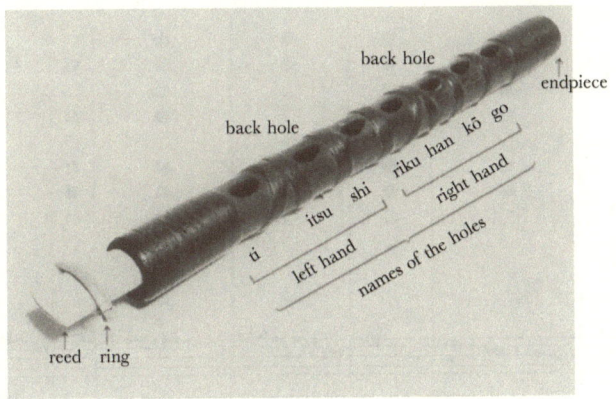

Fig. 1.32. The *Hichiriki*

The *hichiriki*, like the oboe, is a double-reed instrument with the reed made from *ashi*, or mountain bitter bamboo. This reed, the *rozetsu*, more commonly referred to as *shita*, is set in the head of the instrument and secured by a ring (*seme*) made from a folded strip of wisteria bark. The names for each of the nine holes are given in figure 1.33.

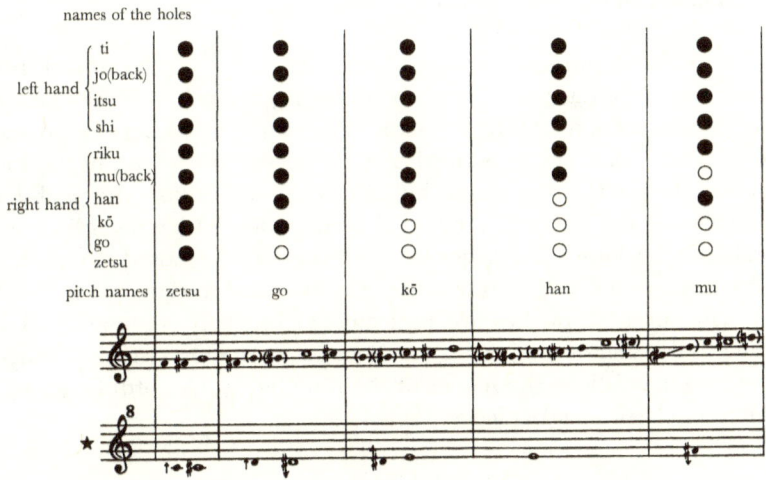

Fig. 1.33. The names of the *hichiriki* holes

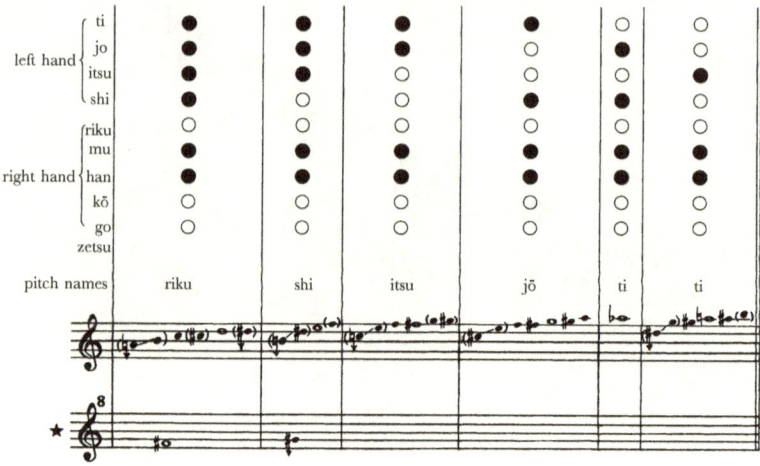

Fig. 1.33. (continued)

The staff marked with a star symbol indicates notes that are produced by blowing when the reed is completely inserted into the performer's mouth. Though piercing, the white notes are stable. Because they are overtones, they are indicated by the symbol 𝄞.

(2) Basic Scales, Derived Pitches, and Fingerings

Using the fingering indicated on the chart, the pitches produced with normal breathing are written as white notes in figure 1.33. These basic pitches of the *hichiriki* are very resonant. Using the same fingering, derived pitches, or *enbai-on*, written as black notes, are produced by holding the reed deep in the mouth, which raises the pitch; if the reed is held in a shallow position, the pitch lowers. Pitch can also be altered by differences in lip pressure. With weaker lip pressure, the pitch can be lowered a major second, but can be raised a minor sixth. Naturally, microtonal pitch inflections can be produced between the basic pitches. The unstable pitches are indicated in brackets, although this varies according to the skill of the performer. There is a notation system for fingering called *te-tsuke* that follows the names of the nine holes. The fifth fingering, *mu*, is not used in classic *gagaku* pieces.

(3) Range and Timbre

The one-octave plus pitch range of the *hichiriki* is extremely narrow, and consequently the tone color is uniform. Naturally, as the pitch is raised, tension increases, resulting is a strained tone. While it depends on the fingering, the pitches f^1, $g^{\sharp 1}$, $e^{\flat 2}$, and f^2 are approached by lowering a higher pitch through embouchure manipulation, rendering the tone quality bad and the intonation poor. The pitch b^2 is outside of the normal range; in order to articulate this note it is necessary to control the reed with the tongue.

(4) Performance Techniques

a) Breathing, reed manipulation, and *enbai*

To play the *hichiriki* properly, the quality of the reed is very important as it directly affects the tone color, the ease of blowing, and the stability: no two reeds are the same. Even for advanced performers, there are times when breath leakage is apparent.

As mentioned above, when the instrument is pushed forward with the reed held in a shallow position, the lowered ornamental inflections added to the melody are called *enbai*. Following are four examples of performance techniques on the *hichiriki*. In figure 1.34, I have given a few phrases that include traditional *enbai* patterns starting on the basic scale tones. The last two phrases are examples starting on the already lowered pitches (characters written in circles), with the reed held in a shallow position at the beginning.

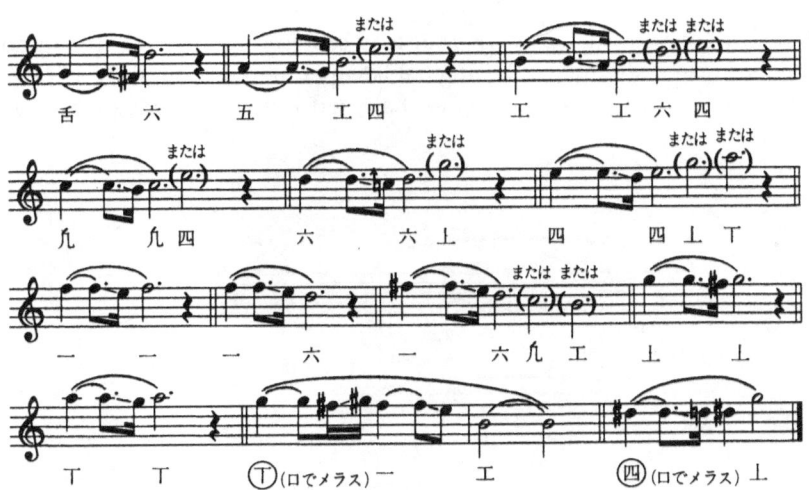

Fig. 1.34. Phrases with traditional *enbai* patterns

Figure 1.35 is the beginning section of *hyōjō-chōshi*.

Fig. 1.35. Beginning section of *hyōjō-chōshi*

Figure 1.36 is an excerpt from *Etenraku*.

Fig. 1.36. An excerpt from *Etenraku*

In the two excerpts in figure 1.37, instead of lowering the pitch, the opposite technique is used, with the reed being held deeper in the mouth to raise the pitch (*karu*). The *katakana* written below the characters is the *hichiriki* solmization.

Fig. 1.37. An example of raised *enbai* on the *hichiriki*

b) Dynamics

When playing the basic scale of the *hichiriki*, a strong, piercing sound is produced. In *gagaku*, the *hichiriki* plays the core melody at all times, the purpose being to lead the ensemble through the heterophonic textures. Even when relaxing lip pressure, with an increase in breath volume and pressure, the sound level will remain unchanged and *forte* can be produced, in spite of the tendency for the sound to weaken. With descending inflections, the volume decreases, and when returning to the original pitch there will be a crescendo. A distinct feature of Japanese wind instruments is the wide dynamic range of the melodic lines, but the volume of the *hichiriki* is truly remarkable. To maintain *pp* requires an extremely skilled performer.

c) Special techniques

1. **Yuri (*yuri-fuki*)**: descending from and returning to a pitch repeatedly is one type of vibrato used in the lower range and used in genres such as *kagura-uta*, *saibara*, and *rōei*. The *hichiriki* plays with the vocal melody, twice for *yōyū* and three times for *iri-bushi*. In modern works, however, there is no restriction on the number of inflections; *yuri* can be indicated in scores by the following symbol: •〜〜. In classical works the finger is never used for vibrato.

2. **Flutter-tongue**: Compared with the transverse flutes or *shakuhachi*, it is difficult to fluttertongue on double-reed instruments. It can be used, however, as an ornament with shorter notes.

3. **Complete reed insertion**: When blowing with the reed completely inserted in the mouth, a strident sound exceeding the normal range is produced. Of course, it is unreasonable to use this in a melodic piece, but it is useful as a sound effect.

(5) Fingering Techniques

The half-hole fingerings so important for the transverse flutes and *shakuhachi* are not used on the *hichiriki*. As mentioned in the paragraph on blowing technique, basic intonation is controlled by reed embouchure. To produce nuances, however, there are special fingering techniques which will be discussed below.

a) Tremolo

The tremolo is not a traditional *hichiriki* technique; however, since tremolos are not impossible, I have indicated them in figure 1.38. It is important to realize that the intonation for tremolos is approximate. The white notes are possible, while the notes indicated by a triangle are difficult. Even if they are impossible to perform as a tremolo, notes that can shift smoothly within a melodic line are indicated with a slur. The stems marked with an X indicate notes with notably poor intonation. Pairs of notes notated in the following manner ♬ indicate that a tremolo is possible when changing fingering.

Fig. 1.38. Tremolo techniques for the *hichiriki*. (a)

e^{b2} is an extremely unstable note, but with new fingerings, it has become possible (figure 1.38b).

Fig. 1.38. Tremolo techniques for the *hichiriki*. (b)

The examples in 1.38c indicated by △ are possible due to new fingerings, but intonation is unreliable.

Fig. 1.38. Tremolo techniques for the *hichiriki*. (c)

In figure 1.38d are possible pitches for tremolos produced by completely inserting the reed into the mouth, including those that require unconventional fingering.

Fig. 1.38. Tremolo techniques for the *hichiriki*. (d)

Above this range, 8va overtones are produced as shown in figure 1.38e.

Fig. 1.38. Tremolo techniques for the *hichiriki*. (e)

b) Miscellaneous techniques and melodic patterns

The upper rear soundhole, *jō*, is controlled by a peculiar technique in which the thumb of the left hand rolls. The first two examples in figure 1.39 are excerpts that correspond to the mnemonic *e-i-ra*. The last three examples illustrate melodic patterns that correspond to the mnemonic *u-ru*, and show the technique of jumping up to a higher pitch by rotating the body of the instrument from below.

Fig. 1.39. Musical excerpts that correspond to the mnemonic *e-i-ra*

1–6: *Shō*

(1) Construction

While many Japanese instruments have their origins in West Asia, the *shō* (figures 1.40 and 1.41) is believed to have originated in Southeast Asia, specifically Indochina. It is said that the *shō* was introduced to China, where is was modified, and then imported to Japan in the eighth century with *gagaku*. An instrument called the *u*, a larger and lower pitched *shō*, came to Japan at the same time, yet disappeared along with the *dai-hichiriki* (large *hichiriki*) during the ninth-century period of musical reformation. Presently, only a small number of *u* survive. The *shō*, however, has gone through a unique structural remodeling in Japan, and also has a unique playing technique not found in the *shō* of China or Southeast Asia. These structural innovations and techniques will be discussed below.

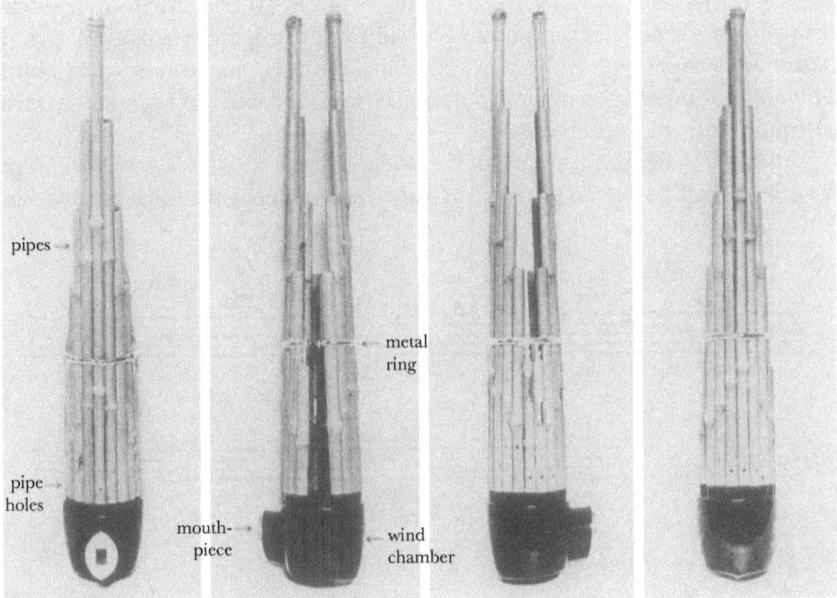

Fig. 1.40. The *shō* from many angles

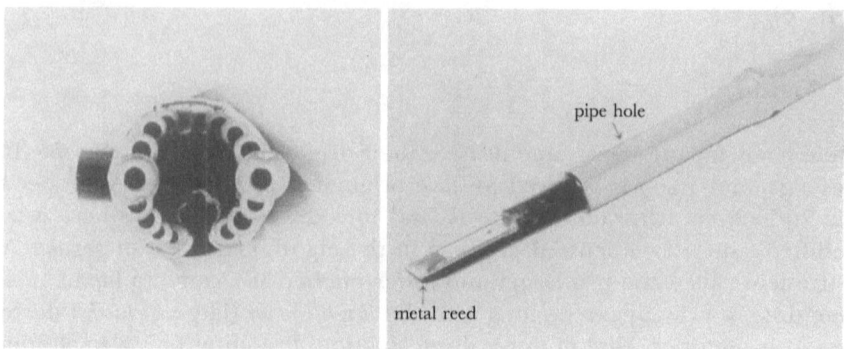

Fig. 1.41. The *shō* seen from above

The pipes of the *shō* are made of thin bamboo tubes of equal thickness. The seventeen pipes are of different lengths, and each pipe has a different pitch except for two pipes that are mute. The upper end of each pipe, known as *take*, is closed at the node, below which there is a rectangular hole. A metal reed is attached to a wooden pipe connected to the bottom of each bamboo pipe. When this reed vibrates, the air between the reed and the node resonates and produces sound. Each pipe has a small finger hole immediately above the reed and only pipes with holes covered emit sound. Uncovered holes are mute.

The ends of these seventeen pipes are set in a circular wind chamber, with a mouthpiece known as the *kashira*.

As illustrated in figure 1.42, each of the seventeen pipes has its own name and produces a fixed pitch. As the two pipes *ya* and *mo* do not have reeds, they produce no sound.

Fig. 1.42. The 17 *shō* pipes, their names, and their fixed pitches

As shown in figure 1.43, specific fingers are assigned to cover each hole. In the notation example, black notes represent the left fingers while white notes represent the right fingers. As can be seen in the figure below the notation example, *hi* (c^3) is covered with the back of the right index finger.

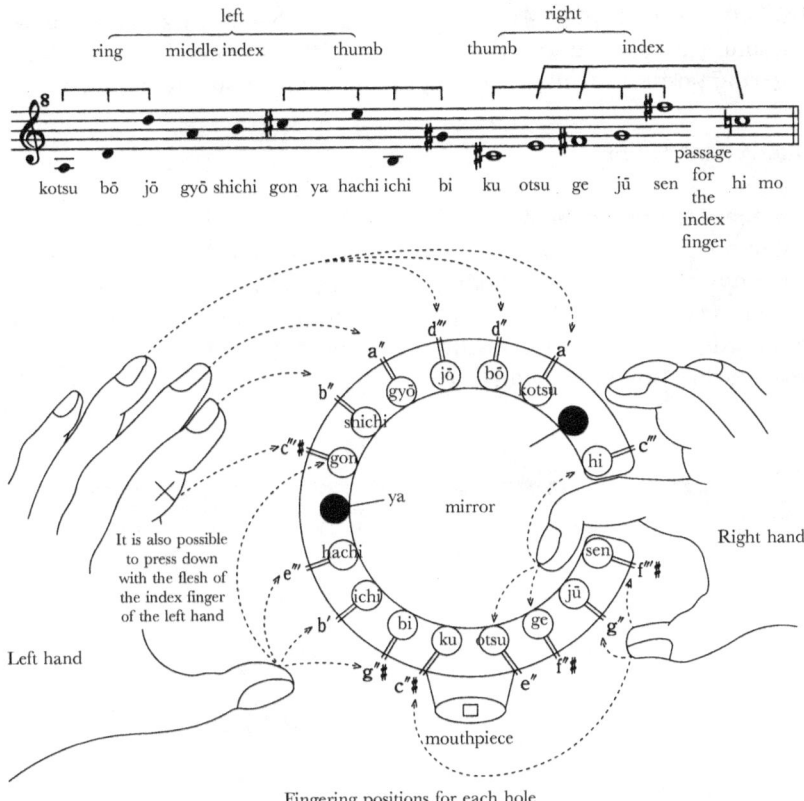

Fig. 1.43. The 17 *shō* pipes, in order based on fingerings

Figure 1.44 illustrates the notes that cannot be produced simultaneously due to the fingering rules. The right index finger, however, can cover both *otsu* (e²) and *ge* (f#²) simultaneously.

Fig. 1.44. Notes that can not be produced simultaneously due to fingering rules

(2) Basic Scales and Fingering

The range of the *shō* is limited (only producing the fifteen tones shown in figure 1.42), and the volume of a single pipe is weak; however, chords with a maximum of six pitches (called *aitake*) can also be produced that have expressive power. Of greater musical significance is the remarkable effect created by the gradual shift of fingering positions (called *te-utsuri*) as one chord flows into another.

(3) Range and Timbre

The fifteen tones of the *shō* share uniform tone colors and characteristics. When played in the *gagaku* ensemble, the lowest pitch of each chord is considered the fundamental tone, and the melody of the *ryūteki* and *hichiriki* proceed in a heterophonic texture with these fundamental tones. Figure 1.45 illustrates the *aitake* chords of the *shō* used in the *gagaku* ensemble, the black note in each chord indicates the fundamental tone.

Fig. 1.45. *Aitake* chords of the *shō* (11 chords used in classic *gagaku*)

(4) Performance Techniques

a) Breathing
The *shō* resembles the harmonica in that inhalation and exhalation, known as *kigae*, are used in alternation during performance. The placement of the breath change is an important element of the instrument's musical expression. With the *te-utsuri* techniques to be discussed later, breath change represents a major characteristic of *shō* playing. In *gagaku*, it is common to play one or two measures of a slow, four-beat passage in one breath, during which one to three *aitake* chords are played.

Sound cannot be produced when the reed is moist, and performers must occasionally dry the area where the reeds are attached. In the past, performers warmed the instrument over a *hibachi* that was placed by their side to dry it; today, however, an electric heater is used. This peculiarity is why the *shō* is not continuously played during a performance. In classical *aitake* performance, the *shō* is able to produce sound continuously for approximately thirty minutes, twenty minutes for contemporary pieces, and from ten to fifteen minutes in *ippon-buki*, or monophonic performance.

b) Dynamic expression
In the classic *gagaku* repertoire, the one-breath *aitake* phrase begins *p*, gradually increases in volume, and then diminishes with the onset of the *te-utsuri*

(fingering change). The beginning of the next phrase, marked by the change of breath, begins at *p* again; this pattern repeats throughout the piece. When composing a new piece, regardless of whether writing in the monophonic *ippon-buki* style or combining it with chords of from two to six tones, it is desirable to enhance expressivity by using these dynamics,

The quick diminishing of volume from *ff* or *f* is also effective (see figure 1.46). As already pointed out, single notes and dyads on the *shō* are weak in volume, thereby making it difficult to be heard in a large ensemble. Dynamic change only occurs with *aitake* chordal playing.

Fig.1.46. An example of a quick diminishing of *shō* volume

c) Special techniques for contemporary pieces

1. Flutter-tongue: This technique can be used in monophonic and chordal playing.

2. Staccato: see above

3. Double and triple tonguing: see above

(5) Fingering Techniques

It is said that the placement of each pipe of the *shō* was determined by visual aesthetics. As shown in figure 1.43, there is no logic in the arrangement of the tones to which the fingers are assigned. Therefore, outside of *aitake* chord performance, composers should confirm the feasibility of fingering by examining the arrangement of the instrument. There is a rule that the left index finger covers *shichi* (b^2), and that the left middle finger covers *gyō* (a^2). These two tones are always added in classical *aitake* playing. By placing those fingers on the designated holes, the instrument can be securely held, making it easier to play.

As an example of monophonic and diaphonic performance techniques, or ways of playing in the classical style other than the *aitake* chords, figure 1.47 illustrates the *shō* part of the *ichikotsu-chō* mode *netori*.

Fig. 1.47. An example of monophonic and diaphonic performance techniques in an excerpt from the *netori* of *ichikotsu-chō*

a) *Te-utsuri* (fingering change)

The most characteristic fingering technique found in the classical *gagaku* repertoire is the *te-utsuri* that occurs when one chord changes to another. As shown in figure 1.48, the performers move their fingers one by one to the next position just before exhaling and produce subtle tonal nuances.

Fig. 1.48. An example of *te-utsuri* (fingering change), excerpt from *Etenraku*

The *shō* introduced from China originally had a long, thin, beak-like curved tube that fit into the mouthpiece, a feature still seen in the contemporary Chinese *sheng*. The remodeling of the instrument and the performance techniques were completed in Japan by the mid-Heian (794–1185) period. Holding the instrument upright in front of the player's face and keeping the lips on the short mouthpiece reduces the technical capabilities of the *shō*. Nevertheless, the Japanese *shō* has achieved an artistic subtlety not found in other countries with the development of the *te-utsuri* and breath-change techniques.

It is difficult to express *te-utsuri* in Western staff notation. The performer, however, will naturally execute the fingering and breath changes if the composer writes the names of the *aitake* chords each time the harmony changes. The player should also be able to perform simplified progressions as shown in figure 1.49.

Fig. 1.49. Simplified *te-utsuri* notation

b) New techniques

Since the arrangement of the *shō* pipes and fingerings is irregular, the composer should avoid scalar passages, vibrato, or sudden jumps. While not impossible, their effect is nevertheless dubious. As new musical ideas and instrumentation require techniques not used in classical pieces, I have provided examples of experimental fingerings used in contemporary pieces.

    a. Cover *gon* ($c^{\#3}$) with the pad of the left index finger instead of the left thumb.

    b. Cover *jo* (d^3), *bō* (d^2), and *kotsu* (a^2)—usually assigned to the third finger of the left hand—by rotating the right third finger around the back of the instrument.

For other techniques not found in classical performance, the composer should study figure 1.43 and the *shō* fingering chart, and should also show the score to the performer and confirm its playability. Figure 1.50 shows three fragments from my compositions. It turned out that excerpts 2 and 3 were difficult to play at the designated tempo.

Fig. 1.50. Excerpt from Minoru Miki's *Yui I*

If the two mute pipes, *mo* and *ya*, are given reeds, or if the visual aesthetics are discarded and the placement of the pipes and pitches changed, a new *shō* can be created with a completely different image. Doubtless, this has already been attempted. I believe the *shō* would be more widely used if someone created a *shō* with the same pipe arrangement as, but pitched a minor second higher than, the present *shō*. Whether new techniques that combine the subtleties of Japanese *shō* techniques with the technical facility of the Chinese *sheng* should be pursued in the upcoming age of Asian cooperation, attempts to modify the Japanese *shō* should be avoided.

The ancient *u*, several of which survive, has a range one octave lower than that of the *shō*, but the disposition of the pipes is the same.

Chapter Two

String Instruments (Lutes)

When classifying string instruments in the West and in Asian countries other than Japan, the norm is to divide them into bowed instruments and plucked instruments. In this book, I have classified string instruments into the lute family and zither family.[1] This chapter deals with the lute family.

With lutes, it is necessary to indicate the string number, which left-hand fingers to use, and the fret number (particularly on the *biwa*). Therefore, in this book, I have adopted the most common method: Roman numerals indicate the string number, Arabic numbers indicate the fingering of the left hand, and encircled Arabic numbers indicate the fret number. The fingers of the left hand are assigned the following numbers following Western string-instrument practice: the index finger is 1; the middle finger is 2; the ring finger is 3; and the little finger is 4. Following Japanese tradition, from lowest to highest, string numbers are indicated by I, II, and III, in contrast to the Chinese and Western systems where I, II, and III are used to number strings from highest to lowest.

While the term *kaihō-gen* is commonly used in Japanese to refer to the open strings—the playing of a string without the left hand pressing any position—the correct term, however, should be *kaihō-gen-on*. In this book, I use the term *kaihō-on*, or "open sound."

Japanese lutes include the *biwa*, the *shamisen*, and the *kokyū*.

2–1: *Biwa*

The Persian *ud* developed into the *pipa* in T'ang China, which was the first *biwa* imported to Japan in the seventh and eighth centuries CE as part of the *tōgaku* ensemble, and is known as the *gaku-biwa*. At the same time, another *biwa*, the *mōsō-biwa* (or *kōjin-biwa*) absorbed the performance techniques of the *vīnā*, an instrument that entered India from Western Asia, and was adapted for use in Buddhist ceremonies before being transmitted to Kyushu via China.

From these two musical currents, the *Heike-biwa*—and its music, *Heikyoku*—arose in the twelfth century, the *Satsuma-biwa* in the sixteenth century, and in the nineteenth century, *Chikuzen-biwa* appeared as instruments to accompany song and narrative. All are depicted in figure 2.1. Each of these schools preserves their traditions to the present day. As the purpose of this book is to describe Japanese instruments rather than classify them, I will mention differences between the different *biwa* only when necessary.

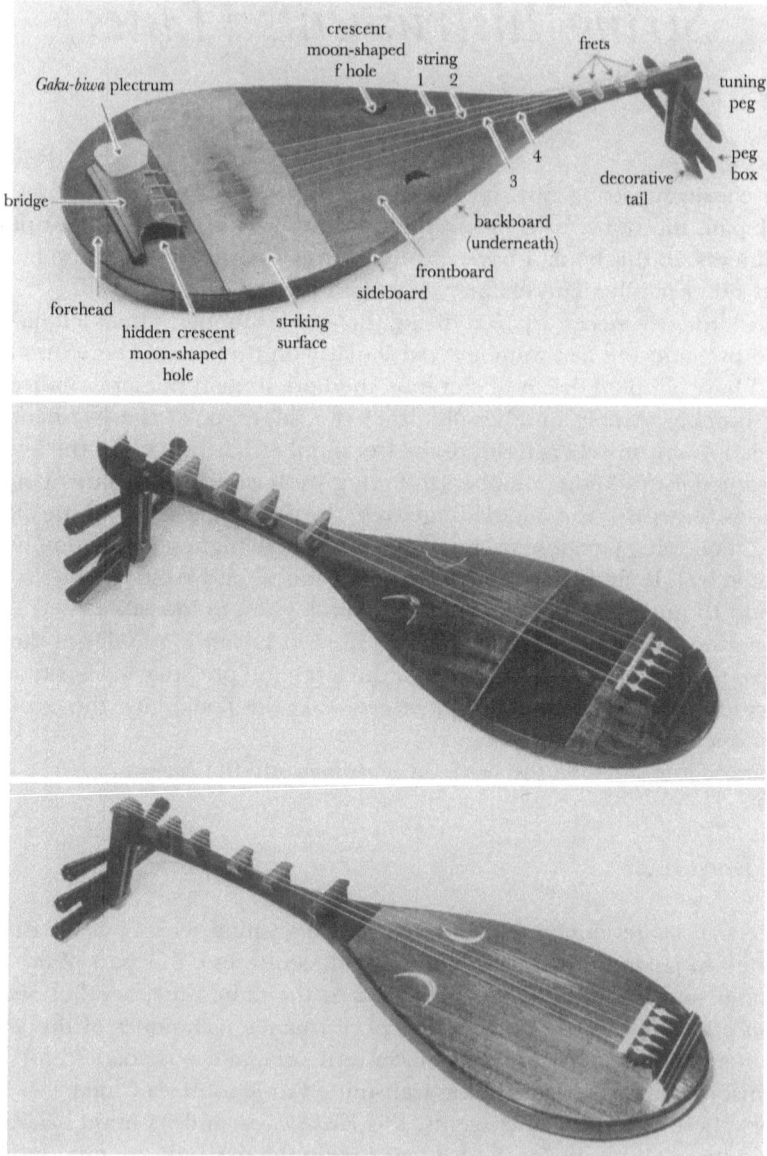

Fig. 2.1. *Gaku-biwa* (top), *Satsuma-biwa* (middle), *Chikuzen-biwa* (bottom)

(1) Construction

The body for the various types of *biwa* mentioned above is almost identical. As shown in figure 2.1, it is pear-shaped with four or five frets on the neck. The neck is topped by a peg-box set at a 90-degree angle; the end of the peg-box is shaped as a decorative tail.

a) Body

The body of the *biwa* is made from a backboard and a frontboard. Traditionally, the backboard—which faces the player's body when performing—is made from quince, red sandalwood, or mulberry, although there are now backboards made from cherry, zelkova, and magnolia. The front of the instrument can be struck with a plectrum, and the sound resonates between the backboard and frontboard of the instrument. The material of the frontboard plays an important role in determining the sound quality; the frontboard of the *gaku-biwa* is made from chestnut, the *Satsuma-biwa* is made from hard mulberry, and the *Chikuzen-biwa* is made from soft paulownia. The front of the *biwa* is flat, except for the *Satsuma-biwa* which is convex. All *biwa* have two crescent moon-shaped holes near the top of the frontboard, similar to the f-hole on a violin. There is also a hole hidden underneath the lower bridge where the strings are tied. *Biwa* come in many different sizes.

Fig. 2.2. *Satsuma-biwa* (left) and *Chikuzen-biwa* (right) viewed vertically from above

b) Frets

Biwa frets are called *chū* and are made from magnolia. The frets of *chikuzen-biwa*, however, are made of the same material as the backboard; the tops of the frets, however, are covered with bamboo. Similar to the Chinese *pipa*, the frets of the *gaku-biwa* are low and close to the body of the instrument. Pitches on the *gaku-biwa* are created by pressing the strings directly over the frets. The frets of the Indian-influenced *mōsō-biwa*, however, are considerably higher above the body, and by pushing the string between the frets, it is possible to raise the pitch as much as a perfect fourth as well as produce subtle pitch inflections. The strength needed to raise the pitch a perfect fourth is such that the space between the frets needs to be wide. Unlike frets for the lute, guitar, or contemporary Chinese *pipa*, frets on the *biwa* are not arranged in half-steps. I discuss below the interval arrangement for *biwa* with four frets; however, most contemporary *biwa* used in ensembles have five frets.

The frets are also thick, sometimes more than one centimeter, which helps create the unique *sawari*[2] of the *biwa*. Figure 2.3—which is exaggerated and distorted in order to illustrate my point—shows the relation of the strings with the frets. *Sawari* is created by pushing and plucking the string at the point marked ↓. The drone is created by the vibration of the string over the bridge under A and B. Along with the pitch created between points A and C, there is a secondary higher pitch resonating between points B and C. These two pitches combine to create *sawari*.

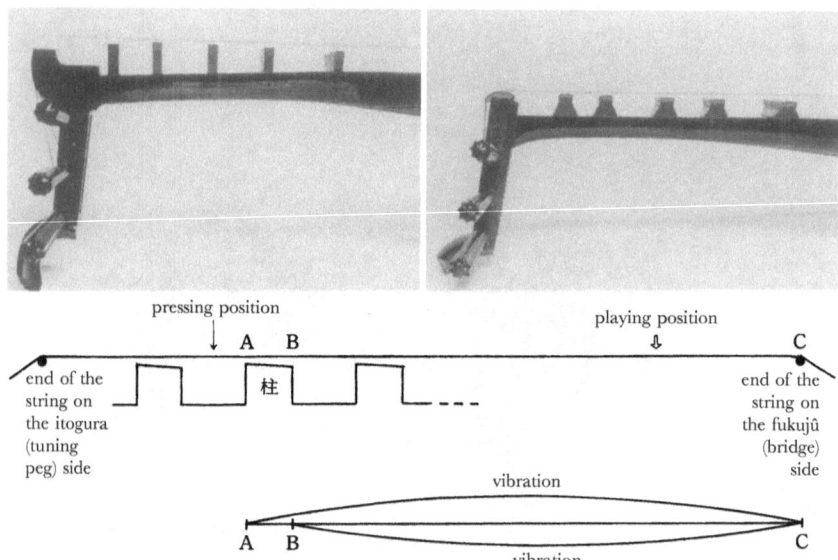

Fig. 2.3. Frets of the *Satsuma-biwa* (left) and *Chikuzen-biwa* (right). The relationship between the strings and frets (illustrated expression)

c) Strings

All *biwa* have four strings of twisted silk; however, the modern *Satsuma-biwa* and *Chikuzen-biwa* generally use five strings in concert settings. The first string is the thickest (on *Chikuzen-biwa* the second string is the thickest), and the strings are progressively thinner towards the fourth string. The fourth and the fifth strings are the same thickness and are always played simultaneously.

There are two important points to be made about the pitches on the *biwa*. First, if the strings should brush the top of the frets, this is not considered problematic; however, in order to produce *sawari*, the length of string that passes over the frets must be more than one centimeter. The pitch produced when the performer presses with the same strength will be higher on the thicker strings that the thinner strings. Second, compared to the *shamisen*, the pitch of the open strings on the *biwa* is unstable because the strength required to press down on the strings exerts great pressure on the tuning pegs. Outstanding *biwa* performers have contrived various ways to solve these problems. Since the construction of the *biwa* is responsible for *sawari*, it is necessary to accept this instability and embrace it as an element that gives the *biwa* its unique timbre.

d) Plectrum

As illustrated in the previous figure, *biwa* plectra come in a wide variety of shapes and sizes. While it is said that boxwood is the best material for plectra, *Chikuzen-biwa* plectra use ebony for the shaft and boxwood or ivory for the edge of the plectrum. *Gaku-biwa* plectra are small and thin; the *Heike-biwa* and *mōsō-biwa* are slightly larger. The playing edge (*hiraki*) of the *Satsuma-biwa* plectrum is sometimes over 30 centimeters in width, which requires different playing techniques. The plectrum for the four-string *Chikuzen-biwa* is about 12 centimeters wide, and resembles the *shamisen* plectrum. The five-string *Chikuzen-biwa* plectrum is about 15 centimeters long; however, the shape is very different from *shamisen* plectra.

(2) Range, Tuning, and Intonation

The range of a string instrument is determined by the length, the thickness, and the tension of the strings. *Biwa* are no exception, and can be classified into two main categories: high-pitched instruments and low-pitched instruments. This distinction depends on the size of the instrument, which, of course, determines the length of the strings, which, in turn, prescribes the range.

Traditionally, women performed *Satsuma-biwa* and men played *Chikuzen-biwa*. In contrast to other Asian countries and the West, the vocal range of female narrators in traditional Japanese music is extremely low. The basic tuning for the *biwa* used to accompany narrative can be adjusted by a third or a fourth, but never an octave. While this principle should not extend to performances of instrumental music, *biwa* performers nonetheless use instruments that correspond to their vocal range. Composers should consult with the performer and determine the range of the instrument before beginning to write for the *biwa*.

a) The range of each *biwa*

Figure 2.4 illustrates the range of each *biwa*. The white notes represent the readily available range in terms of the string tension, while the black notes indicate the extreme limits of the range. *Biwa* music can be written in either bass and treble clef (with the corresponding octave designation); in general, however, I recommend the latter.[3]

Fig. 2.4. Range of each *biwa*

The question as to whether or not a score should be written at the actual sounding pitch or transposed is, of course, a source of continual debate. I believe that for an ensemble work, the composer should indicate the actual sounding pitch (or its octave transposition). When making the parts, however, the composer should use notation to which the performer is accustomed, whether it be transposed, based on numbers, or tablature. This is the best way to ensure that the performer is not inconvenienced.

Example 2.4 indicates the normal range for each of the open strings; however, this can change according to the type of string.

b) Tunings

There are many tunings for the *biwa* and figure 2.5 shows several tunings for each type of *biwa*. While there are traditional tunings for the *gaku-biwa*, the *mōsō-biwa*, and the *Heike-biwa*, there are also experimental tunings for the *Satsuma-biwa* and *Chikuzen-biwa* that were developed for use in contemporary compositions. I have given a few examples of these new tunings below. It is safe, however, to consider the tuning c′–g–c′–c′–g′–g′ as a standard for ensemble pieces, as indicated with a ★ mark.

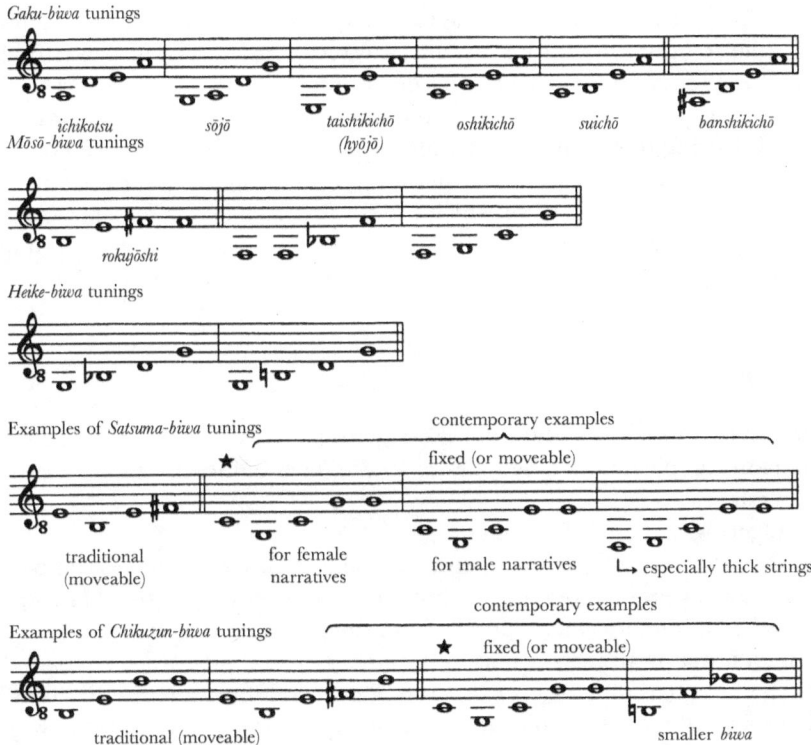

Fig. 2.5. Tunings for many *biwa*

Usually, the first and third strings are tuned to the same pitch. The first string of the *Satsuma-biwa* is very thick. Primarily played in open position, it functions as a drone. The second, third, and fourth (and fifth with the five-string *biwa*) are used for melodic passages. As mentioned above, the fourth and fifth strings are also tuned to the same pitch. Both are thin, and appropriate for delicate, expressive musical passages.

The most common tuning found in contemporary pieces is *hon-chōshi*. Ignoring the first string, the second and third strings are a perfect fourth apart, and the fourth—and possible fifth—are tuned to a perfect fifth above the third. Preserving the resonance of traditional *biwa* tunings, the *nakakari-chōshi* tuning is based upon the neutral sound of an augmented fourth. I created this tuning for performers accustomed to traditional fingerings, as it facilitates the creation of contemporary musical intervals on the second string. In 1964, I first used this tuning on the *shamisen* and since then have used it frequently with the *biwa* as well. When using *nakakari-chōshi* tunings with the *biwa*, it is unnecessary for the first and third string to be tuned to the same pitch. Tuning the first to a perfect fourth or fifth against the second string allows for a wide range of musical expression, including for solo performance.

In an ensemble work, it is possible to change the tuning during the performance while temporarily shifting the musical focus to another instrument. The pitches for a re-tuned *biwa* strings will slip, as they have a propensity to return to their original pitches. They require frequent adjustment after they have been changed. During this time, it is difficult for performers to concentrate on their playing. It takes approximately one minute for a string to stabilize after being readjusted. Unlike the *shamisen*, which will be discussed below, *biwa* players have to be careful when adjusting the tuning. In solo *biwa* compositions, it is impossible for performers to change their tuning until the piece is over.

(3) Left-hand Techniques

Rather than discuss the different *biwa* genres or its role as an instrument accompanying narrative, I will describe the possibilities of the *biwa* as an instrument.

a) Fingering and pitch formation

On the *biwa*, the pitch of the open string determines what pitches can be produced by each fret, what pitches can produced by applying pressure between the frets, and what pitches can be produced on the neighboring strings.

As mentioned in the section on frets, pitches on the *gaku-biwa* are created by pressing the strings directly over the frets. Figure 2.6 illustrates the five possible pitches—including the pitch of the open string—for each string in the various tunings. The intervals that can be produced above the open strings are a major second, a minor third, a major third, and a perfect fourth.

STRING INSTRUMENTS (LUTES) 79

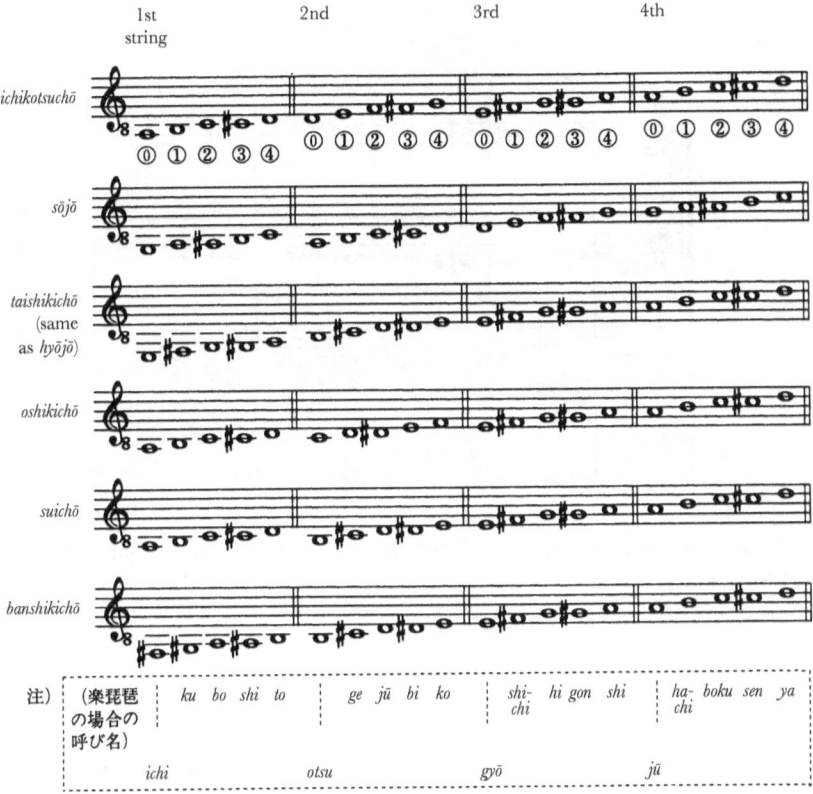

Fig. 2.6. Intervals produced above open strings for various *gaku-biwa* tunings

On the *Satsuma-biwa*, the interval produced by the first fret is slightly wider than a minor second (some schools change the position of the first fret to produce a major second). The second fret is a minor third from the open position, the third fret is a perfect fourth, the fourth fret is a perfect fifth, and the fifth fret is a minor seventh. Using the wide minor second produced by the first fret in an equal-tempered melody requires caution as it can sound unnatural.

On the *Chikuzen-biwa*, the interval produced by the first fret is a major second from the open string. The second fret is slightly higher than a minor third from open position, while the remaining frets are the same as the *Satsuma-biwa*. With the *Chikuzen-biwa*, the position of the second fret—which is based on unequal temperament—is problematic in an equal-tempered melodic passage.

Figure 2.7 shows the pitches that can be produced in a representative tuning for the *Satsuma-biwa*.

Fig. 2.7. Frequently produced pitches produced for the *Satsuma-biwa, oriented for a male voice*

Figure 2.8 illustrates the same for the *Chikuzen-biwa*.

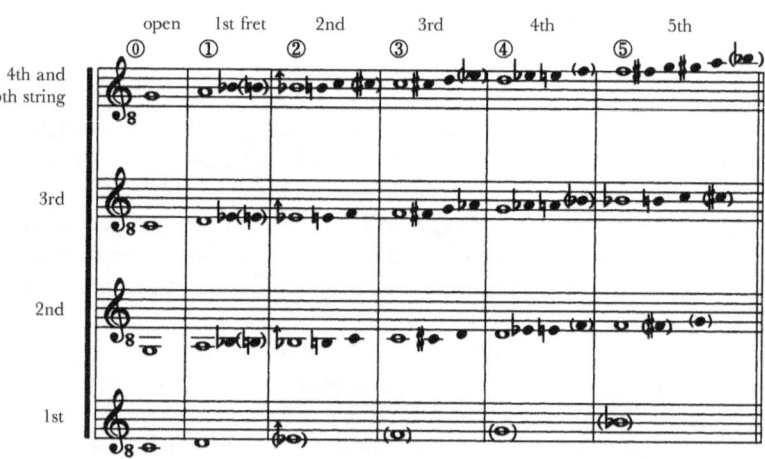

Fig. 2.8. Frequently produced pitches for the *Chikuzen-biwa*

The most important thing to remember for either *biwa* type is that it is impossible to produce an equally tempered half step above the open strings.

The first, second, and third fingers of the left hand are used to press the strings. There are two methods to execute this technique. The first, the standard way of making a musical interval, is to lightly press the strings on or next to the fret (with the *gaku-biwa*, this is the only way to create intervals). Pitches produced in this manner are represented by white note heads in figures 2.7 and 2.8. The second way is to apply pressure and press the strings between the frets, raising the pitch a minor or major second above the open position. One school of *biwa* playing calls this technique *oshikan*. Depending on the fret, it is possible to raise the pitch even higher, from a minor third to a perfect fourth. The timbre, however, becomes quite hard and brittle, and these pitches are difficult to use as musical sounds. These pitches are represented by black note heads in figures 2.7 and 2.8 (the black note heads in parentheses are rarely used). This method of producing pitches does not exist for the Persian *ud*, but developed as a technique in ancient India. With the Japanese *biwa*, the strings are pushed vertically between the frets; however, with the Chinese *pipa* and the Indian *sitar*, the strings are pushed horizontally across the frets rather than towards the neck. Producing pitches wider than a major second above the open strings requires the use of two or three fingers.[4]

b) Large intervallic jumps

Large intervallic jumps are not problematic when leaping from an open string or a pitch produced by a light pressing to another lightly pressed pitch. It is also possible to leap from a strongly pressed position to one more lightly pressed. When jumping to a pitch produced from a strongly pressed position, however, the composer should carefully consider the finger position to ensure the possibility of it being played with correct intonation. When playing a musical passage characterized by wide leaps at a fast tempo, frequent use of open strings in alternation is effective.

c) *Jūon* (multiple stops)[5]

In traditional Japanese string music, the norm for multiple stops is to use one or more open strings with a maximum of two stopped notes. There is never an instance of stopping three notes at the same time with the left hand. Because the use of open strings in multiple stops weakens the harmonic implications, a percussive element is introduced into the music for plucked lutes. Various intervals can be produced on the *biwa* by pressing the fourth and fifth string, and dyads can be easily created by adding the open third string, or triads by adding the open second and third strings. Finally, the first string can be added to produce rich and resonant four-note chords. It is important to remember that as the number of notes increases, there is a corresponding increase in the volume according to how the plectrum is used. Of course, it is possible to create chords by simultaneously pressing two or three strings. Unlike guitarists or violinists, however, *biwa* players are unaccustomed to playing consecutive chords that require multiple altered pitches. Composers need to calculate the amount of time necessary to prepare for playing one multiple stop. Also, it is necessary to carefully consider hand span, since the distance between each of the frets is 4 to 6 centimeters.

d) Vibrato

Except when playing open strings, the fingers of the left hand can be used to create vibrato at any time. Also, after producing a pitch, the reverberating sound can be freely manipulated by changing the pressure of the fingers. I recommend using the following graphic symbols in the score: •⌣─── or •⌣⌣─. As illustrated in figure 2.9, vibrato can be applied effectively with double stops. Unlike the *koto*, however, the strings of the *biwa* do not reverberate for a long period of time; hence, it is best not to expect too much from this technique.

Fig. 2.9. Sample *yuri* on *biwa*: the G is an open string; the F is played on an adjacent string

e) Glissando and portamento

It is possible to execute a glissando or portamento by sliding the finger between two pressed positions. Considering, however, the duration of the reverberation of *biwa* strings, this type of sliding gesture should be considered as a glissando rather than a portamento. As with other instruments, the symbol for this technique is two pitches connected with a straight line and a slur between the note heads. When a slur is present, the performer should not re-attack the second pitch. See figure 2.10.

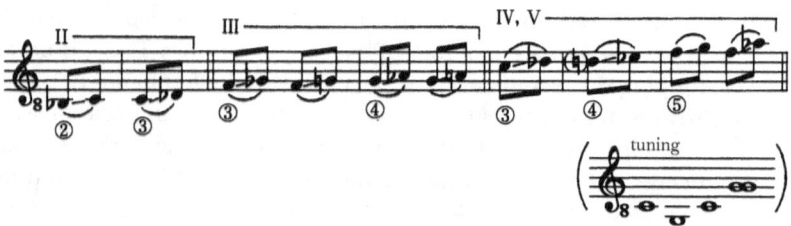

Fig. 2.10. *Biwa* glissando and portamento patterns (pressing technique)

Rather than using two pressed positions, a smooth glissando-like gesture can be made by quickly sliding the fingers of the left hand along the length of the string starting from a position on top of one of the frets. The technique is most effective when moving toward higher pitches. See figure 2.11.

Fig. 2.11. *Biwa* glissando and portamento patterns (sliding technique)

Using the same technique, but avoiding a glissando, any pair of notes in a melodic passage can be connected in a portamento-like manner. This type of portamento is very effective on instruments like the guitar. In the score, one simply notates "port." between the two pitches.

f) Left-hand pizzicato

A left-hand pizzicato on the *biwa* is similar to one on the violin or other instruments. For notation, the symbol "+" should be used, which is recognized internationally (see figure 2.12, measure a). In principle, left-hand pizzicato is executed by pressing down with the first finger and plucking with the third finger. Normally, however, left-hand pizzicato is only done on the open strings. When playing in standard positions, it is also possible to pluck with the left hand directly after striking a string with the plectrum. This effective technique is found in classical Japanese repertoire (see figure 2.12, measure b).

g) Striking (*utsu*)

After the string has been struck with the plectrum, the top of the fret in the next position is lightly stopped with one of the fingers of the left hand. In the score, mark either *utsu* or indicate the technique with the symbol ⊤. See figure 2.12, measure c.

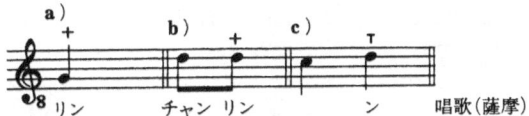

Fig. 2.12. Left-hand pizzicato *biwa* technique

(4) Right-hand Techniques

a) Normal use of the plectrum

Plectrum technique differs according to the type of plectrum being used, but the basic playing technique is nonetheless the same. The plectrum is held facing the body and the strings are struck as the hand moves away from the body. It is unnecessary to indicate this in the score, but when emphasizing the downward motion, the symbol ⊓ can be used. Plucking the string with an upstroke can be indicated with the symbol ∨.

b) Striking the body of the *biwa*

An important technique for *Satsuma-biwa* is striking the dense playing surface of the instrument with the plectrum. The body of the *Chikuzen-biwa* is made of soft paulownia, and striking it harms the instrument without delivering an effective sound; hence, it is better not to use this technique. The symbol "X" is used to indicate percussive-like striking. There are many ways to approach this technique. See figure 2.13.

Fig. 2.13. Striking the body of the *biwa* technique

Measure a shows striking all of the strings and the body of the instrument at the same time. This technique is used when a strong accent is needed.

Measure b shows striking the first string and the playing surface at the same time.

Measure c shows striking the playing surface of the body next to the fifth string with the plectrum and then playing the fourth and fifth strings with an upstroke followed by a downstroke.

Measure d shows striking the first string and then playing the remaining strings.

Measure e shows striking the fourth and fifth strings.

c) Tremolo

The *biwa* excels at playing tremolos on the fourth and fifth strings. The sound of the *biwa* tremolo, colored by the characteristic *sawari* drone, is rarely masked within an ensemble setting and will always stand out from the texture. The acute-angled *Satsuma-biwa* plectrum is superb for this. Of course, the *Chikuzen-biwa* is also capable of performing a surpassing tremolo, and I can imagine that other instruments, such as a mandolin with two strings tuned to the same pitch, can produce expressive tremolo. In figure 2.14, measure a indicates that the performer should strike all of the strings but only tremolo strings four and five. Measure b indicates that all strings should be played with tremolo. Measure c indicates that only strings four and five should be played with tremolo.

Fig. 2.14. *Biwa* tremolo

d) Dynamic expression

It is impossible to play one note at *forte* on the *biwa*. As the number of strings that the plectrum strikes increases, however, the sound combines with the overtones of the lower strings and the dynamic expression can be expanded to *ff*. Figure 2.15 illustrates an effective way of using tremolo while emphasizing dynamic contrast. This passage is also effective when performed with consecutive downstrokes.

Fig. 2.15. Dynamic expression, *biwa* example

e) Arpeggio

Normally, if the arpeggio mark ⸘ is absent, this indicates that the strings should be strummed quickly. In contrast, when the arpeggio mark is present, it indicates that the strings should be strummed slowly. On the *gaku-biwa*, arpeggios should be played even more slowly, each string firmly plucked with the plectrum in a slicing movement. The same principle can be applied to other kinds of *biwa*. Figure 2.16 measures a and b illustrate two ways of indicating arpeggio in the score. In example c, the right hand rotates in the shape of a figure eight, and is thus called the "figure-eight" (*hachi noji*).

Fig. 2.16. Ways of indicating *biwa* arpeggio in a score

f) Pizzicato (*tsuma-biki*)

The fingers of the right hand pluck the strings rather than playing with the plectrum. This is indicated by writing "pizz." in the score.

g) Plectrum scrape (*suri* or *suri-bachi*)

The performer rubs or scrapes the string lengthwise with the open face (*hiraki*) of the plectrum. Originally a *Satsuma-biwa* technique, *suri* is indicated by the graphic symbols given in figure 2.17. In addition to graphics, the *biwa* performer will understand the composer's intention if "suri" is written in the score. As illustrated in figure 2.17, measure g, I make an effort to use symbols such as △↗ or △⌢ at the beginning of the measure, which indicates various shapes and directions for the plectrum. In figure 2.17 measures e and f can also be written like measures h and i, which are clearer and easier to understand. It is also possible to perform this technique by using the side of the plectrum. After scraping the string the performer can easily connect a *suri* gesture to normal playing technique.

a) Scrape all of the strings
b) After attacking all of the strings, scrape strings four and five
c) Scrape the first string only
d) Scrape strings four and five
e) Start from a high pitch and scrape to a low pitch without a tremolo-like effect
f) Start from a low pitch and scrape to a higher pitch without a tremolo-like effect

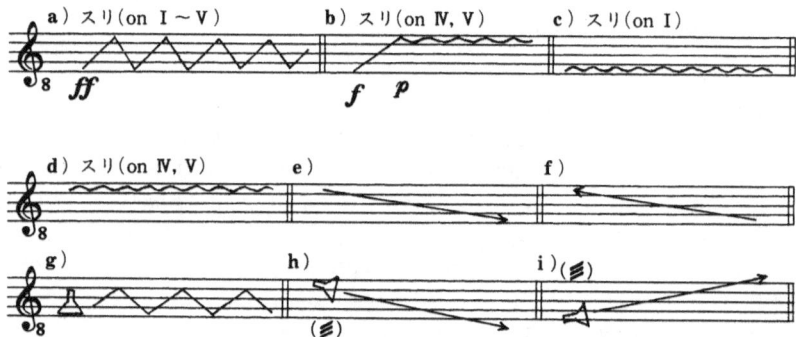

Fig. 2.17. Various *biwa suri* techniques

h) *Kuzure* technique

In the instrumental sections of *biwa*-accompanied narratives, there is a technique called *kuzure*. It is unclear when this technique was established, but it is characterized by a combination of fast triplet rhythms, plectrum movement in the shape of a figure eight, and tremolo within a mixed-meter passage. Figure 2.18 illustrates the triplet rhythm pattern.

Fig. 2.18. *Kuzure* technique triplet rhythm pattern in the *biwa*

The fourth and fifth strings of the five-string *biwa* are made from thin silk and, while tuned to the same pitch, slight imperfections in the tuning produce beats in the pitch. Combined with the *sawari* of the *biwa*, these two elements contribute to the unique sound of the instrument. This is why the *biwa* is rarely masked in an ensemble work. Moreover, when this timbre is combined with similar techniques used with other instruments—for example, the swiping nails (*chirashizume*) technique of the *koto*—the result is even more distinctive.

In this book, I discuss the playing techniques for each instrument, but I do not address effective combinations of different instruments, the possibilities of which are limitless; not only new combinations of different Japanese instruments, but also Japanese instruments with other East Asian instruments, Western instruments, and electronic instruments such as the synthesizer are possible. It will be exciting to see how young composers approach orchestration for these instruments, which will lead to new discoveries. As an author, it is not my intention to evade responsibility for discussing this subject in this book; for the reader to see some of the ideas I have tried, I have included a selected list of my compositions for Japanese instruments at the end of this book.

Due to the influence of the *Heike-biwa* and tragic narratives, there is a tendency for the *biwa* to be perceived as the darkest and most negative of all Japanese instruments. Certainly, the *biwa* is a wonderful instrument for dramatic expression. When used as a solo instrument, it is capable creating a unique atmosphere by using non-tempered scales, similar to the *nōkan*. In the Edo period, however, the *biwa* also acquired a humorous aspect. Figure 2.19 is a comic piece that I composed in 1969. The tuning should not be considered standard, as it was intended for a small four-string *Chikuzen-biwa* that was used by the performer who premiered this piece. This tuning should be considered the limit of high-pitched tunings for modern *biwa*.

Fig. 2.19. The limit of high-pitched tunings for modern *biwa* in a excerpt from Minoru Miki's *Kuse*

2–2: Shamisen

Most instruments entered Japan via China or Korea before the Nara period (710–94) and were then significantly modified, as they were adapted to indigenous tastes. The history of the *shamisen*, however, begins in the mid-sixteenth century CE, during the Eiroku period (1558–70), the last years of the Muromachi period (1333–1573). Some documents claim the Ryūkyū *sanshin* was introduced to Sakai[6] in 1562, after which changes were effected in the construction of the instrument. At this time, the organ had already been imported to Japan and was being performed. Due to religious strife with Christians, however, Western music was banned, and the *shamisen* became the center of Edo period musical culture, and developed amidst a policy of national isolation. The original form of the *sanshin*, which is derived from the Chinese *sanxian*, can be traced to the Middle East and the traditional instruments of Tibet. The commonly accepted explanation is that the instrument was established in Yuan dynasty China (1271–1368) and later entered Okinawa.

The *shamisen* was an instrument that accompanied the voice, and two distinct musical styles developed. The first musical style, *katarimono* (narrative), was practiced by *biwa*-playing monks, the first group to encounter the *shamisen*. *Katarimono*, also known as *jōruri*, includes the following popular genres: *Gidayū, Itchū, Katō, Miyazono, Kiyomoto, Shinnai* (the suffix *bushi* can be added to all of the previous genres), *sekkyō-bushi and rōkyoku*. The second musical style is *utaimono*, or *utamono* (lyric), which gave rise to genres such as *jiuta, nagauta, Ogie-bushi, hauta, Utazawa*, and *kouta*.

The *shamisen* is classified into three groups according to size: the *hosozao* (small), the *chūzao* (medium), and the *futozao* (large) (figure 2.20). *Nagauta* is the most representative *hosozao* genre. The Yamada *koto* school, and genres such as *hauta, Utazawa, kouta, Katō*, and *Ogie* also use *hosozao shamisen*. *Jiuta, Tokiwazu, Kiyomoto, Shinnai, Itchū*, and *Miyazono* all use *chūzao shamisen*. The *futozao* is used in *bunraku* (puppet theater) and *Tsugaru shamisen*. In the world of *jiuta* and *sōkyoku* it is customary to refer to the *shamisen* as *sangen*. To avoid confusion in this book, however, I will use the term *shamisen*. As the purpose of this book is to explain the musical possibilities of Japanese instruments, I shall not discuss in any depth the *shamisen* music of the different schools or instrument types. I will, however, briefly touch upon those differences when necessary, and have included supplemental discussions of the *futozao* used in *bunraku*, the *Tsugaru shamisen*, and the Okinawan *sanshin*.

STRING INSTRUMENTS (LUTES) 89

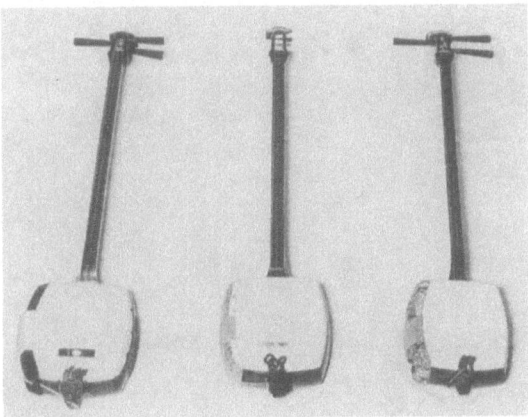

Fig. 2.20. The three *shamisen* classification groups: *futozao* (left), *chūzao* (middle), *hosozao* (right)

(1) Construction

The physical appearance of the various types of *shamisen* is similar. Figure 2.21 shows how the *shamisen* is shaped from a neck and body. The dimensions of various sections of the *shamisen*, such as the thickness of the neck and the size of the body, differ according to the genre.

   a) **Body**

   The body of the *shamisen* is hollow and made from quince, mulberry, or zelkova, and is a squarish frame, each side with a slight bulge, over which cat or dog skin is stretched. In recent years, however, *shamisen* skin has also been made from synthetic materials such as plastic. The neck and body of the *shamisen* increase in size from *hosozao* through *chūzao* to *futozao*. The Chinese *sanxian* and the Okinawan *sanshin* are covered with snakeskin, but due to the impossibility of replacing the snakeskin and the Japanese preference for a different sound quality, the materials discussed above were substituted.

   A small and very thin piece of leather called the *bachi-kawa* is pasted on the playing surface where the plectrum strikes the skin. The position and size of this area differs according to the type of *shamisen*. The side of the body that falls underneath the performer's arm when supporting the instrument on the right knee is covered with a paper guard covered with silk.

   b) **Neck**

   In order for the fingertips of the left hand to create pitches by pressing on the string, the front and rear of the neck must be uniformly smooth. The neck

90 STRING INSTRUMENTS (LUTES)

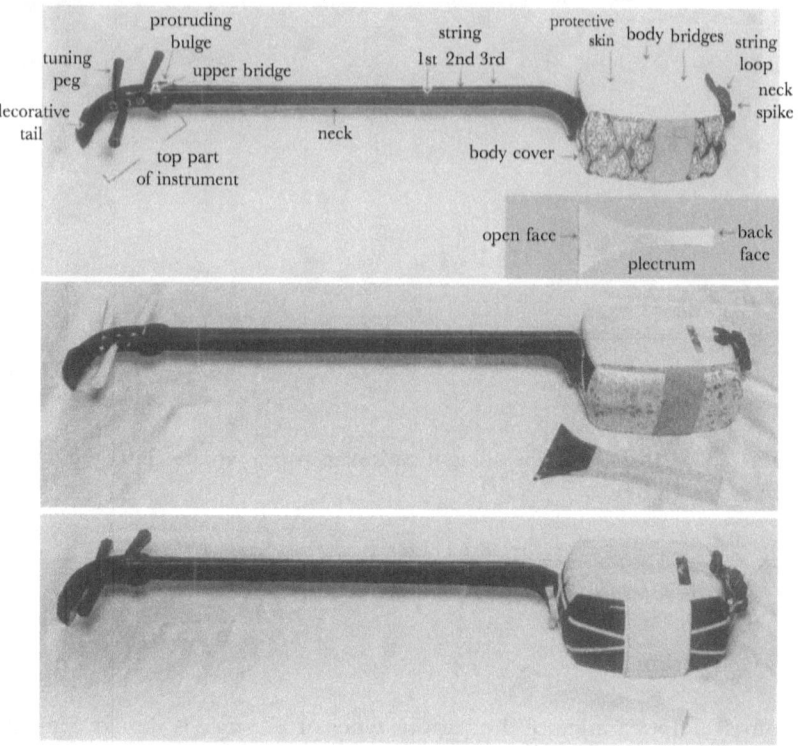

Fig. 2.21. The groups shown with details: *hosozao* (top), *chūzao* (middle), *futozao* (bottom)

and curved tail (*tenjin*) of the *shamisen* are made from rosewood, red sandalwood, or oak. The end of the neck passing through the body and protruding from the bottom is known as the *nakagosaki*. A stylized knot of thick silk cords to which the strings are tied is looped over the *nakagosaki*. The other ends of the strings are wrapped around ebony or ivory pegs, which are used to adjust the tension of the three strings. There is a bulge, known as the *chibukuro*, on the sides of the neck immediately below the peg box. The second and third strings pass over the top of a metal or bamboo bridge, known as the *kamigoma*, which is affixed to the edge of the peg box; the thick first string, however, does not. The first string vibrates over a shallow depression, which creates the distinct drone known as *sawari*. When playing the second and third string, those pitches that are part of the overtone series of the first string make the first string resonate. As the *shamisen* was first played by *biwa* monks, it is said that the changes they effected in the structure of the *shamisen* were to recreate the sound of the *biwa*. The proper balance of this drone note is a great concern for *shamisen* performers.

While the thickness of the neck is classified into three groups, the length of the entire instrument is one meter.

c) Bridges

Shamisen bridges, similar to violin bridges, transmit the vibrations of the strings to the body of the instrument and are made from a variety of materials and come in a variety of sizes, which play an important role in determining the timbre and volume. The *hosozao shamisen* of *nagauta* and *kouta* use small bridges made from ivory, while the *jiuta shamisen* and *Gidayū shamisen* use large bridges made from water buffalo horn. Genres such as *Tokiwazu*, *Kiyomoto*, and *Shinnai* use medium-size bridges made from ivory. Some performers use bridges with lead implants to make a heavier sound. Bridges designed to mute the sound made from bamboo and other materials have existed since the Edo period (1603–1868), primarily so that musicians can practice without disturbing the neighbors. It is possible for performers to change bridges during a performance provided there is a sufficiently long period of rest. The composer may indicate the size and material of the bridges desired in the score; however, if they wish to avoid this, they can allow the performer to select the appropriate bridge for the musical passage in question.

d) Strings

The strings of the *shamisen* are always made from silk and performers are often concerned that a string may snap during performance. To circumvent this problem, they occasionally use nylon or tetron strings. There is no comparison, however, to the touch and the give of silk strings. Strings come in many different weights and gauges. Regardless of the type, all *shamisen* have three strings. The lowest string is the first string, the middle string is the second string, and the highest string is the third string. The length and material is the same for each strings; however, the ratio of the string weight and the ratio of the string gauge are both 3:2:1. The weight and gauge of the strings to be used, however, are determined by the size of the instrument, as well as the performer's tastes.

Since the strings sometimes break during performance, many performers prepare an extra *shamisen*, especially for solos. Should a string snap during a group performance, however, rather than using a second *shamisen* or restringing the instrument anew, the performer can use the excess string coiled on the tuning peg.

e) *Kase*

Kase serve the same function as guitar capos. A small bar made from bone, wood, or metal, the *kase* is firmly attached by a cord to the neck of the *shamisen*. Pressing down on all three strings in the same position traditionally raises the pitch of the open tuning a perfect fourth or perfect fifth, this higher tuning being called the *uwa-jōshi*.

f) Plectrum

The *sanshin* introduced from Ryūkyū in the sixteenth-century became the *shamisen*. In adapting the *sanshin* to Japanese tastes, the *biwa* monks developed new performance techniques, one of these being the use of a large and heavy plectrum rather than the pick used for the *sanshin*. *Shamisen* plectrum are made from high-grade ivory, water buffalo horn, deer horn, or tortoise shell, but are sometimes made from less expensive materials such as boxwood, oak, or plastic. The size and weight of a *shamisen*'s plectrum correspond proportionally to the thickness of its neck. The shape of the plectrum, however, differs according to the type. As indicated in the previous illustration, the front of the plectrum is called the *hiraki*, while the back is called the *saijiri*.

From the above discussion, it must be understood that the *shamisen* is a percussion instrument as well as a string instrument. The body of the *shamisen* is a *taiko* drum, and when the plectrum strikes the strings and produces pitches, it is also simultaneously striking the head of the drum. In composing for the *shamisen*, the composer must always be aware of this aspect of the instrument.

(2) Range, Tuning, and Intonation

Like the *biwa*, the *shamisen* developed as an instrument to accompany voice, and the pitch of the tunings is adjusted to the vocal range of the performer. Regardless of the size of the *shamisen*, each of the strings has a sizable intervallic range to correspond to various tunings. The range covered by the *futozoa*, however—as well as low-pitched *shamisen* used in *nagauta*—is typically a fourth or fifth below that of the *hosozao* and *chūzao*.

a) The ranges of various *shamisen*

In figure 2.22, I have indicated the ranges for three types of *shamisen* (the *Tsugaru shamisen* and the *sanshin* of Okinawa will be discussed below). The white pitches indicate the range at which the tension is natural, while the black pitches indicate the limits of the range. Normally, the following clef is used to indicate the octave where the resulting pitch will actually sound: 𝄞. For the *futozao*, using the bass clef is more accurate, but it is impractical due to the frequency of ledger lines that would appear above the staff.

In the figure, the most commonly used range is indicated on the right side for each string.

STRING INSTRUMENTS (LUTES) 93

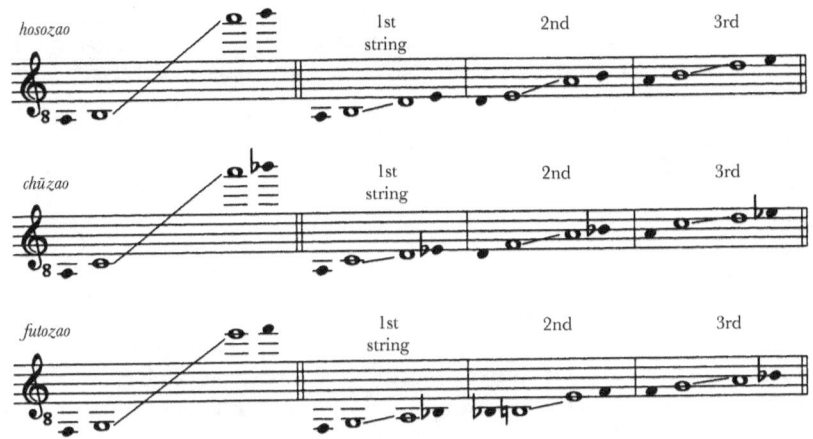

Fig. 2.22. Sample ranges for the three *shamisen* groups

Thus far, I have discussed the range of the *shamisen* in terms of actual sounding pitches. A full score should use the actual pitches or with an octave designation symbol. For performers, however, tablatures are easier to use as they indicate the fingering of the left hand. When writing a *shamisen* part, choose notation to which the performers are accustomed. This will be referenced in the following section on tuning.

b) Tuning

The traditional tunings used in *shamisen* music are *hon-chōshi, ni-agari, san-sagari, roku-sagari,* and *ichi-sagari,* the first three being the most common. Using the natural overtone series, these tunings are very resonant and are the most often used in the classical *shamisen* repertoire. Since there is music that cannot be expressed by these traditional tunings, I created, in 1964, a tuning based on the interval of an augmented fourth and called it *nakakari-chōshi*. This tuning is appropriate for pieces that contain multiple stops based on the augmented fourth. It also gave traditionally trained performers an opportunity to use an interval not found in classical pieces.

Showing the actual sounding pitches in Western staff notation for the various tunings is a laborious undertaking. In this section, I shall use the transposed notation to which *shamisen* players are accustomed. In this system, the first string is B (notated as b, the note below c^1), one space below the first ledger line beneath the treble clef. With the first string as B, the most frequently played notes in first position can be indicated without using accidentals. It also has the advantage of being easily sung with solfège. Figure 2.23 illustrates this method of indicating various tunings.

In classical *shamisen* music, there are times when the performer changes the tuning in the middle of a piece. The traditional method of tuning changes is

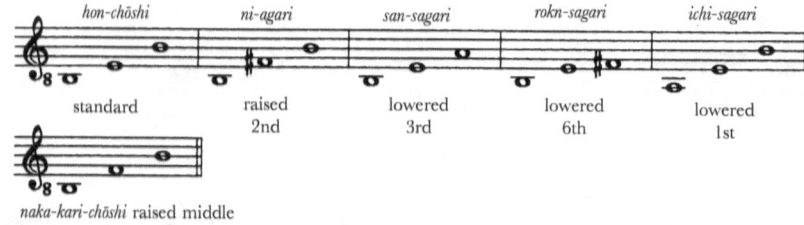

Fig. 2.23. Various *shamisen* tunings

illustrated in figure 2.24. Of course, in order to change the pitch of a string, the performer must check the intonation as they tighten or loosen the tuning pegs with their left hand. During this time, the performer must either stop playing and allow someone else to play, or continue playing while adjusting the pitch.

As mentioned in the *biwa* chapter, the adjusted strings tend to return to their original pitch during a performance, and usually require re-tuning until they settle into the new pitch. The strings of the *shamisen* are, however, more stable than those of the *biwa*.

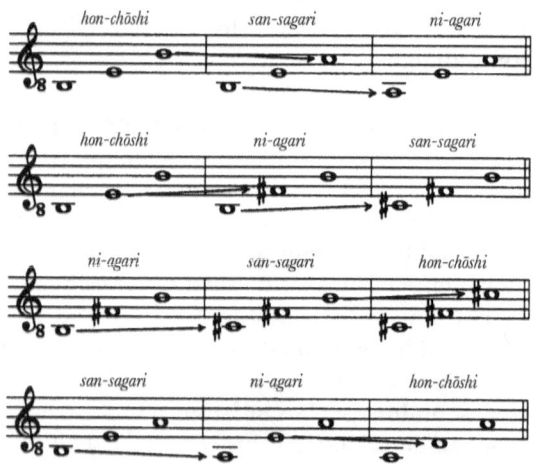

Fig. 2.24. Adjusted tunings for *shamisen*

(3) Left-hand Techniques

a) Fingering

Unlike the *biwa* and the guitar, the *shamisen* is fretless, and playing with the correct intonation requires the performers to rely on their sense of pitch. The violin and cello are also fretless; however, intonation adjustments can be made immediately after sounding the pitch. In addition, compared to the *shamisen*, the fingering technique for the different playing positions on the violin has been perfected. Having a long neck, the *shamisen* is similar to the cello, and the distance between minor and major seconds is therefore wider, making it more difficult to achieve correct intonation. A seam on the neck of the *shamisen* indicates the position for a perfect fourth or perfect fifth (depending on the neck), but otherwise there is no other mark on the neck to orient the performer.

Figure 2.25 illustrates notes and their positions for *hon-chōshi* with the first string tuned to B. Each string has a range of one-and-a-half octaves above the open string. The neck of the *jiuta shamisen* has a different construction that adds a major second to the range of each string.

Fig. 2.25. Various notes and their positions for each string

The first, second, and third finger of the left hand are used when playing the *shamisen*. The interval created by the distance of the natural placement of the first and second finger on the neck is a minor second; however, the higher positions become consecutively narrower. In traditional *shamisen* performance, when playing a melodic passage, it is common to slide from one pitch to another on the same string with the same finger. While this can be interpreted as searching for the correct pitch, it is a vital part of the aesthetics for the *shamisen*. Musical passages performed on easily reached positions on adjacent strings are not nearly as "*shamisen*-esque" as sliding from one pitch to another on the same string. One reason this is effective is that the timbre remains the same when a melody is played on one string.

b) Large intervallic jumps

It is very difficult to achieve accurate intonation when playing melodic lines containing wide intervals; in fast passages these can be more effectively executed with the insertion of open strings into the melody.

c) Multiple stops

Theoretically speaking, like the cello and other string instruments, it is possible to pluck two or more strings at the same time while using a combination of left-hand fingerings. As mentioned in section 3–9 (fingering) above, playing the correct intonation with one finger is difficult; double stops are thus more difficult. Moreover, multiple stops are not part of classical *shamisen* training. Multiple stops are nonetheless musically very powerful and leave a strong impression. Whether the performer plays double stops or triple stops, it is possible to deliver an effective multiple stop by pressing one string with one finger of the left hand and leaving the remaining strings open. This technique is effective for maintaining volume and *sawari*.

Of course, it is possible to create double and triple stops through various combinations of left-hand fingering. It is necessary, however, to provide the performer with ample preparation time, and to confirm whether the particular fingering required for the multiple stop is in fact possible. Normally, with string instruments, the position of the first minor second is 1/18 the length of the string (in this instance, the margin of error is 1 cent or 1/100 of a minor second). The next minor second is another 1/18 up the string; a fingering chart for the neck makes this clear. The strings of the *shamisen* are 80 centimeters in length, so the first equal-tempered minor second is 4.4 centimeters from the upper bridge. With a progression of minor seconds on the neck, the distance gradually becomes narrower. At the perfect fifth above the open string, the distance is about 3 centimeters, while at the octave the distance has narrowed to 2.2 centimeters, a normal fingering width. When writing double stops (for the performer), it is advisable to assume this degree of distance. Playing in thumb position as with the cello, or using barré techniques like those on the violin and guitar, do not exist for the shamisen.

d) Vibrato (*yuri*)

Skilled performers of any stringed instrument can add different types of vibrato to the notes they produce. The *shamisen* is no exception, and all performers can add subtle nuances to a sounding pitch (except for open strings) by using the fingertips or the fingernails. It is unnecessary to indicate vibrato in the score, as this should be the responsibility of the performer. If, however, there is a particular kind of vibrato shape the composer wishes to emphasize while a note is resonating, it must indicated in the score using graphic symbols such as the following: •⁔ or •〜. The same holds true for multiple stops.

e) Glissando and portamento (*koki, suri*)

If a performer slides the left hand up or down after a pitch has sounded, with the fingers remaining pressed on the string, the pitch, of course, changes (see figure 2.26). The composer should indicate the desired shape of the glissando or portamento and track the resonance via a graphic symbol.

Fig. 2.26. Glissando and portamento for *shamisen*

There are two traditional classifications for these two techniques: *koki* and *suri*. The distinction, however, between these two terms is unclear. As I understand it, a glissando produced by immediately altering the pitch after a note has sounded is called *koki*, while a portamento-like gesture that is produced by moving the fingers just before the sounding of the next pitch is called *suri*. If the second pitch is not re-articulated, a single slur connecting the two pitches suffices to render these techniques clear. It should be noted that the terms "*agari*" and "*sagari*" used by performers refers to vertical movement with the fingers on the neck of the *shamisen* and does not refer to pitch.

f) Ornamental sliding (*koki-otoshi*, *koki-oroshi*, or *suri-otoshi*)

This is an ornament unique to traditional Japanese music, and illustrated in figure 2.27. The plectrum strikes the same string twice in rapid succession. The first note is played with the left hand placed on the string at an indefinite position, the pitch of which is within a minor third of the open string. After the initial strike, the left hand slides up the neck, again, to an indefinite position, after which the second stroke enters immediately. It is also possible to execute this technique on two adjacent strings, from lower to higher, with the sliding pitch functioning as a leading tone to the next pitch on the open string. This technique is indicated with the following symbol:

Fig. 2.27. Ornamental sliding *oshide* for *shamisen*

g) Left-hand pizzicato (*hajiki*)

1. Normal *hajiiki*

As explained in the *biwa* chapter, a left-hand pizzicato is indicated by the international symbol "+." In traditional *shamisen* notation, however, the symbol ⌒ is more commonly used. Normally, the third finger plucks while the first finger presses down on a string in any position. *Hajiki* are also played on the open strings, in which case plucking is done with the first finger.

2. Alternating *hajiki* (*kake-hajiki*)

After a right-hand stroke with the plectrum, the fingertip of the ring (third) finger of the left hand immediately plucks the string in a pressed position in alternation. It is possible to perform this technique with the second pitch being either a minor or major second lower than the original pitch. Some *shamisen* genres do not use this term to describe this technique.

3. Reverse *hajiki* (*ura-hajiki*)

Rather than a downward action with the finger of the left hand, the *ura-hajiki* is executed with the back of the fingers in an upward motion. The fingers unfold from their position against the side of the neck, flicking the string consecutively, from fourth or third finger to first. In measure c of figure 2.28 the curved fingers of the left hand flick the string in order from the third, second, to first finger. *Ura-hajiki* is executed on the third string. When conducted on the first string it is called *soto-hajiki* (outside *hajiki*).

Fig. 2.28. *Hajiki* techniques for *shamisen*

h) Striking (*uchi*)

The flesh of all of the fingers of the left hand (except for the thumb) lightly strike the strings. It can also be executed by holding a position with the first finger and striking with the third finger. It is usually indicated with the symbol T, but in traditional *shamisen* notation it is written ウ (see figure 2.29.)

Fig. 2.29. An example of *uchi* (striking technique) for *shamisen*

i) Left-hand portamento

After striking the string with the plectrum, the left hand slides up or down while the string is still resonating; the interval can be either narrow or wide (figure 2.30). The volume is extremely soft when this technique is conducted in combination with the *uchi* technique discussed above rather than with the plectrum.

Fig. 2.30. An example of left hand portamento for *shamisen*

j) Staccato

Normally, staccato is played with the open strings. A staccato dot is all a performer needs to understand the composer's intention, although the symbol ケ is used in traditional *shamisen* notation.

k) Harmonics

To produce the octave and other overtones, the flesh of a finger of the left hand lightly touches the string before plucking (figure 2.31). Harmonics are ineffective in higher positions, and only half the length of each string can be used.

Fig. 2.31. Harmonics in *shamisen*

(4) Right-hand techniques

a) Normal use of the plectrum

The basic right-hand plectrum technique is to raise the plectrum above the body of the instrument and strike the string in a downward gesture. Use the symbol ⊓ only when necessary. With an upstroke, an upward pluck away from the body of the instrument, known as *sukui*, the following symbol should be used: ∨

b) Different places to strike with the plectrum

The *shamisen* is partly a percussion instrument. The plectrum strikes the body of the *shamisen* in an area covered with a thin piece of leather called the *bachi-kawa*. The position and size of this area differs according to the type of *shamisen*. With *jiuta shamisen*, the plectrum strikes the body of the instrument on the wooden frame, producing a timbre suitable for playing in a *koto* ensemble.

c) Striking the body

The symbol ϯ is used when directly striking the wooden body of the *shamisen*. The composer should include an annotation for clarification.

d) Tremolo

In contrast to the *biwa*, the *shamisen* is unsuitable for producing tremolo. While not impossible, the sound is unclear, ill balanced, and not uniform. Also, it cannot be played continually over an extended period of time. Tremolo, however, is one of the special techniques of the *Gidayū shamisen*. That instrument will be discussed in detail in the next section of this chapter.

e) Dynamic expression

The *hosozao* used in *nagauta* and the *futozao* are loud instruments and they can produce extremely percussive sounds. As the *chūzao* used in *jiuta* is considered a chamber instrument, not much can be expected in terms of volume. In the hands of an excellent performer, by lightly striking with the plectrum and avoiding the percussive sound quality, the *shamisen* can perform effectively at soft dynamic levels.

It is possible to change bridges during a performance and obtain a mute-like effect; it is, however, impossible to do this while the performer is playing.

f) Arpeggio (*kokashi-bachi*)

There are two types of arpeggios. If the symbol ⦃ is absent, it indicates that the strings should be plucked simultaneously, similar to a multiple stop. When an arpeggio symbol mark is present, it indicates that the notes should be plucked slowly. Figure 2.32 illustrates a combination of left-hand pizzicato with an arpeggio that is written out in strict time

Fig. 2.32. Left hand pizzicato combined with an arpeggio in strict time

g) Reverse arpeggio

It is possible to play an arpeggio in the reverse direction by playing with the back side of the plectrum. The symbol [⦃] should be used to indicate this technique. A melodic variation on the reverse arpeggio is illustrated in figure 2.33.

Fig. 2.33. Reverse arpeggio in *shamisen* playing

h) Pizzicato (*tsuma-biki*)

The fingers of the right hand, instead of the plectrum, pluck the strings. It is sufficient to write "pizz.," but in order to clearly distinguish this technique from the left hand pizzicato, it is clearer to write "pizz. (R.H.)."

i) Special plectrum techniques
1. *Suri*

Like the *biwa*, it is possible to play the *shamisen* by scraping the strings with the open face (*hiraki*) of the plectrum. With ivory plectra, however, performers are reluctant to use this technique as it damages the playing edge of the plectrum. It is possible to request this technique with less expensive plectra. With ivory, it is better to use the end (*saijiri*), non-ivory part of the plectrum, although this is awkward for the performer to execute. The symbols ↙ or ↘ indicate this technique, but it can also be shown by simply writing *suri*. In this case, however, the composer should include an annotation.

2. *Kakebachi* (*keshi-hajiki, ate-hajiki*)

The tip of the plectrum is placed underneath the third string while it is plucked by the fingertips of the left hand. It is used to imitate the sound of monkeys and called *kya-kya* in the *geza* (background music) of *kabuki* (figure 2.34).

Fig. 2.34. *Kakebachi* in *shamisen* playing

3. *Soto-hazushi*

The string is pushed off the neck to the side with the thumb (in *Gidayū shamisen*, the first finger) of the left hand while plucking with the plectrum. In the world of *Gidayū shamisen*, this technique is referred to simply as *hazusu* (figure 2.35).

Fig. 2.35. *Soto-hazushi* in *shamisen* playing

4. *Sukui-hajiki*

The tip of the plectrum is placed under the string and then the string is plucked with the fingertips of the left hand. If a *sukui* on the first or second open string is executed at the same time as *hajiki* on the third string it is called *sukui-hajiki* (figure 2.36).

Fig. 2.36. *Sukui-hajiki* in *shamisen* playing

5. *Kokema*

This is a right-hand technique and the most effective way of adding a traditional rhythmic sense to a passage. If, for example, a performer divides one beat into two eighth notes, the second eighth note in the pattern will sound irregularly late. Similar to Viennese waltzes where the second and third beats are rushed, *kokema* should be understood as a rhythmic technique unique to the *shamisen*.

This concludes the discussion of general techniques for the *shamisen*. There are other techniques unique to *Gidayū*, *Tsugaru*, and *sanshin* that will be discussed in the following section. Figures 2.37 and 2.38 consist of excerpts from several of my compositions for the *hosozao shamisen*; I have provided these as examples of contemporary compositions. Also in these figures, referencing section 4f (arpeggios) is an instance of multiple stops being performed at an extremely fast tempo. At ♩=98 most performers can pluck all three strings; at ♩=120, however, this takes intensive training. Performers who are able to play this passage softly are truly rare.

Fig. 2.37. Excerpt for *hosozao shamisen* from Minoru Miki's *Tan no Mai*

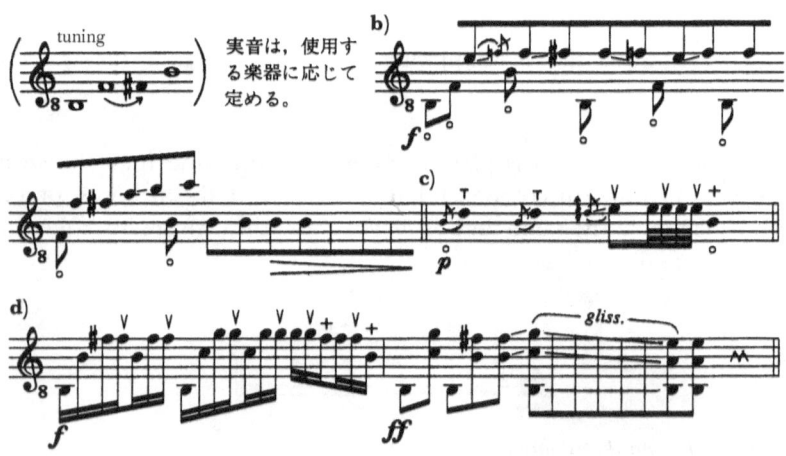

STRING INSTRUMENTS (LUTES) 103

Fig. 2.38. Excerpt for *hosozao shamisen* from Minoru Miki's *Honjū* (the actual sounding pitch will depend on the instrument used)

I would like to conclude this section by introducing, as a representative example, the mnemonics for the *shamisen* (figure 2.39). It is necessary to mention that mnemonics may differ according to the school and genre. Otherwise known as *kuchi-jamisen*, these mnemonics do not indicate positions and intervals, but are used to assist the oral transmission of works and their memorization through syllabic representation of the melody.

2–3: Special *Shamisen*

Like many Edo-period (1603–1868) Japanese performing arts, the *shamisen* underwent a unique development. Morphologically, *shamisen* can be classified according to other perspectives than the size of the neck. Each *shamisen* is distinct, and it is difficult to say which is the most representative. In this section,

Description	Mnemonic	Durations shorter than an eighth note
First string:		
Playing the open string normally	*don*	*do*
Holding a position and playing normally	*tsun*	*tsu*
Playing *sukui* on an open string	*ron*	*ro*
Second string:		
Playing the open string normally	*ton*	*to*
Holding a position and playing normally	*tsun*	*tsu*
Left-hand pizzicato	*ron*	*ro*
Playing *sukui* on an open string	*ren*	*re*
Holding a position and playing *sukui*	*run*	*ru*
Holding a position and alternating upstrokes and downstrokes	*tsuru-tsuru*	*tsuru-tsuru*
Third String:		
Playing an open string normally	*ten*	*te*
Holding a position and playing normally	*chin*	*chi*
Left-hand pizzicato	*rin*	*ri*
Playing *sukui* on an open string	*ren*	*re*
Playing an open string and alternating between upstrokes and downstrokes	*tere-tere*	*tere-tere*
Holding a position and playing *sukui*	*run* or *rin*	*ru* or *ri*
Holding a position and alternating upstrokes and downstrokes	*chari-chari*	*chiri-chiri*
Double stop on the first and second string	*jan*	*ja*
Double stop on the second and third string	*shan*	*sha*
Striking (*uchi*)	*u*	*u*

Fig. 2.39. Mnemonics for the *shamisen*

I will discuss elements of the special *shamisen* that I was unable to cover in the previous section.

(1) *Futozao (Gidayū Shamisen)*

The *futozao* shamisen used in the *bunraku* puppet theater is known as the *Gidayū shamisen*. This instrument was used in earlier *jōruri* forms before it became the accompanying instrument for *Gidayū-bushi*. Its appearance and function are similar to the *hosozao* and *chūzao*, but it is tuned a perfect fourth or fifth lower. I have never heard a clear explanation for this discrepancy in range. When an instrument is used to accompany song and narrative, I can objectively understand the necessity for the instrument to be paired with the low-pitched range of the chanter. Compared to the founders of Kantō[7]-style narrative genres, the range of the *futozao* must have been based on the range of the voice of Takemoto Gidayū, whose influence all but monopolized narrative genres in Kansai.[8] Several documents note that Takemoto Gidayū had a large voice that covered a wide range. In order to match the power and range of his voice, the corresponding instrument must have been large, thick, and heavy; the same can be said about the bridges, strings, and plectrum. The *futozao* requires great strength, and when performers accustomed to the smaller *shamisen* try to play the *futozao*, they feel as if they are being repelled by the instrument and it is difficult for them to produce a full sound. It is extremely rare for performers to have equal facility on smaller *shamisen* as well as *futozao shamisen*.

There is a lower-pitched *shamisen* that covers the range of the *futozao* used by *hosozao nagauta* performers. The *nagauta shamisen*, however, is an instrument that was developed to accompany song rather than narrative. On the other hand, the *futozao* is an instrument with distinctive techniques that are tied to its function as an accompanying instrument in the theatrical narrative tradition of *bunraku*. In terms of timbre, power, tension, its comical expression, and overall affect, the low-pitched *shamisen* should not be considered as a substitute for the *futozao* shamisen. The existence of a *shamisen* pitched a fourth or fifth lower than normal *shamisen* offers such expressive power and encourages both solo performance and use within a large ensemble.

In conjunction with the fingering position chart in figure 2.25 in the previous section, figure 2.40 is a convenient diagram that illustrates the range of the *futozao* as well as the most frequently occurring pitches and patterns.[9]

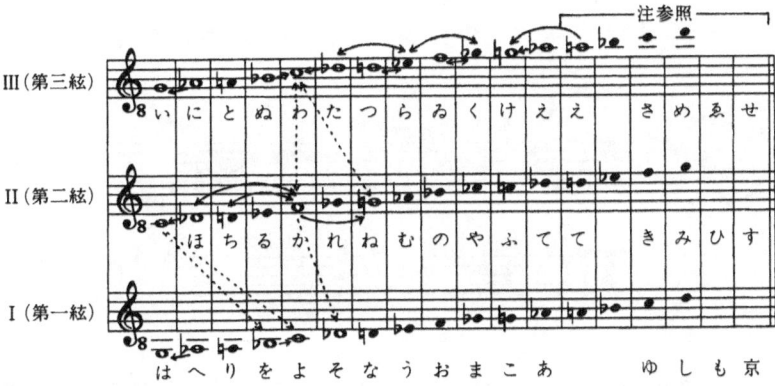

Fig. 2.40. Various notes and their positions for each string of the *futozao* (*gidayū*) *shamisen*

There are several significant differences between playing techniques for the *Gidayū shamisen* and other *shamisen*. Due to the thickness of the strings, the volume, the power, the left-hand glissando, and the portamento are unrivaled.

In the previous section, I stated that the *shamisen* is unsuitable for producing tremolo with the plectrum. The *Gidayū shamisen*, however, is an instrument with outstanding technical capabilities and a formidable presence. There are three reasons for this. First, the open end (*hiraki*) of the plectrum that plucks the strings is extremely thick and close to a right angle rather than an acute angle; second, the plectrum is heavy and prevails over any resistance created by the vibrations of the strings; third, because the bridges are high, the strings are further away from the skin, making it easy to rapidly shake the plectrum and produce an effective tremolo.

The *Gidayū shamisen* has the ability to produce sounds that depart from standard tuning. This rarely occurs in the lyric genres, but is more common in the narrative genres in which the music gives an expressive voice to the drama. I have often been astonished at how ingeniously *Gidayū shamisen* players are able to execute a musical passage of continuous pitches that subtly departs from standard intonation. The musical results are remarkable and similar to the *nōkan*. If the composer wishes to takes advantage of this unique characteristic, however, rather than attempting to explain in the score the physical production of the sound, it may be better to consult with the performer and ask them to depart from the standard tuning, leaving the details to them.

The *Gidayū shamisen* is also known for its ability to produce a sharp and exaggerated percussive sound. In contrast to a normal stroke, the string is attacked in a large gesture and the sound of the plectrum striking the skin of the instrument can be clearly heard. There is no special symbol used to indicate this technique; the composer can provide an annotation in the score that reads "*tataki-bachi*," with a short explanation.

Figures 2.41a–f and 2.42 a–c show a variety of representative patterns.[10]

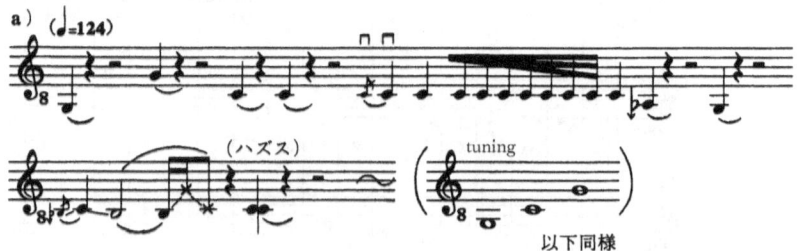

Fig. 2.41. Techniques for the *Gidayū shamisen* with excerpts from the classical *gidayū* repertoire. (a) A technique for the *Gidayū shamisen* with an excerpt from *Sonae*

Fig. 2.41. Techniques for the *Gidayū shamisen* with excerpts from the classical *gidayū* repertoire. (b) A technique for the *Gidayū shamisen* with an excerpt from *Nozakimura*

Fig. 2.41. Techniques for the *Gidayū shamisen* with excerpts from the classical *gidayū* repertoire. (c) A technique for the *Gidayū shamisen* with an excerpt from *Hidakagawa*

Fig. 2.41. Techniques for the *Gidayū shamisen* with excerpts from the classical *gidayū* repertoire. (d) A technique for the *Gidayū shamisen* with an excerpt from *Yūrei*

Fig. 2.41. Techniques for the *Gidayū shamisen* with excerpts from the classical *gidayū* repertoire. (e) A technique for the *Gidayū shamisen* with an excerpt from *Inori*

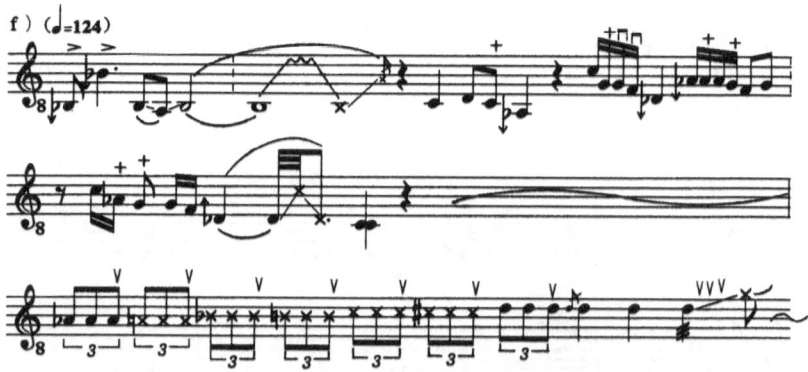

Fig. 2.41. Techniques for the *Gidayū shamisen* with excerpts from the classical *Gidayū* repertoire. (f) A technique for the *Gidayū shamisen* with an excerpt from *Kitsunebi*

Fig. 2.42. Techniques for the *Gidayū shamisen* with excerpts from Minoru Miki's works for *Gidayū shamisen*. (a) A technique for the *Gidayū shamisen* with an excerpt from Minoru Miki's *Paraphrase After Ancient Japanese Music*

Fig. 2.42. Techniques for the *Gidayū shamisen* with excerpts from Minoru Miki's works for *Gidayū shamisen*. (b) A technique for the *Gidayū shamisen* with an excerpt from Minoru Miki's *Kuse*

Fig. 2.42. Techniques for the *Gidayū shamisen* with excerpts from Minoru Miki's works for *Gidayū shamisen*. (c) A technique for the *Gidayū shamisen* with an excerpt from Minoru Miki's *Jōruri*—An opera in three acts

(2) *Futozao (Tsugaru Shamisen)*

While the *Tsugaru shamisen* is also a *futozao shamisen*, unlike the *Gidayū shamisen* that was the main instrument associated with *bunraku* and the traditional arts in the urban centers, the strong technique and rough sound of this *shamisen* was born in the poor, isolated villages of northern Japan (figure 2.43). These characteristics contribute to its appeal for the people of today. In dictionaries and other sources for Japanese music, there are no entries for the *Tsugaru shamisen*. It is a true folk instrument.

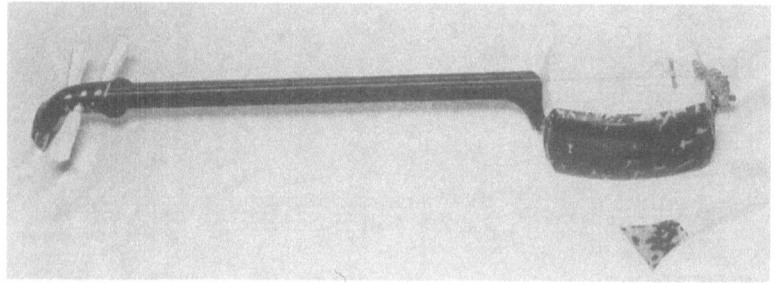

Fig. 2.43. The *Tsugaru shamisen*

The history of the *Tsugaru shamisen* begins in 1877, when a blind entertainer named Nitabō obtained a secondhand *Gidayū shamisen*. Nitabō—who had artistic sensibilities—transposed the *Tsugaru* lyric and narrative genres performed to the accompaniment of the *hosozao shamisen* to the *futozao shamisen*. He also rounded the thick *Gidayū shamisen* plectrum to resemble a rice paddle, changed the playing position to a vertical one, and expanded the playing area to include the region close to the bridge. His most distinctive modification, and what now characterizes *Tsugaru shamisen*, was his beating and slapping[11] the strings like a percussion instrument rather than using the normal plectrum technique. As discussed in the previous section, the *Gidayū shamisen* has a technique called "*tataki-bachi*," but this technique differs from that of the *Tsugaru shamisen*. Using a combination of vigorous left-hand techniques of glissando, portamento, pizzicato, and upstrokes that were codified during the Meiji era (1868–1912), after World War II, the *Tsugaru shamisen* moved into the limelight of the folk-music music boom throughout Japan and *Tsugaru shamisen* performers become popular. Keeping with historical trends, however, many virtuosic reformers appeared and took the technique of *tataku*, for example, to create schools that promoted even stronger performance techniques. Other schools consciously promote a technique closer to the playing technique of normal *shamisen*.

While modern-day *Tsugaru shamisen* are considered *futozao shamisen*, the thickness of the neck and the strings can be adjusted to the performer. The range of the first string of the *Tsugaru* shamisen can be set anywhere between G and f♯ to match the range of amateur singers, although professional performers prefer that the first string be set between c and d for the desired tension.

There are many differences between the body of the *Tsugaru shamisen* and the *Gidayū shamisen*. The biggest difference is the bridge. *Tsugaru shamisen* bridges are quite short and close to the skin (which is primarily dog skin). As a result, the distance between the bridge and the skin is very narrow, this proximity accounting for the effectiveness of the *tataku* technique. As illustrated in figure 2.44, the playing, or rather, striking area of the *Tsugaru shamisen* is extremely wide. There are *Tsugaru shamisen* where the *bachi-kawa* is stretched over the entire area.

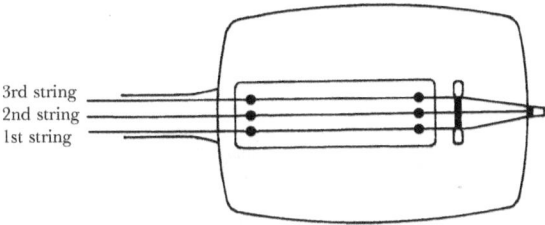

Fig. 2.44. Striking area of the *Tsugaru shamisen*: the places marked ● indicate the margins where the plectrum may be struck

The plectrum of the *Tsugaru shamisen* is similar to those used in *nagauta*. As discussed in the previous section, therefore, tremolo never occurs with *Tsugaru shamisen*. The characteristic playing technique of the *Tsugaru shamisen* is to continuously strike the strings and skin with all one's strength. Even through it is an instrumental genre, the playing technique differs from the *Gidayū shamisen*. For example, within a pattern of eighth notes that either repeats the same pitch or moves without leaping over wide intervals, a *Tsugaru shamisen* performer can impress the audience by the seemingly endless strength and endurance required to perform steady hits and strikes. Within this pattern, performers commonly use upstrokes and a dynamic playing technique called *sute-bachi*. All three strings are struck rapidly, creating an extremely fast arpeggio. It unnecessary to use the arpeggio marking ⸸. Rather, the composer should use a symbol like [, indicating that the three notes should be considered as a single unit. In the *tataku* school of *Tsugaru shamisen*, there is a style of playing called *oshi-bachi* in which the plectrum presses down on the *bachi-gawa* of the instrument to accent the percussive quality of the instrument. This technique is indicated by the symbol ⌈.

Normally, expressive dynamic contrasts are not made by adjusting the striking force of the plectrum, although there are some contemporary performers who can do this. While not the case with all performers, in general the *Tsugaru* shamisen is played with one uniform level of strength. Differences in dynamics and timbre can be heard by the audience depending on where the performer strikes the surface of the instrument. When playing close to the bridge, the volume is loud and the timbre bright. When playing farther from the bridge, the volume decreases and the timbre becomes darker. In order to create these dynamic and timbral differentiations, the plectrum must be moved quite frequently. Various patterns are noted in figure 2.45.[12] Even with the same type of pattern, there are schools of *Tsugaru shamisen* playing that begin playing close to the bridges, while other schools start the pattern as far from the bridges as possible. When notating these contrasts in Western staff notation, it is too complicated to write instructions like "near bridge" or "off bridge" to indicate the playing position. Instead, it may be easier to understand if the composer simply uses the dynamic markings of *f* and *p*.

Fig. 2.45. An excerpt from the *kyūbushi Tsugaru-jongarabushi*, transcribed by Mitsugu Koyama

Fig. 2.45. An excerpt from *Chūbushi*, transcribed by Mitsugu Koyama

Fig. 2.45. An excerpt from *Shinbushi*, transcribed by Mitsugu Koyama

The first string of the *Tsugaru shamisen* is especially thick, although thinner than the first string of the *Gidayū shamisen*. The second and third strings, however, are about the same gauge as those of the *hosozao shamisen*. In the *tataku* playing style, in order to restrain the resonance of the third (and sometimes the second) string, the tip of the fourth finger of the right hand presses on the second of third string where it passes over the bridge to create mute-like effect. When performing with more power and strength the finger is removed.

(3) *Sanshin*

As explained in the beginning of section 2.2, the history of the *shamisen* began in the mid-sixteenth century CE with the introduction of the Ryūkyū *sanshin* to the Japanese mainland and its subsequent modification. It is said the *sanshin* was transmitted from China to the Ryūkyū kingdom through cultural exchange between the two countries 150 years before it entered Japan. The *sanxian* of Yuan-period (960–1368) China differed considerably from the *shamisen* of today. It was much smaller and closely resembled the *sanshin*. Many items from China, like their counterparts in the Ryūkyū islands, used python skin. There are many people who refer to the Ryūkyū *sanshin* as the "snakeskin instrument," but this term is not used in Okinawa.

The *sanshin* that came to Japan and developed into the *shamisen* was reimported to the Ryūkyū islands in the early seventeenth century CE. It is said this influenced the *sanshin* to resemble the *shamisen*. Despite this shared history, there are still a number of major differences between mainland *shamisen* and the *sanshin*.

As indicated in figure 2.46, many parts of the *sanshin* have different names. The neck of the *sanshin* is thinner and shorter, with a length of seventy-six centimeters. As discussed above, the skin of the *sanshin* is different, and there is no *bachi-kawa*. Also, there are no incisions made above the bridges on the peg box to create *sawari* similar to the *biwa*. The bridge, called the *uma*, is positioned high on the body of the instrument. Its shape also differs from those of *shamisen* bridges. The right hand does not hold a plectrum, and instead, the first finger is fitted with a long pick made of ebony or water buffalo horn.

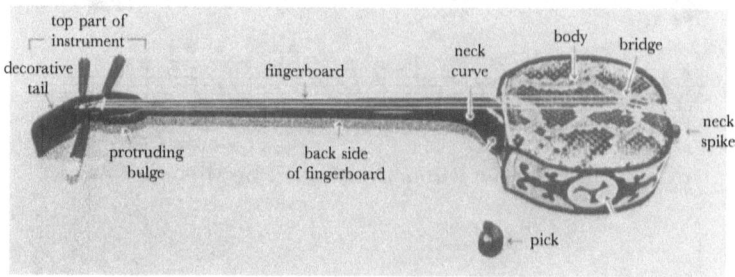

Fig. 2.46. The *Sanshin*

To play the characteristic Ryūkyū scale that appears in classical Ryūkyū music, the playing positions differ from the *shamisen*. Figure 2.47 illustrates this in Western staff notation.[13] The characters beneath the staff are the names assigned to various positions in Ryūkyū *sanshin* music.

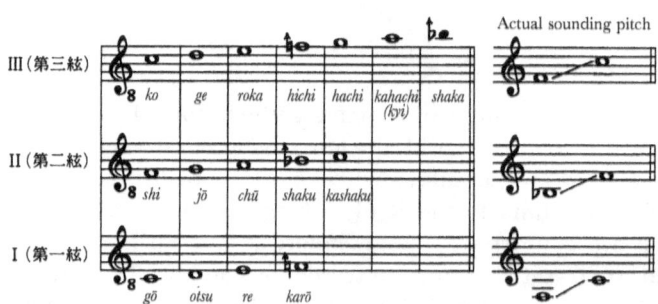

Fig. 2.47. Various notes and their positions for the Ryūkyū scale for the *sanshin*

While there are regional differences, the pitches used when playing classical works, *rō, karō, chū, shaku, roku,* and *hichi,* deviate from equal temperament. Performers can, however, also use equal temperament when performing modern works.

The range of the *sanshin* is set to the range of the vocalist. When playing instrumental music, however, the first string is usually set between f and c^1. The second string is set a perfect fourth above the first string. If the first string is set to F, the second string would therefore be tuned to a b♭ (a♯). In the past, there was some confusion as to whether the pitch of the second string, *shi,* was b♭ or c, the confusion apparently stemming from the Japanese pronunciation of the English C, read *shi* in Japanese.

Except for the difference between the *shamisen* plectrum and the *sanshin* pick, the *sanshin* should be capable of most *shamisen* techniques. It is better, nonetheless, to limit *sanshin* techniques to those derived from its function as an instrument accompanying the unique song traditions of traditional Ryūkyū music, such as simple quarter-note or eighth-note accompanying patterns in a relatively slow tempo. Figure 2.48 illustrates several characteristic patterns of the *sanshin*.[14]

Fig. 2.48. Characteristic *sanshin* patterns in excerpts from the *sanshin* repertoire. (a) A characteristic pattern of the *sanshin* in *Kagiyate-kazebushi,* transcribed by Haiko Otsuka

Fig. 2.48. Characteristic *sanshin* patterns in excerpts from the *sanshin* repertoire. (b) A characteristic pattern of the *sanshin* in *Akatsukibushi,* transcribed by Haiko Otsuka

Fig. 2.48. Characteristic *sanshin* patterns in excerpts from the *sanshin* repertoire. (c) A characteristic pattern of the *sanshin* in *Shimodashi-jakaibushi,* transcribed by Haiko Otsuka

In Okinawa, many popular music groups have begun to attract attention as they integrate elements of traditional Okinawan music, and infuse it with a contemporary sensibility. Some groups lead prosperous and active careers all over Japan. Most of the *sanshin* performers in these groups approach the instrument and its techniques freely, and through contact with their audience, devise new techniques not found in classical Ryūkyū repertoire. It is said that the progress of the *shamisen* has stopped, but with the trends and currents of the *Tsugaru shamisen*, it is no mistake to say that these two remote and isolated traditions have combined to make significant contributions in reforming, changing, and revitalizing the potential of the *shamisen*. I look forward to seeing what the future holds for them.

2–4: *Kokyū*

The *kokyū* is the only bowed instrument in Japan. The origin of bowed instruments is conjectured to be India. The Arabian *rebab*—originally a two-stringed instrument, which later became three-stringed—was the first bowed instrument to spread throughout the world. The representative, vertically performed, two-stringed bowed instrument that traveled eastward to Asia became the Chinese *erhu*. With twice the number of strings, the violin was perfected in Europe, and marks the beginning of string instruments placed on the shoulder. Three-stringed instruments advanced eastward through Islamic countries along the coast of Asia and entered Ryūkyū. The Ryūkyū *kokyū* originally had a round sound box, and this instrument was introduced to Japan during the Bunsei period (1592–96), thirty years after the arrival of the *shamisen*. A widely accepted explanation is that the same group of musicians that modified the *shamisen* improved the Ryūkyū *kokyū* in a similar fashion. A four-stringed *kokyū* also appeared; this instrument, however, can be considered a three-stringed instrument as the third and fourth strings are tuned to the same pitch.

From the Edo period (1603–1868) until the beginning of the Meiji period (1868–1912), the *kokyū* was closely associated with *sōkyoku* (*koto* music), and performed with *koto* and *shamisen* as part of the *sankyoku* ensemble. The *shakuhachi* later replaced the *kokyū*, at which point the popularity of the *kokyū* waned. Some musicians made a conscious effort to revitalize the *kokyū*. Michio Miyagi, in particular, included the *kokyū* in new compositions during the *shin-nippon ongaku undō* (the New Japanese Music Movement). Miyagi also expanded its capabilities by designing a lower-pitched *kokyū*, which I tentatively call the *chū-kokyū*. Another important figure in Japanese music history, Hisao Tanabe (1883–1984), turning to the *rebab*, invented an instrument known as the *reikin* for lower registers. As the only Japanese bowed instrument, I firmly believed that the *kokyū* should be included in the *Nihon Ongaku Shūdan* (Pro Musica Nipponia). I convinced Keiji Azechi, who originally wished to study *koto*, to switch to the *kokyū*. He took my advice and over the last twenty years has been a pivotal figure in establishing contemporary performance techniques for the *kokyū*. Azechi has improved the instrument, and also designed a *dai-kokyū* (large *kokyū*). Nevertheless, compared to the number of Western string and Chinese *erhu* players, there are significantly fewer *kokyū* performers. In many instances, we must ask Chinese *erhu* players to participate in large *kokyū* ensembles. The timbre of the *kokyū*, however, is different from the violin or *erhu*, and displays a unique sensibility and humor. I expect further development of the *kokyū*.

(1) Construction

As shown in figure 2.49, the main body of the *kokyū* resembles that of the *shamisen*. The *kokyū* invented by Miyagi has the same shape as the regular *kokyū*, but is larger, and is tuned a fifth lower. Azechi's *dai-kokyū* is even larger than Miyagi's.

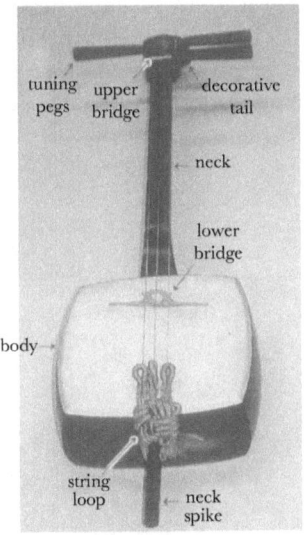

Fig. 2.49. The *kokyū*, seen from above

a) Body

The body of the classic *kokyū* is smaller than that of the *shamisen*. Cat skin is used for the membrane, but the Okinawan *kokyū* employs snakeskin.

b) Neck

The neck of the *kokyū* is shorter than that of the *shamisen*. Unlike the *shamisen*, however, the *kokyū* is held upright like a cello. The section of the neck that penetrates the sound box and protrudes from the bottom (the *nakagosaki*) is considerably longer than on the *shamisen*, and is placed between the performer's knees to stabilize the instrument. The standard length of the instrument is 69 centimeters. There are no modifications to the neck of the *kokyū* to produce *sawari*.

c) Bridges

The bridge of the *kokyū* is placed on the upper side (closer to the neck) of the skin stretched over the body. The shape of the bridge differs from *shamisen* bridges, which have a trapezoidal shape. To bow each string without sounding a neighboring string requires their placement in an arc, and the bridge is rounded much like a violin bridge.

d) Strings

Kokyū employs *shamisen* strings, but the tension of the *kokyū* is higher than that of the *shamisen*.

e) Bow

The bow of the *kokyū* is very different from that of the violin; as shown in figure 2.50, it truly has a bowed shape and uses twenty or thirty strands of white or black horsehair. The *kokyū* bow ranges from 96 centimeters to as much as 110 centimeters in length making it 20 to 30 centimeters longer than a violin bow. The tension of the *kokyū* bow is extremely loose, and unlike violin bows (which have a screw), the *kokyū* player creates the desired tension by pulling the hairs with the right middle and ring fingers while playing.

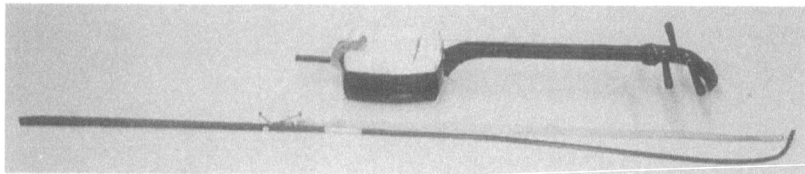

Fig. 2.50. The *kokyū* and bow

(2) Range and Tuning

Figure 2.51 shows the ranges and basic tunings of the traditional *kokyū* and *chū-kokyū*, as well as the tuning of the *reikin*, which has not been reconstructed since its loss during World War II. As with *shamisen* tunings, there are numerous tuning possibilities for the *kokyū*. The traditional repertoire is usually tuned to *san-sagari*: eleven of the twelve *honkyoku* of the *Fujiue-ryū*, a representative *kokyū* school, use *san-sagari*, the tuning for the twelfth piece being *ni-agari*. *Hon-chōshi* is not used. Of course, newly devised tunings can be used for contemporary pieces.

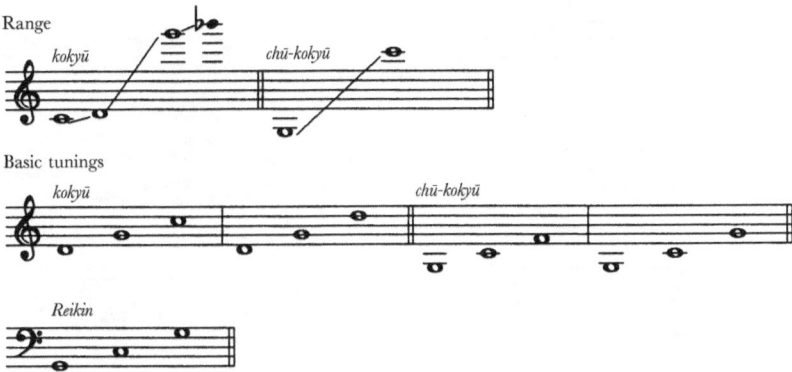

Fig. 2.51. Tunings of the traditional *kokyū* and *chū-kokyū*

(3) Left-hand Techniques

Bowing techniques for the *kokyū* and the cello are fundamentally different. For the cello, the player changes the angle of the bow, held in the right hand, against the body of the instrument body as the bow moves from one string to another. With the *kokyū*, however, the bow is always kept parallel to the front of the player's body and to the floor. Rather than change the angle of the bow to play different strings, the instrument is twisted so that the appropriate string moves to the correct position under the bow.

a) Fingering

The fingering technique for the *kokyū* is equally unique. Positions on the fingerboard (called *kandokoro*) are reached by sliding, in a fashion similar to the *shamisen*. In traditional *kokyū* performance, there are no fixed fingering positions such as those used for the violin, which still holds true for contemporary performance. Judging from the history of the *kokyū*, the fingering perhaps developed in tandem with the *shamisen*, as the same group of musicians performed both instruments. The first, second, and third fingers of the left hand are used. Despite the similarity of the finger position on the neck for both the *kokyū* and the cello, which arises from a similar distance between pitches on both instruments, the two are fundamentally different. Thumb techniques, which are commonly used on the cello, are never used on the *kokyū*. On rare occasions, the fourth finger is used, but the composer should consult with the player before incorporating this technique. Figure 2.52 illustrates an example of classical fingering. In *kokyū* music, the symbols for the left hand are 人 (first finger), 中 (second finger), 工 (third finger), and 小 (fourth finger). In this book, the more international 1, 2, 3, and 4, as explained in the section on the lute-type instruments, are used.

Fig. 2.52. Classical fingering for the *kokyū* in an excerpt from *Yachiyo-jishi* by Fujinaga Kengyō, transcribed by Keiji Azechi

The first and second strings of the *kokyū* are used less frequently than the third string. The tonic in *san-sagari* tuning, however, is the open second string, and the sound of this string is important in the classical tradition.

b) Multiple stops

Multiple stops, impossible on the Chinese *erhu*, are particularly suited to the *kokyū*; they also increase the volume. Following *kokyū* practice, however, I recommend that multiple stops make use of an open string, as illustrated in figure 2.53. Of course, it is possible to create a multiple stop by pressing more than one string; depending on position, however, there are instances in which the desired sonority may be impossible to obtain. A firm knowledge of fingering sequences is necessary. As with the *shamisen*, when using multiple stops, it is necessary to allow time for their preparation.

Fig. 2.53. Multiple stops technique for the *kokyū*

c) Vibrato
When indicating vibrato in the score, it can be drawn graphically as •⁓ or •⁓. There is no need to indicate the player's natural vibrato.

d) Glissando and portamento (*suri*)
This technique is the same as on Western bowed instruments. It is important to note, however, that the *kokyū* often employs glissandi beginning with the open string. As illustrated in figure 2.52, a prominent characteristic of traditional *kokyū* performance technique is the slide from c^2—the open position of the third string in *san-sagari*—to d^2, which accounts for the prevalence of this tuning in the classic *kokyū* repertoire.[15] The ornamental technique which employs the pitch sequence of $d^{\flat 2}$–c^2–$d^{\flat 2}$, and resembles the *nayashi* of the *shakuhachi* or *hiki-iro* of the *koto*, is called *yuri* in *kokyū* performance. Calling the regular vibrato *yuri* will lead to confusion, and is best avoided.

While the frequent use of the *suri* in the lower register may create an odd, unsettling effect, its use in the high register results in a delicate expression.

e) *Kokiotoshi* or *Kokioroshi* (sliding down)
This is a representative *shamisen* technique; unlike the *shamisen*, however, there is no sound decay with bowed instruments (see figure 2.54). The sound stops abruptly as the downward gliding finger is lifted from the fingerboard. A smooth decrescendo is an extraordinarily difficult technique on all bowed instruments, including the violin or the cello. A performer with an intuitive understanding of this technique, however, can produce it correctly.

Fig. 2.54. The *kokiotoshi* or *kokioroshi* (sliding-down) technique for the *kokyū*

f) Left-hand pizzicato
The international symbol "+" suffices. In the Japanese music world, ⌒ is used.

g) *Uchi* or *uchite* (striking)
Uchite is the same technique used in *shamisen* performance, and is commonly used in *kokyū* performance to create a unique atmosphere. It occurs with great frequency on d^2 immediately above the open c^2 of the third string in *san-sagari*. I indicate *uchite* with the symbol T, but in the classical repertoire △ or ウ is used. As can be seen in figure 2.52 and in figure 2.55 below, *uchi* is central to the melodic expressiveness of the *kokyū*. For example, with repeated sixteenth notes, rather than using the bow, the insertion of *uchite* creates a lighter and more interesting sound.

h) Left-hand *suri*

As with the *shamisen*, *suri* are glissandi created by a finger of the left hand sliding on the neck after a pitch has been articulated. On the *kokyū*, however, *suri* are difficult to execute effectively as the neck is considerably shorter than on the *shamisen*.

i) Harmonics (*soto-osae*)

Harmonics do not occur in traditional *kokyū* performance, but it is possible to obtain octave overtones by playing an open string and lightly touching a position with the back of the fingernails. This technique, however, is not overly effective, so the composer should consult with the player before using it in a composition.

(4) Right-hand Techniques

a) Regular bowing techniques

The right hand primarily engages in bowing, the grip for which is similar to the German style of holding the bow for the double bass. The shape of the bow and the grip also resemble those for the viola da gamba. As mentioned above, the bow of the *kokyū* moves parallel to the front of the performer's body and the floor. As with the cello, the bowing symbols ⊓ to indicate rightward bowing and V to indicate leftward bowing are written when necessary. In the past, the sustained sound of bowed instruments was not popular among Japanese, hence the *shakuhachi* replaced the *kokyū*. I nonetheless believe that a well-trained *kokyū* performer's bowing can express an artistic rigor or sensibility that will make contemporary listeners forget this former stigma.

b) Tremolo

Tremolo performed on the *kokyū* are extremely effective, and traditional *kokyū* music often uses this technique.

c) Dynamic expression

As the *kyokyū* is a bowed instrument, it is capable of remarkable dynamic expression. In figure 2.54, an effective use of dynamics is to have the performer execute an extended crescendo that abruptly changes to *p* or diminuendo with the return of the bow. A stimulating effect may also be achieved by playing a sustained pitch with tremolo.

d) Pizzicato

Pizzicato cannot be used effectively due to the short length of the *kokyū* strings; depending on the position, however, it is possible to create a clear and strong sound. Since the right hand grip of the bow is different from that of the violin, it may appear impossible to execute pizzicato while holding the bow. It is nevertheless possible, and there is no need to put down the bow.

e) *Sul tasto, sul ponticello*

Sul tasto, playing at a position away from the bridge, like the violin, produces a soft timbre and weak stress. If the playing position is too far from the bridge, it makes the string unstable. Executed near the bridge, however, *sul ponticello* creates a piercing sound quality and strong stress.

f) Playing beyond the bridge

This is a technique of playing at a position on the other side of the bridge above the membrane of the sound box. It creates a remarkably intense sound of indeterminate pitch and is used as a sound effect.

Finally, I have included several excerpts from classical and contemporary *kokyū* pieces in figure 2.55a–c.

Fig. 2.55. Techniques for the *kokyū* from the classical *kokyū* repertoire. (a) An example of techniques for *kokyū* in an excerpt from *Mushi no Ne* by Fujio Kōtō, transcribed by Keiji Azechi

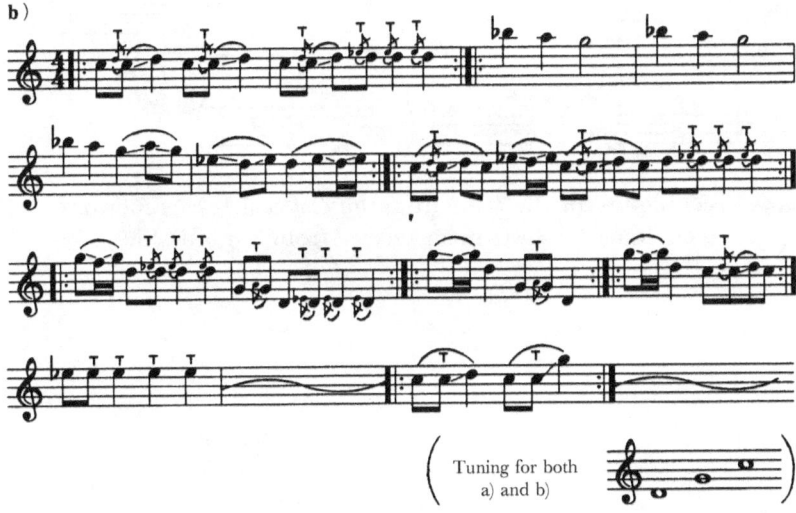

Fig. 2.55. Techniques for the *kokyū* from the classical *kokyū* repertoire. (b) An example of techniques for *kokyū* in an excerpt from the classical repertoire *Tsuru-no-sugomori* by Kengyō Yoshizawa, transcribed by Keiji Azechi

Fig. 2.55. Techniques for the *kokyū* from the classical *kokyū* repertoire. (c) An example of techniques for *kokyū* in an excerpt from Minoru Miki's *Hote*

Chapter Three

String Instruments (Zithers)

In Japan, there are two Chinese characters that are read "koto," 琴 and 箏, both of which are classified as zithers in the category of plucked instruments. The difference between the two characters is that 箏[1] indicates instruments with movable bridges while 琴 is used for instruments without bridges. There is, however, one exception to this rule: an ancient six-stringed *koto* known as the *wagon*, in spite of having movable bridges, uses the characters 和琴.

With zithers, it is necessary to indicate the number of the string to be plucked as well as the fingers to be used on both hands. In traditional notation for the 13-string *koto*, string numbers are indicated by the Chinese characters for the numbers one though ten, while three non-numeric characters are reserved for strings eleven through thirteen: 一、二、三、四、五、六、七、八、九、十、斗、為、巾. *Kotos* with more strings use this numbering system as a base from which symbols are derived to indicate the remaining strings. These symbols are shown in the following examples of various tunings. Fingerings for the right hand are indicated by the numbers 1 through 5, and the same numbers enclosed in circles indicate fingerings for the left hand.

Presently, the zither used in concerts is predominantly the *koto*. I have regretfully omitted discussion of the *ichigen-kin* (1-string *koto*) and *nigen-kin* (2-string *koto*) in this book. There is also a unique instrument called *taisho-goto*, modeled after the *nigen-kin*, which has push buttons arranged in the order of piano keys so that people can play the instrument easily. Even now, it is an extremely popular instrument. Pitches are produced by pushing buttons with the left hand, while the right hand holds a plectrum; the two strings can be played simultaneously. The instrument is a very simple, melodic instrument. This is all one need know about the *taisho-goto*, so I have not made a separate entry for this instrument.

3–1: *Koto*

The history of the 13-string *koto* begins with its importation from China as a *gagaku* instrument (*gakusō*) in the seventh and eighth centuries CE. The *gakusō* is still used today in the *gagaku* orchestra and retains its original shape and form. Use of the *gakusō* spread to temples and ordinary citizens. With the development of a new genre in the sixteenth century, the *gakusō* was referred to as the *chikusō*. In the seventeenth century, with Kengyō Yatsuhashi's (1614–85) popularization of the instrument among the common classes, it came to be known as the *zokusō*. The *zokusō* developed into two distinct traditions, the Ikuta and the Yamada, which still remain the two major *zokusō* traditions.[2]

Historically, there were very few instrumental pieces in the *koto* repertoire, most pieces being vocal works in which the *koto* provided accompaniment. In the 1960s, however, the *koto* began to develop an extensive body of instrumental works. Today, the *koto* is the most active Japanese instrument.

An instrument that now plays an important role in ensemble works, the 17-string bass *koto* was developed in 1921 by Michio Miyagi (1894–1956) in a cooperative effort with Hisao Tanabe. Miyagi also experimented with the construction of an 80-string *koto*; this instrument, however, was too impractical for use. In the early 1960s, Shūretsu Miyashita combined the 13-string *koto* and the 17-string *koto* to create a 30-string *koto*. What few 30-string *kotos* exist are all played by Miyashita's students. The 20-string *koto* was born in 1969 through the collaborative efforts of Keiko Nosaka and myself, and two years later, in 1971 the number of strings was increased to twenty-one. The repertoire for the 21-string has soared in numbers: there are hundreds of performers and many times that number of instruments. Beginning with China, 21-string zithers have been adopted by every country in East Asia. As a result, the repertoire for this instrument can be played throughout East Asia; it is my belief that the 21-string zither will become an international standard.

Many performers, however, have created zithers with different numbers of strings. In Japan, *kotos* with fifteen strings, eighteen strings, twenty-two strings, and Keiko Nosaka's 25-string *koto* have appeared, each of these instruments being actively promoted by their creators.

The first section of this chapter discusses the basic 13-string *koto* and the characteristics that all *kotos* have in common. The second section discusses some of the distinctive characteristics of different-sized *kotos*.

(1) Construction

The construction of the 13-string *koto* has hardly changed for over 1,000 years. In the twentieth century, strings have been added, the size has been increased, and different modifications have been effected through the ingenuity of performers, composers, and instrument makers; nonetheless, the construction of the koto remains fundamentally the same.

a) Body of the instrument

The names for the parts of the 13-string *koto* are given in figure 3.1. Paulownia is the best wood for constructing the body of the instrument, and *kotos* constructed from straight-grained paulownia are reputed to have the highest sound quality, grained paulownia being the level below. Recently, the number of *kotos* made from plywood and other inferior materials has increased, but in the world of Japanese music where timbre and quality of sound are of primary importance, these instruments have yet to be widely accepted.

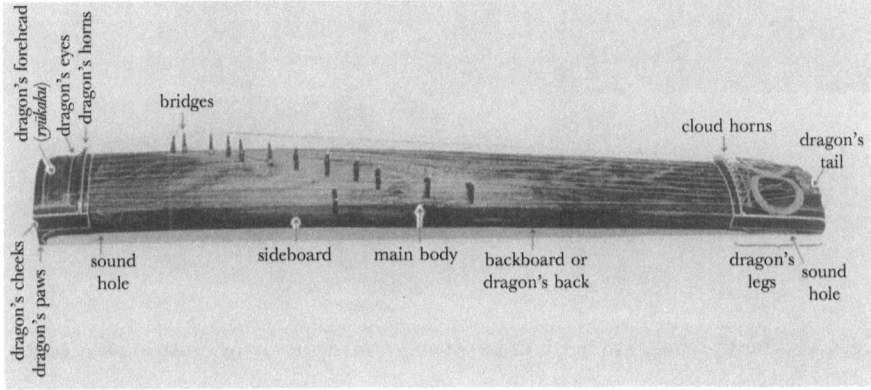

Fig. 3.1. The *gakusō*

Some parts of the *koto* must be made from harder wood, and the head, the tail, the *ryūkaku*, and the *unkaku* are made from *kōki* wood. Many exquisite *koto* found in museums are decorated with mother-of-pearl and other materials. It is believed that a *koto* produces its best sound for a period of ten or twenty years after its construction.

The length of the 13-string koto is 6 *shaku* (181.8 centimeters); however, the 21-string *koto* is 190 centimeters while the 17-string bass *koto* is 210 centimeters. The oldest *gakusō* is 194 centimeters in length. The width of the 13-string *koto* is 25 centimeters, the 21-string *koto* is 36 centimeters, and the 17-string *koto* is 31 centimeters. The height or thickness of the 13-string *koto* is 4.8 centimeters, the 21-string *koto* is 6 centimeters, the 17-string is 10.3 centimeters, and the *gakusō* is 4.3 centimeters. Figure 3.2 illustrates the three basic types of *kotos*.

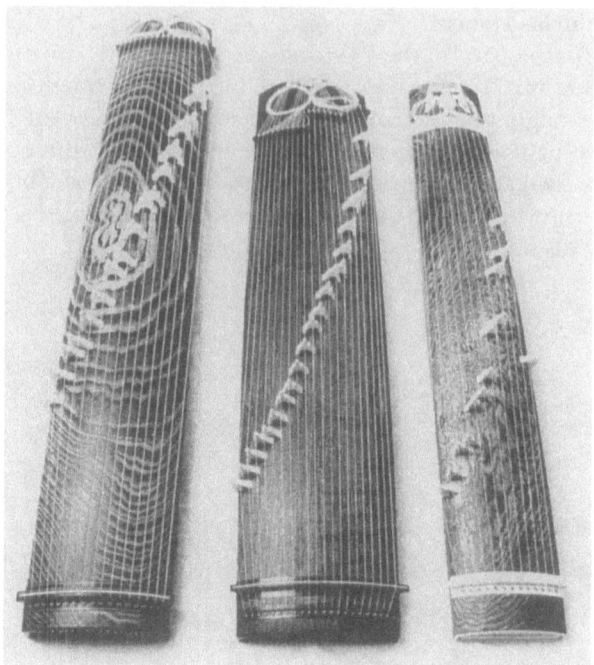

Fig. 3.2. The 17-string *koto* (left), the 21-string *koto* (center), the 13-string *koto* (right)

b) The strings

Traditionally, silk is considered the highest quality material for the strings. The gauge for the strings of the 13-string *koto* is the same, and the performer's plucking in a predetermined area gives the *koto* its characteristic sound quality. The techniques used in contemporary music, however, require an increased string tension, which causes the silk strings to snap more easily. Thus, performers have replaced the silk with strings made from synthetic materials—nylon and tetron—that approximate the timbre of silk strings. Synthetic strings are made in numerous gauges; for example, the strings of the 13-string *koto* come in gauges from 17 to 19 *monme*[3] (the total weight of thirteen strings). The strings of any individual 13-string *koto* are the same gauge. According to the register, the strings of the 17-string bass *koto* use between seven and eleven types of gauges that range from 30 to 80 *monme*, while the strings of the 21-string *koto* come in seven gauges of thickness, ranging from 17.5 to 45 *monme*.

Traditionally, the strings for the 13-string *koto* are white, while those for the 17-string *koto* are yellow. With more than seventeen strings of the same color, it becomes extremely difficult for performers to distinguish one string from another. In order to avoid this problem with the 21-string *koto*, it was decided that certain strings should be colored differently.

c) Bridges

The bridges of the koto are called *ji* or *kotoji*. The bridges of the *wagon* were originally made from the joints of tree branches, but have been replaced with rosewood. Bridges for the *koto* are made from inexpensive Chinese wood or plastic, although the recent opinion is that ivory bridges produce the best sound. The bridges of the 13-string *koto* are 6 centimeters in height. There are also bridges 4.7 centimeters in height that are used when needed: depending on the tension of the strings, these small bridges are used to tune a string when the correct pitch is impossible to obtain without being obstructed by a neighboring bridge. With the development of the 17-string *koto*, the largest bridge has a height of 8.5 centimeters. For 20 or 30-string *kotos*, one instrument may have a set of bridges of different sizes; the 21-string *koto*, for example, normally has four different sizes of bridge between 6 and 7 centimeters in height.

d) The picks (*tsume* or plectra)

Normally, a performer attaches three small picks called *tsume* to the thumb, first, and second fingers of the right hand. *Gakusō* picks are made from bamboo, bone, or deer horn, but *zokusō tsume* are made from ivory. Due to the difficulty of obtaining ivory, however, *tsume* have recently been made from plastic. The picks are set into paper strips, which are then set in leather rings or bands coated with lacquer. The rings tend to slip off, and *koto* players have been using egg whites as an adhesive for many years. Today, it is time-consuming and troublesome to prepare egg whites for every performance, and performers have devised various ways of solving this problem.

The shape of the *tsume* differs depending on the school of performance. The Ikuta school uses square-shaped *tsume*, while the Yamada school uses a rounded *tsume* (figure 3.3). Each has distinctive merits, but the rounded *tsume* are ineffective for tremolos.

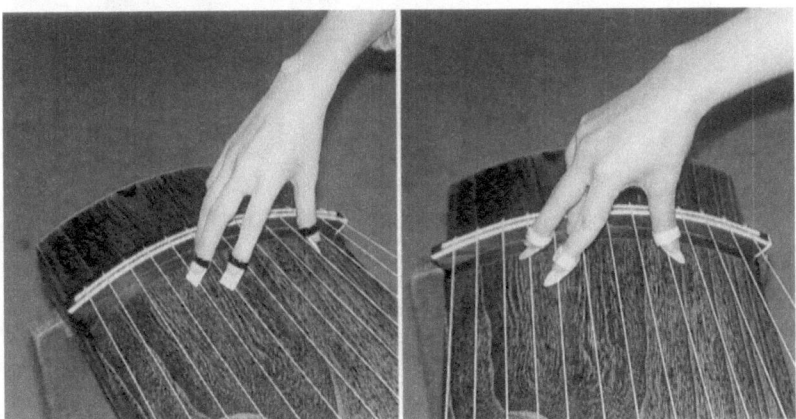

Fig. 3.3. Illustrations of the Ikuta plectra and the Yamada plectra

In *koto* music, pizzicato with the third and fourth fingers of the right hand is indicated by "pizz." Pizzicato played with the left hand may be indicated by writing "+" above the note.

e) The *koto* stand

Gakusō players perform cross-legged, while *zokusō* players in the nineteenth century performed while sitting on their heels. Today, performers commonly sit in a chair with the *koto* on a stand. When performing with pop musicians, they are often requested to play standing.

Since the twentieth century, many methods have been contrived to raise the *koto* when performing while sitting on one's heels. A simple pair of legs called *uma-no-ashi* was placed underneath the head and tail to support the body. Later, vertical boards were placed in the same position with a horizontal board to stabilize both ends. In 1952, a large, resonating *koto* stand was designed by Utashito Nakashima and Yukio Tanaka.

When the strings of the *koto* are played, the sound is amplified by the resonating cavity of the hollow body; some of the sound is transmitted through the wooden parts of the instrument. In concert halls, where the sound resonating through holes underneath the head and the tail is more pronounced, the shape and quality of the stand's vertical board under the instrument greatly influences the sound quality (figure 3.4). In the early 1970s, just as the 21-string *koto* began to be manufactured in larger numbers, I conducted blind tests at several different halls with the cooperation of many *koto* players. The results of these tests showed conclusively that the volume and power of the sound transmitted to the seats in a concert hall are unmistakably affected by instrument quality, string quality, and stand quality.

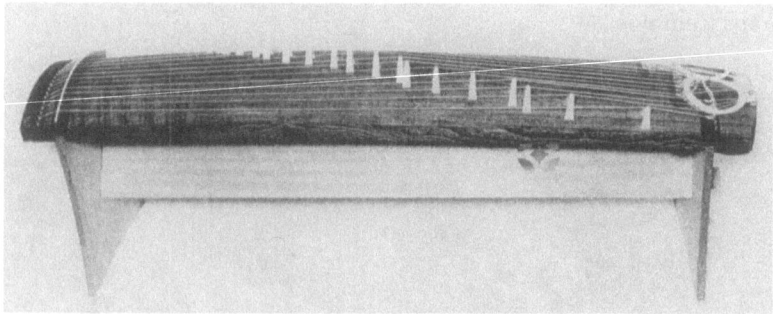

Fig. 3.4. A 20-string (21-string) *koto* placed on a standard *koto* stand

(2) Range and Tuning

By moving the bridges on the *koto*, it is possible to tune each string to either of its extremes. In the extreme registers, however, the reverberation is poor and an expressive sound is difficult to produce. In addition, a composer should be aware that the use of the left hand in the lower range is limited.

a) The range of different-sized *koto*

It is difficult to compare the 13-string *koto* with strings of the same gauge to the larger-sized *kotos* such as the 17-string bass *koto* and 21-string *koto*, where string gauge differs according to the range. The usable range of each *koto* is illustrated in figure 3.5. The range between the white whole notes is the normal range. Other *kotos* have special-sized strings, so the composer should consult with individual performers to determine the ranges of these instruments.

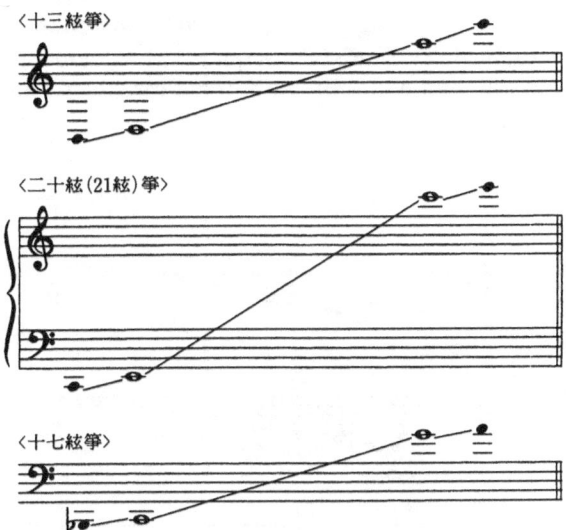

Fig. 3.5. The range of different-sized *koto* (from top to bottom: 13-, 21-, and 17-string *koto*)

b) Tuning

The 13-string *koto* has numerous traditional tunings. These tunings, illustrated in figure 3.6 with the *Ryūkyū*, or Okinawa tuning, were compiled by Hisao Tanabe, and correspond to the pentatonic scales used in Japanese music. The names of these scales, however, differ according to the school of *koto* playing, which often leads to confusion. To the right of the first tuning in the figure is the range in which the first string can be set. As explained at the beginning of this chapter, the *zokusō*, like the *shamisen*, was originally an instrument that accompanied song. Hence, all of these tunings can be transposed to match the range of the singer.

For *koto* music, the notes in the score should be the actual sounding pitch, as with all the instruments discussed thus far. For solo pieces and parts, each performer should use the notation to which they are accustomed. Each school of *koto* playing has its own tablature, all of which indicate the name of the string rather than the sounding pitch. While effective for indicating what strings should be plucked, traditional tablature is ineffective for notating complex rhythms. Like a vocal part that indicates both music and words, the easiest notation for a *koto* performer to read is Western staff notation with traditional *koto* tablature indicated above the staff. There is even a *koto* school that places special symbols above Western staff notation to indicate strings one through five. While useful within the confines of one school, since the system of tablature notation varies between schools of playing, *koto* players from one school may not be able to interpret other tablature systems. Consequently, I recommend using Western staff notation with numbers above the staff to indicate the string to be plucked, as shown in figure 3.6.[4]

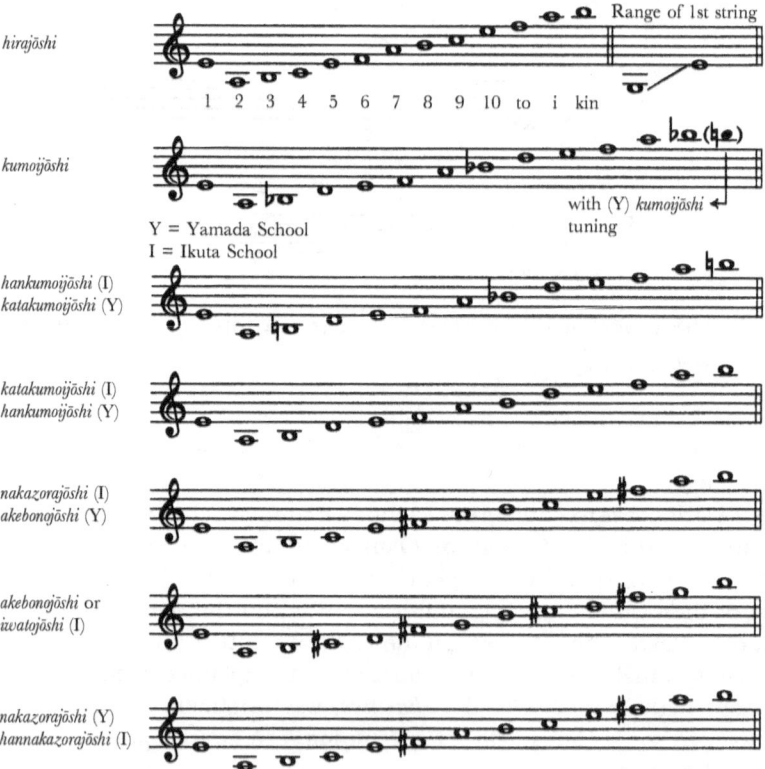

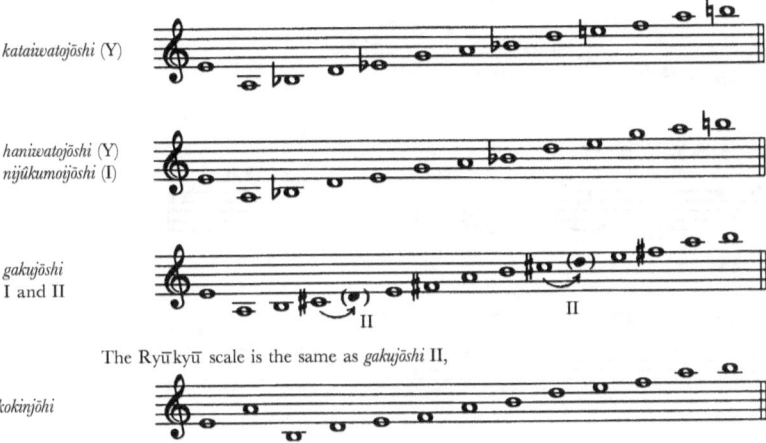

Fig. 3.6. Traditional *koto* tunings

In contemporary music for the *koto*, it is common for a bridge to be moved during a piece in order to change the tuning. With the exception of the lower strings, a bridge can be moved within a few seconds. If a composition calls for a tuning change, the *koto* performer will mark the strings to be moved before the performance. Many contemporary pieces for *koto* call for harmonics (which will be discussed below), a technique that also requires marking the strings. As a result, *koto* performers require substantial preparation time before a performance. The bridges must be set for the tuning used at the beginning of the piece, and markings must be made to indicate both the harmonics and the bridges to be moved throughout the piece. As an example, in my opera *Ada*, commissioned by a British opera company, I had originally written for a part to be played by a solo harp; at the opera company's request, however, I rewrote the harp part for a 21-string *koto*. As a result, the 21-string *koto* performer had to move the bridges over 200 times. This is, of course, an extreme example, and as a well-trained, professional 21-string *koto* player played the part there were no problems during the performance. Changing the bridges during a performance takes great care and concentration, and often results in the player losing focus. Needless to say, this is not a desirable condition. Also, it is important to remember that when a performer is changing a bridge with the left hand, it is impossible to manipulate the resonance of notes plucked with the right hand or to perform any left-handed pressing techniques.

With the 13-string *koto*, it is possible to use tunings based on diatonic scales, 12-tone rows, as well as modes (figure 3.7). Tunings based on modes are particularly well suited for the 13-string *koto*.

134 ◆ STRING INSTRUMENTS (ZITHERS)

Fig. 3.7. Tunings for the 13-string *koto* based on diatonic scales (a) and modes (b) tuning of the first *koto* part in Yoshiro Irino's *Music for Two Kotos* (c), and tuning of the second *koto* part from Minoru Miki's *Aya II* (d)

The tunings for the bass 17-string *koto* are normally based on the diatonic scale illustrated in figure 3.8. In this case, even if string numbers are not indicated in the music, the performer should be able to make a connection between the notation and the actual string to be plucked (sharps or flats can be added any of these pitches without difficulty).

Fig. 3.8. Tunings for the 17-string *koto*

The basic tuning for the 21-string *koto* is indicated in figure 3.9a. The performer should understand the relationship between the notation and the actual string to be plucked. The five string numbers circled in the graph represent the yellow strings on the 21-string *koto*, which, in the basic tuning, correspond to the pitches c, g, c^1, g^1, and c^2.

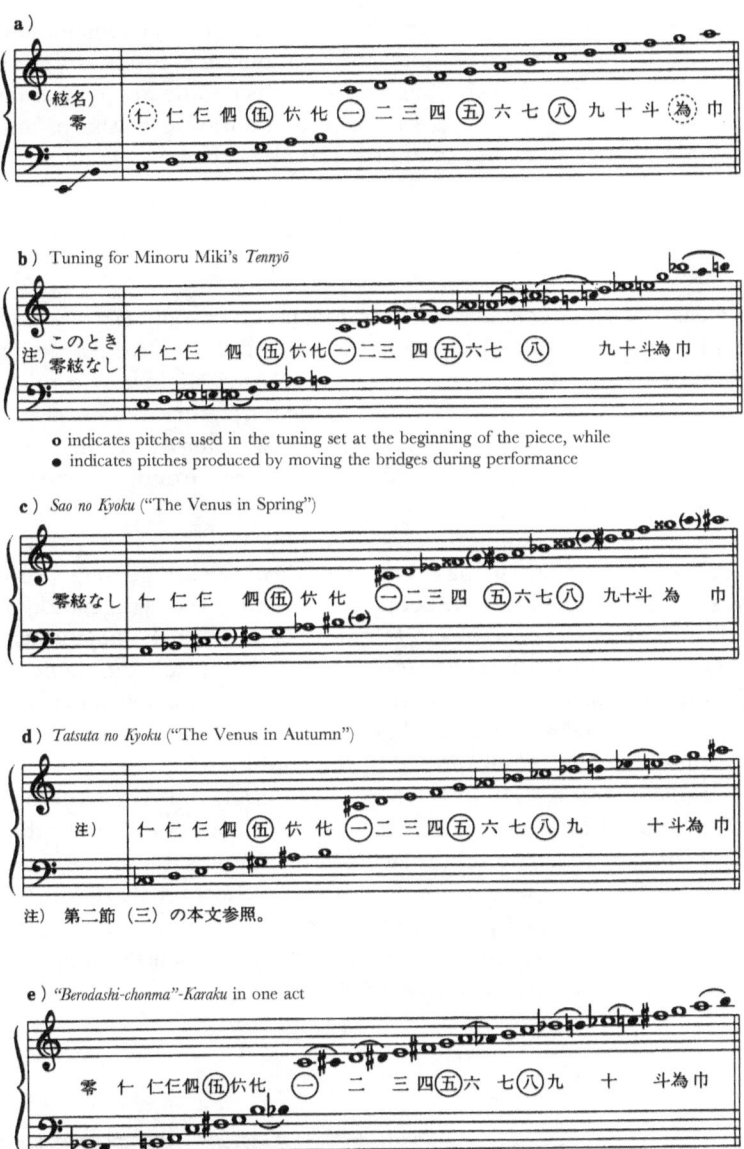

Fig. 3.9a–e. Tunings for the 21-string *koto*

One intent in creating the 21-string *koto* was to facilitate sight-reading by establishing a clear relationship between Western staff notation and the sounds produced on the instrument. Because of this, I think the scope and range of musical situations in which the *koto* can participate has expanded greatly.

A decided advantage is that 21-string *kotos* can be tuned to any imaginable scale structure. While there are exceptions (for example, the strings at the extreme registers), the 21-string *koto* was designed so that its middle range would use the basic tuning as much as possible, with a free application of sharps and flats. Figure 3.9b–e illustrates several examples of such tunings.

(3) Left-hand Techniques

Until the early twentieth century, left-hand technique on the *koto* was limited to changing the timbre and pitch by using the area on the left side of the bridges. With the influx of Western music into Japan, Miyagi Michiyo and other composers began imitating techniques found in the harp and other Western instruments. With the influence of contemporary music after the 1960s, numerous possibilities on the *koto* were explored. The following examples illustrate left-hand techniques and their notation.

a) *Oshide* (pressing technique)

The left hand presses the string on the left side of the bridge to raise the pitch a minor or major second before being plucked with the right hand. When a piece calls for a pitch outside of the tuning designated at the beginning of the score, the decision rests with the performer as to what means should be utilized. Either raising the pitch on a string immediately below the desired pitch by an *oshide*, or moving a bridge, are possible. For complicated compositions, these decisions should be made beforehand by the composer.

Arrows indicate this technique as shown in figure 3.10a. The written pitch is the pitch produced when pressing the string, and does not indicate the string that should be plucked. The solid black arrow indicates a minor second alteration, while an empty white arrow indicates a major second alteration.[5] To indicate a return to the original pitch, a small circle is sometimes used as in figure 3.10b, but normally this is unnecessary. A similar circle is used to indicate harmonics, and using both may lead to confusion.

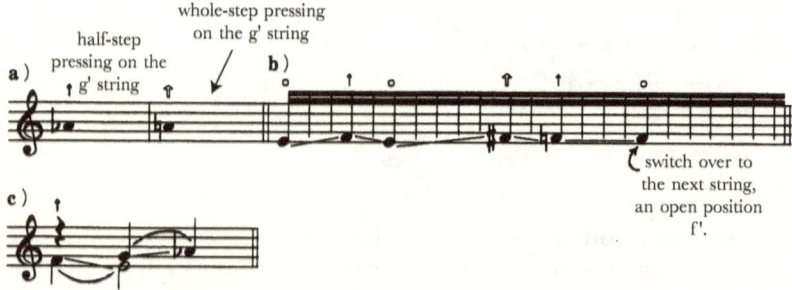

Fig. 3.10. *Oshide* technique

Normally, an *oshide* alters one string. It is possible, however, to execute this technique while pressing two strings simultaneously. One effective way to do this is illustrated in figure 3.10c, but it is best to limit it to a minor second at most (for professionals, it is possible to execute this technique in the lower range and press up a major second).

b) ***Oshibiki*** **(glissando pressing technique)**

After plucking a string with the right hand, the left hand presses a string to the left of the bridge and raises the pitch a minor or major second. If the symbol ╱ is used between the two pitches, it is unnecessary to use arrows indicating the change in pitch. If, however, the composer wants the performer to pluck an open string and then rearticulate a higher pitch on the same string without the glissando, an arrow placed above the next note will make this as clear as using a symbol. It is more practical to consider this kind of technique as an *oshide* rather than an *oshibiki* (see figure 3.11c). In general, when the raised pitch is not rearticulated by plucking, a slur should connect the two pitches. A line should also be inserted between the two pitches. The shape of this line serves as a graphic representation of the movement of the reverberating pitch. See figure 3.11f.[6]

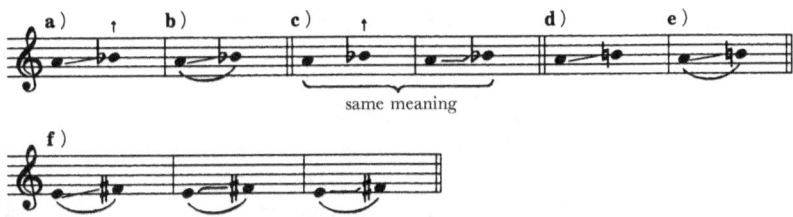

Fig. 3.11a–f. Some *oshibiki* techniques

c) ***Ato-oshi*** **(ornamental pressing technique)**

Similar to *oshibiki*, after a right-hand pluck, the left hand presses the string to the left of the bridge to raise a pitch (figure 3.12). The degree of pressing and the resultant interval, however, is indeterminate. Moreover, after raising the pitch a lower-pitched string is immediately plucked.

Fig. 3.12. An *ato-oshi* technique

d) ***Oshi-hanashi*** **(pre-pressing release technique)**

For *oshi-hanashi*, the left hand presses the string to the left of the bridge before plucking, and then releases after the string has sounded (figure 3.13). Similar to *oshide*, an arrow must be placed above the note to be plucked. A slur should be used to connect the two pitches and a line placed between them, similar to *oshide*.

Fig. 3.13. The *oshi-hanashi* technique

e) *Yuri* (vibrato)

Yuri is the application of a vibrato with the left hand after a string is plucked. A clear, definite vibrato should be indicated with the following type of graphic ﾍﾍﾍﾍﾍ. See figure 3.14. It is not necessary to indicate a common vibrato.

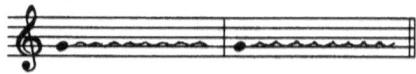

Fig. 3.14. The *yuri* technique

f) *Hiki-iro* (pulling technique)

After a string has been plucked, a *hiki-iro* lowers the pitch by the left hand pulling on the string on the left of the bridge to the right. As shown in figure 3.15, this technique is indicated by using a graphic line in combination with the character ヒ or ひきいろ. The technique is ineffective in the higher register and difficult to execute in the lower register. In the middle register, the pitch can be lowered about a minor second, but it is better not to consider this technique as a method for lowering a pitch. Rather, *hiki-iro* should be considered a delicate ornamentation. It has the same nuance as the *nayashi* technique of the *shakuhachi*.

Fig. 3.15. The *hiki-iro* technique

g) *Tsuki-iro* (quick pressing technique)

The left hand quickly presses and immediately releases a note after it has been plucked with the right hand. If the technique is executed very quickly, the reverberating pitch can be ornamented at quite a loud volume. This technique is very elegant when the string is plucked and the note is allowed to reverberate for a few seconds. As illustrated in figure 3.16, a graphic line is used to indicate the reverberating pitch, and the symbol ツ may also be written directly above the ornament.

Fig. 3.16. The *tsuki-iro* technique

h) *Keshizume* (muting technique)

The back of the nail of the forefinger of the left hand is placed underneath the string to the right of the bridge and lightly touches the string before plucking. When the string is plucked, it creates a deadened, buzz-like timbre. A small black triangle is placed to the right side of the pitch to indicate this technique (figure 3.17).

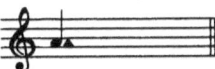

Fig. 3.17. The *keshizume* technique

i) Muting

When muting the *koto*, one of the fingers of the left hand is placed on a string where it passes over the top of the bridge. When the string is plucked with the right hand, the resulting timbre lacks brightness and resonance; it is nonetheless effective. As it is very easy to confuse this technique with *keshizume*, this technique should be clearly indicated by writing "mute" above the selected pitches (figure 3.18).

Fig. 3.18. The technique of muting

j) Staccato

Staccato on the *koto* is normally produced by damping the string on the right side of the bridge with the left (sometimes the right) hand after it has been plucked. A normal staccato dot should be placed above the note to indicate this technique.[7]

k) Pizzicato

On the *koto*, pizzicato is used to refer to pitches produced with the tips of the fingers, in contrast to the normal method of plucking with the *tsume*. When producing pizzicato with the left hand, it is possible to use all of the fingers. When left-hand pizzicato is desired, the composer should mark "+" above the notes to be plucked. There are some schools of koto that use the symbol "⌢," the same symbol used to indicate pizzicato for the *shamisen*. See figures 3.19 and 3.29. It is also possible to perform a "Bartók pizzicato" on the lower strings.

Fig. 3.19. Pizzicato in an excerpt from Minoru Miki's *Ame-zanzan* ("A Squall")

l) Harmonics

On the *koto*, it is only possible to perform harmonics at the second partial, which produces a pitch an octave higher than the open string. See figure 3.20a. *Koto* performers will mark the middle of strings on which harmonics are to be played in preparation before a performance. There are several ways to produce a harmonic. The *koto* player places the tip of a finger or the side of the palm of the left hand on the marked area, and plucks with either the right hand or an available finger on the left hand. Harmonics have a pure and distinct timbre, but lack the power and volume found in a normally plucked note. In classical *koto* music, harmonics are called *fuene*, or "flute sounds."

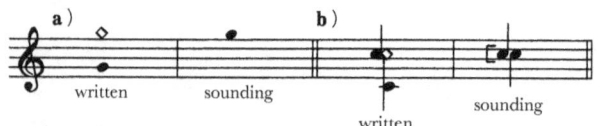

Fig. 3.20. Harmonic effects on the *koto*

A unique effect can be produced by playing a harmonic in the manner mentioned above while simultaneously plucking another string with the same pitch as the harmonic with the *tsume*. The result is a subtle change in both pitch and timbre. As this is an advanced technique, it should be used with caution (see figure 3.20b).

m) *Voix céleste*

On the Western harp, a doubling effect can be produced by changing the pedals. On the *koto*, the same effect can be produced by setting two strings to the same pitch, but then adjusting one of them to create a slight difference between their frequencies (figure 3.21). By plucking both strings at the same time, the difference between these frequencies creates beats, producing a rich *voix céleste* effect.

Fig. 3.21. The *voix céleste* effect in an excerpt from Minoru Miki's *Sōmon*

(4) Right-hand Techniques

The basic technique used to produce a sound on the *koto* is to pluck the string with the plectrum on the thumb of the right hand a few centimeters from the *ryūkaku* (the fixed bridge on the performer's right), and stopping the movement of the hand when the plectrum strikes the next string. According to one explanation, the most resonant place to pluck the string can be found by dividing the string into eight equal parts and by playing at the distance 1/8 from the *ryūkaku*, which is rich in overtones. The first finger and second finger pluck in the opposite direction of the thumb. The remaining two fingers are used for pizzicato. In composing passages for the *koto*, one must consider how to use the first three fingers naturally. To indicate a normal pluck with the fingers, a down-bow symbol similar to that for the violin is sometimes used, but normally this is unnecessary.

Among the right-hand techniques to be introduced, there are several that are considered traditional. In the musical examples, the letters below the staff indicate the accompanying mnemonics, or *shōga*, the Japanese equivalent of the solfège system.

a) *Awasezume* (playing together)

Awasezume is the simultaneous plucking of two strings with the thumb and middle finger of the right hand. In classical koto repertoire, this technique is most often used to play octaves or unisons. When employing this technique in contemporary music, the first finger can be added to play three-note chords (figure 3.22). It is, of course, possible to play even richer harmonies by incorporating the remaining fingers without tsume attached. As it requires time, however, to prepare the finger positions on different strings, I recommend limiting this technique to six-note harmony. Also, if the thumb of the right hand takes the highest note within a chord, the overall balance will improve.

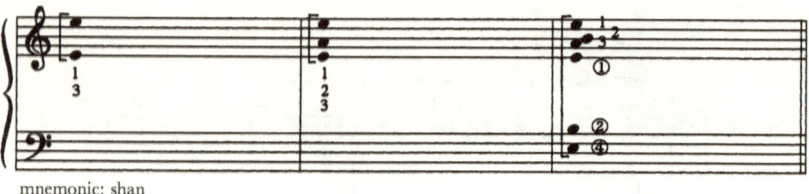

Fig. 3.22. The *awasezume* technique

b) *Kakite* (adjacent string plucking)
Two adjacent strings are plucked in a rapid gesture to create a roll-like effect using the third finger. See figure 3.23a.

c) *Warizume* (adjacent string plucking with repetition)
A traditional performance technique similar to *kakite*, except that the strings are plucked twice, first with index finger, and then with the second finger. See figure 3.23b.

d) *Oshiawase* (pressing and plucking together)
The pitch of a lower string is raised to the pitch of the upper neighboring string and both strings are played quickly like an arpeggio. See figure 3.23c.

e) *Kakezume* (middle finger grace note technique)
Common patterns from traditional repertoire. See figure 3.23d.

f) *Kakizume* (technique of alternating fingers 3 and 1)
Another classic pattern. See figure 3.23e.

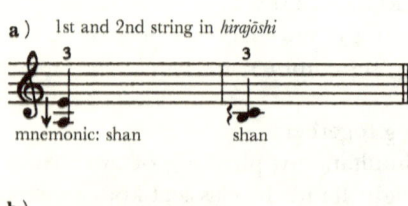

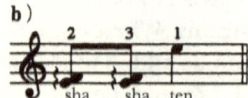

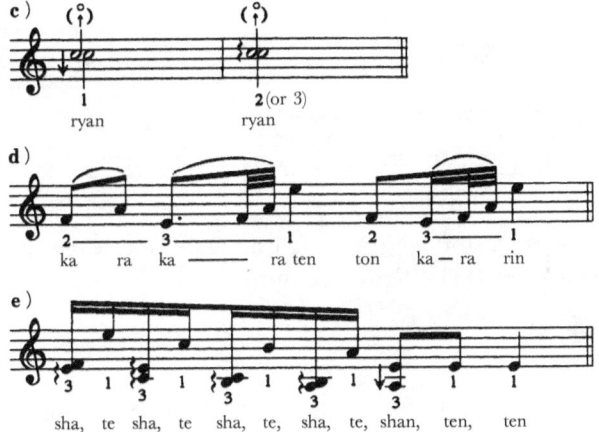

Fig. 3.23a–e. Various right-hand *koto* techniques: *kakite, warizume, oshiawase, kakezume,* and *kakizume*

g) *Sukizume* (upstroke)

The back of the plectrum is used in a scooping motion and is most commonly performed with the thumb. This technique is indicated by the symbol V, used to indicate an up-bow for the violin. *Sukuizume*—figure 3.24a—is most often performed in conjunction with normal downward plucking while 3.24b is from *Tatsuta no Kyoku* ("The Venus in Autumn"), a composition based almost entirely on this technique. The symbol ✓ is used to indicate a strong accent created by quickly scraping the string alongside the edge.

Fig. 3.24a, b. Examples of *sukizume*. Figure 3.24b is an excerpt from Minoru Miki's *Tatsuta no Kyoku* ("The Venus in Autumn")

h) *Kozume* (flicks)

Producing a timbre similar to *sukuizume*, the front of the plectrum flicks the string and plucks upwards (figure 3.25). The symbol ↗ is used to indicate this technique.

Fig. 3.25. The *kozume* technique

i) *Chirashizume* (swiping plectra)

The first or second finger (or both in the case of two strings) of the right hand quickly swipe the string (or strings) from right to left with the side of the plectrum (figure 3.26). This technique is indicated by the symbol ← or ↙. The symbol ⇐ is used to indicate when the performer scrapes the top edge of the plectra on the string, while the symbol ⇒⇐ is used to indicate a back-and-forth gesture.

Fig. 3.26. The *chirashizume* technique

In the classical repertoire, *chirashizume* performed on first and second strings is known as *waren*.

j) *Surizume* (plectrum scrape)

The back of the plectrum on the index and middle fingers are firmly placed on adjacent strings, and a lengthy scraping gesture is executed along the strings (figure 3.27). Normally, the performer returns to the initial position. The effect is one of timbral modification, as no sensation of pitch is heard.

Fig. 3.27. The *surizume* technique

k) *Uchizume* (plectrum strike)

The face of the plectrum is used to hit the strings. The symbol ▼ is placed above the note to indicate this technique (figure 3.28). At lower dynamic levels, the pitch can be heard clearly.

Fig. 3.28. The *uchizume* technique

l) *Uchikaki* (plectrum strike/scrape)

Three or four strings are scraped rapidly like a glissando. Symbols like ↗ or ↗ are placed above the note to indicate this technique (figure 3.29). This technique has a distinctive sound quality with a strong impact.

Fig. 3.29. The *uchikaki* technique in an excerpt from Minori Miki's *Tatsuta no Kyoku* ("The Venus in Autumn")

m) Glissando

A *koto* glissando may be performed with any of the three fingers on the right hand with plectra or with the remaining fingers (figure 3.30a). The same symbol used to indicate glissando on the piano or harp should be used. Using both hands simultaneously is similar to the harp's glissando technique. More unique is the *koto*'s ability to produce a glissando of undefined pitch by playing on the untuned left side of the bridges. It is possible to play both types of glissando simultaneously. There is also a glissando played on the strings outside of the *ryūkaku*, a section of a few centimeters that performers normally do not use. Playing a glissando in this area with the plectra produces an extremely high nonpitched sound effect (figure 3.30b).

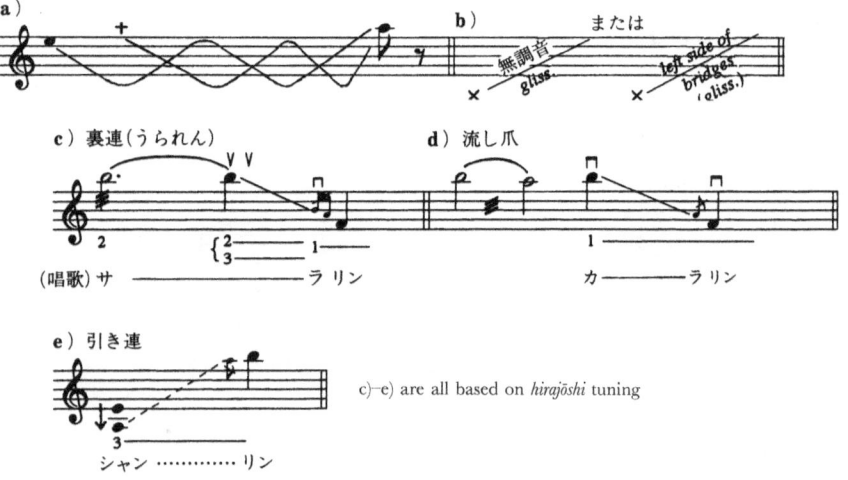

Fig. 3.30a–e. Glissandi in the *koto* repertoire

Additionally, in the classical *koto* repertoire, glissandi are often played in conjunction with other patterns and techniques, most commonly *unren* (indicated by the mnemonic *sararin*), *nagashizume* (indicated by the mnemonic *kararin*), and *hikiren*. See figure 3.30c, d, and e.

n) Tremolo

A tremolo can be executed by placing the plectra of the first finger at a right angle to a string and playing with a rapid cutting gesture. Since the *koto* is incapable of playing sustained lines, melodies performed with tremolo tend to stand out. If not handled properly, it sounds simplistic, but the effect is acceptable. Tremolos can be produced effectively and easily with Ikuta school picks, but are more difficult to execute with Yamada school picks.

o) **Repetition of the same pitch**

Because strings vibrate after a note is played, it is best to avoid playing two consecutive notes on the same string on instruments, such as the harp, that are played with the fingers. This generalization holds true for pizzicato on the *koto*. Playing with the *tsume* of the *koto*, however, is completely different, and repetition of the same pitch on the same string is extremely effective. This is one of the advantages that the *koto* has over the harp.

p) **Playing with a bow**

In the past, the *koto* was also played with a bow (a contrabass-type bow) similar to how the Korean *ajaeng* is played. This technique, however, is no longer used, necessitating research and familiarity with the *aejeng* before attempting this on the *koto*.

q) **Striking the strings of the *koto***

It is possible to execute a kind of *uchizume* (see above) technique by striking the strings of the *koto* with percussion sticks. The timbre and effect will vary greatly depending on the sticks used.

r) **Striking the body of the *koto***

As the *koto* has a large body, it is also possible to create a percussive effect by hitting it with the plectrum or a stick. The bottom board is often used in this manner. As there is no standard notation for this technique, it is necessary to provide an annotation.

s) **Playing position on the strings**

As explained in the beginning of this chapter, in traditional *koto* performance the player plucks the strings in the same fixed position, 1/8th of a string length from the *ryūkaku*. After the 21st string was added to the 20-string *koto*, I applied a technique used on the violin and other string instruments, and assigned different playing positions to obtain the timbres I wanted. The composer should only request that the performer play in a certain position on the string if they have a specific timbre in mind. Normally, it is best to leave the playing position to the performer. Below figure 3.31 I have explained what the terminology over the music indicates.

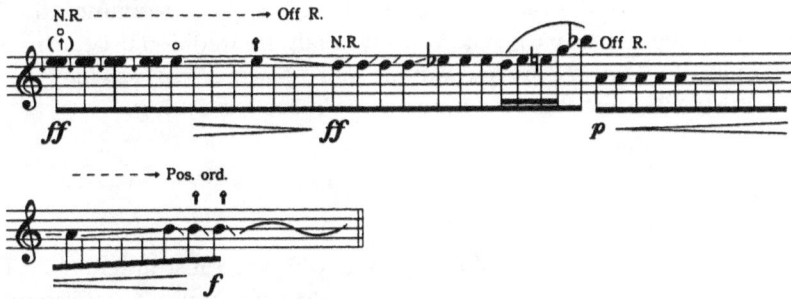

Fig. 3.31. Various *koto* playing positions in an excerpt from Minoru Miki's *Tennyo*

a) N.R. (Near the *Ryūkaku*)

This indicates that the performer should pluck the strings close to the *ryūkaku*, producing a hard timbre.

b) Off R. (off the *ryūkaku*)

This indicates that the performer should pluck the strings away from the *ryūkaku*, in the direction of the bridges, producing a soft timbre.

c) Pos. ord. (ordinary position)

This indicates that the performer should return to the normal playing position.

In the *shamisen* section, I introduced a right-hand rhythmic technique called *kokema*, in which the weak beats feel rushed. In contrast, on the *koto* there is a rhythm called *kinutamono*,[8] where the weak beats drag. This rhythm is also used for *jiuta shamisen*,[9] and, for example, in the *shamisen* part to the *Awa* dance.[10] I want the reader to know that a combination of ⊓ and ∨ creates a bouncy and relaxed rhythm that provides a distinct color, as in figure 3.32.

Fig. 3.32. *Kinuta mono* rhythm in *koto*

3–2: Special *Kotos*

In the first section, I discussed characteristics common to all *kotos*. In this section, I will first discuss the *gakusō*, which is used in *gagaku* court music, and then other newly designed *kotos* with more strings than the traditional 13-string *koto*. Even though they are recent innovations, the 17-string bass *koto* and the 21-string *koto* have become standard instruments in concert settings.

(1) *Gakusō*

In *gagaku*, since the *gakusō* plays in ensemble with wind instruments that have fixed ranges—the *shō*, the *hichiriki*, and the *ryūteki*—the tunings are also predetermined. For an instance of this, see figure 3.33.

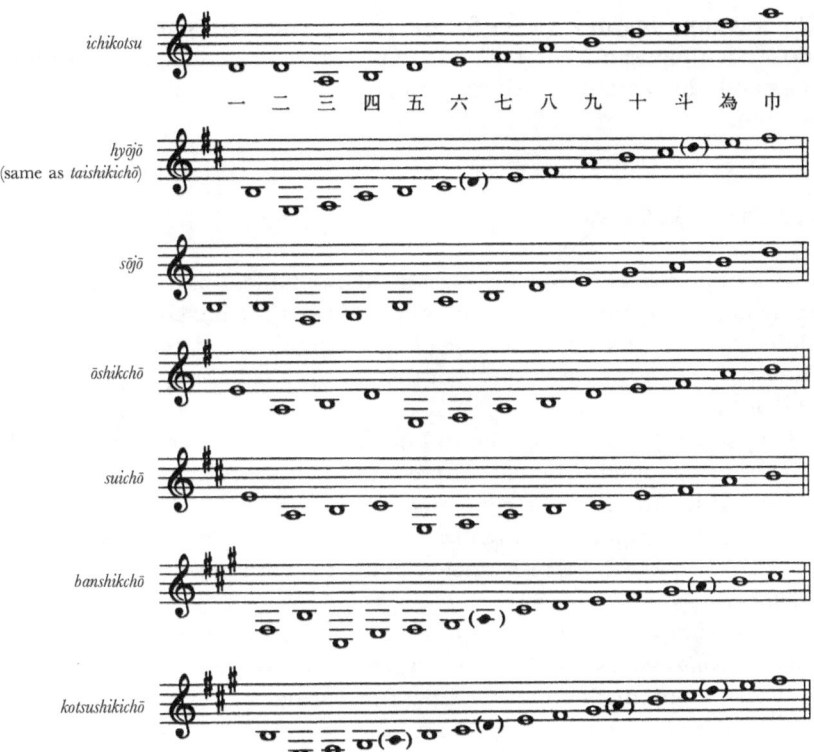

Fig. 3.33. Various tunings of the *gakusō*

In traditional *gagaku* performance, the *gakusō* is limited to playing distinctive patterns, *kakite* and *kozume*. The first technique is a pattern in which two adjacent strings are plucked with the middle finger and index finger in a fixed order. There are two ways to play the *kakite* pattern, depending on the tempo of the composition. Slower compositions use the term *shizugaki* while faster compositions use the term *hayagaki* (figure 3.34). The second technique, *kozume*, was discussed in the previous section's discussion on right-hand techniques: the thumb plucks a string without touching the next string. The symbol ↗ can be used to indicate this technique, but this is not an established rule.

Fig. 3.34. *Kakite* and *kozume* on the *gakusō*

When composing new pieces for the *gakusō*, composers are, of course, free to do what they want, but I recommend consulting with the performer to understand the extent to which they are able to execute the techniques requested.

(2) 17-string Bass *Koto*

The 17-string bass *koto* is the low voice in an ensemble. I have already discussed the origin, construction, tuning, and range of the 17-string koto in the previous section. The 17-string *koto* is capable of executing nearly all techniques as effectively as the *koto*. There are aspects of the 17-string bass *koto* not previously covered that I wish to discuss.

The 17-string *koto* was designed to function like a cello; and like the cello, it also is used as a solo instrument. There is now a large body of well-known compositions written for the 17-string *koto* as well as performers who specialize in this instrument. It is important to realize that the lower range, the thicker strings, and the larger body of this instrument require greater physical strength than the 13-string *koto*.

Effective compositional techniques for the 17-string *koto* include pizzicato, *hiki-iro*, and *ato-oshi*, as all allow the strings to reverberate for long periods of time. When manipulating the left side of the strings in the low range, it is necessary for the performer to stand and fully extend the left arm. Intricate passagework in the low range can therefore be problematic as the sounds of the resonating strings overlap, resulting in a muddy texture. Do not oversimplify writing for the 17-string *koto*.

The middle range of the 17-string *koto* is brighter and fuller than the same range on the 13-string *koto*, and can be considered the "chest voice." To ignore the extraordinary expressive potential of this range by limiting the role of this instrument to providing the bass line in ensemble works is to squander a wonderful opportunity. Figure 3.35a–c includes several excerpts from my compositions.

Fig. 3.35. Patterns for 17-string bass *koto*. (a) An excerpt from Minoru Miki's *Kagai*

Fig. 3.35. Patterns for 17-string bass *koto*. (b) An excerpt from Minoru Miki's *Hote*

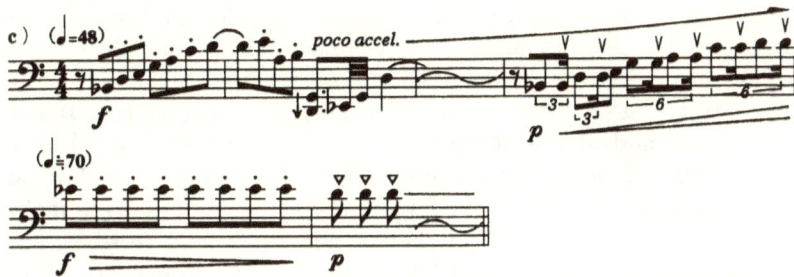

Fig. 3.35. Patterns for 17-string bass *koto*. (c) An excerpt from Minoru Miki's *Wa*

Normally, this instrument is called the 17-string *koto*, but there are many professional performers who have added an 18th string. This instrument has not yet become standard, so I recommend limiting compositional efforts to the 17-string koto.

(3) *Nijūgen* (21-string Koto)

As noted in the beginning of this chapter, the 20-string *koto* was designed in 1969, and two years later, in 1971, it became the 21-string *koto*. The reason for the addition of this extra string was illustrated in figure 3.24b, where a repeated *sukizume* pattern appears at the beginning of the composition *Tatsuta no Kyoku* ("The Venus in Autumn"). In order to execute a repeated *sukizume* pattern, one plucks rapidly with the *tsume* attached to the thumb, stops briefly on the next string and then plucks backwards with an upward stroke of the thumb. Before the addition of the extra string, playing a *sukizume* pattern on the lowest string required the performer to strike the body of the *koto* instead. An extra string, referred to as the "zero string," was added to the bottom for the sole purpose of allowing the thumb to strike an adjacent string rather than the surface of the instrument. Since then, the instrument originally created as the 20-string *koto* became the 21-string *koto* and composers write for the 21-string instrument even though it is still called the 20-string *koto*. The intent at the time was not merely to increase the range of the *koto*. It was also the idea that, in adding extra strings to increase the expressive potential of the instrument, we were creating a solo instrument that reflected contemporary sensibilities. Just as in contrast to the period in which the 13-string *koto* was built, our lives today are, in every sense, larger in scale. In the previous section, 13-string *koto* tunings were illustrated in Western staff notation. The 21-string *koto* was designed to incorporate the range of these traditional tunings, and thus preserve the unique timbre of the 13-string *koto*.

By coincidence, in 1974 I realized that zithers in China, and other countries with large Chinese populations, such as Vietnam and Indonesia, came to have twenty-one strings. The experiment in China consisted of taking the three-octave, 16-string *koto*[11] with its pentatonic scale (e.g., C–D–E–G–A, C–D–E–G–A, C–D–E–G–A–C), and adding another octave, resulting in a 21-string instrument. The concept was simple and clear; however, as can be seen in the traditional *koto* tunings in the previous section, the addition of strings to the *koto* to make the 21-string *koto* was more complicated. Following China's lead, North Korea created a twenty-string *kayagum*. In 1995, South Korea started to make *kayagum* with twenty-two strings with a seven-note diatonic scale of three octaves and one extra pitch.

As noted at the beginning of this chapter, the 20-string *koto* came to have twenty-two strings, and then Keiko Nosaka's twenty-five string *koto* appeared. Once a solid repertoire for the 25-string *koto* is established, there will surely be a new voice in the music community with the 25-string *koto* as a standard. On the other hand, people who have purchased a 21-string *koto* cannot perform compositions for a 22-string *koto*. Even now, there are many pieces composed under the assumption that all *kotos* must have 21 strings. The Chinese version of the 21-string *koto* is recognized as the modern *koto*, and what was previously referred to as the "classic" *koto* is now simply called *koto*. If a 21-string zither is established as a pan-Asian instrument, performers will then be able to freely play compositions from other countries, and scores will be widely circulated. My composition for 21-string *koto*, *Hanayagi* ("The Greening") was recently printed in a Chinese music textbook, and is now frequently performed in China. As a result, performance technique has improved and, according to what I have been told by instrument makers and performers, the exchange of information between various Asian countries has progressed.

It is difficult for Westerners to understand why an instrument called the 20-string *koto* has 21 strings. I simply say "*koto*," and in documents, I usually write "*koto* (21 strings)." Since 2004, however, I have referred to this instrument as the *nii-goto* (新箏), the Chinese characters literally meaning "new *koto*."

As shown in figure 3.9, the first eight strings have special names, and the names for the remaining thirteen strings are the same as for the 13-string *koto*. Traditional 13-string *koto* pieces can be played on the 21-string *koto* by using the top thirteen strings, one through thirteen. Figures 3.36a–c are all excerpts from my 21-string *koto* compositions. Figures 3.19, 3.22, 3.24b, and 3.29 were also composed for the 21-string *koto*.

Fig. 3.36. Excerpts from Minoru Miki's 21-string *koto* works. (a) The beginning of Minoru Miki's *Mebae* ("A Young Sprout")

Fig. 3.36. Excerpts from Minoru Miki's 21-string *koto* works. (b) An excerpt from Minoru Miki's *Hanayagi* ("The Greening")

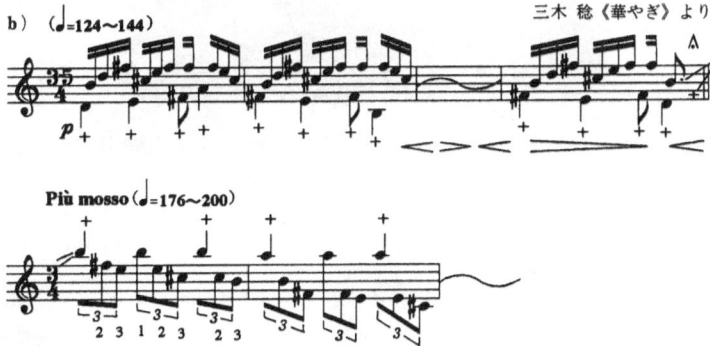

Fig. 3.36. Excerpts from Minoru Miki's 21-string *koto* works. (c) The beginning of Minoru Miki's *Autumn Fantasy*

(4) Three Types of 21-string *Kotos*

Besides the standard 21-string *koto*, there is also a shorter and a longer version of this instrument (figure 3.37). The shorter *koto* may be considered a soprano *koto*, as all of the basic tunings are one octave higher than normal. In the score, this can be indicated with 𝄞 or 𝄢. The longer *koto*, on the other hand, is one octave lower than written and can be considered a bass 21-string *koto*, or a 17-string *koto* with an expanded upper range.[12]

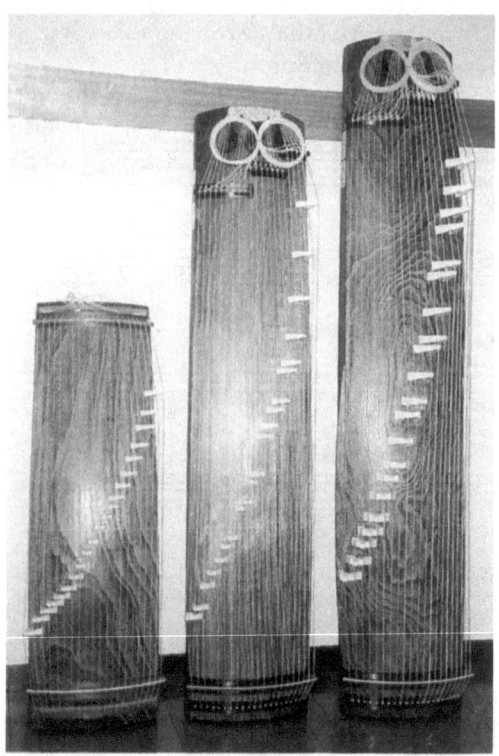

Fig. 3.37. The soprano 21-string *koto* (left), the 21-string *koto* (center), and the bass 21-string *koto* (right)

Figure 3.38 is the tuning for each of the 21-string *kotos* used in my *koto* quintet *Cassiopeia 21*.

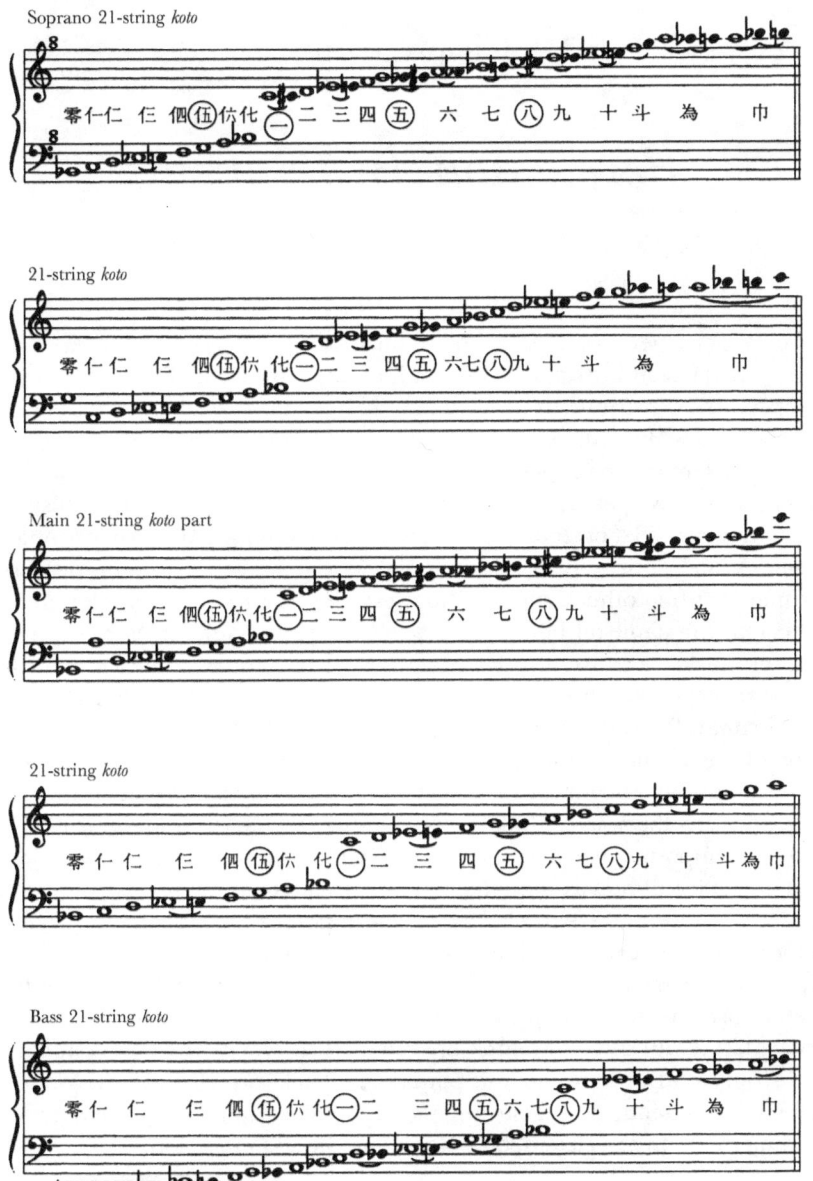

Fig. 3.38. Tunings for each 21-string *koto*—the soprano, 21-string, and bass *koto*s—used in Minoru Miki's *koto* quintet, *Cassiopeia 21*

Chapter Four

Percussion Instruments

Unlike Western percussion instruments such as the timpani or the xylophone, Japanese percussion instruments do not have definite pitch.[1] There are, however, many percussion instruments where different, if still undefined, pitches can be produced by striking the instrument in different areas. Instruments such as the *shamisen* can be considered a type of percussion instrument. The *koto* and *biwa*, the *shakuhachi* and *nōkan* also have percussive sounds that are an integral part of their music. This concept has exerted a profound influence on contemporary Western instruments.

Some Asian cultures, particularly India, have peerless membrane percussion instruments, while others, such as Indonesia, have remarkably developed metal percussion, the gamelan being the representative instrument. Some aspects of Japanese musical culture also focus on percussion; for example, the aesthetic concept of expressing the sounds of natural phenomena through the sound of a *taiko* drum reflects the pleasure Japanese take in rhythm.

One distinguishing feature of Japanese percussion performance is the rallying cries and shouts of encouragement by the performers. In some percussion ensembles, particularly the *hayashi*, these cries play more than an expressive role as the voice is also an important element in the formation of rhythmic patterns. The cries also function as musical cues as conductors are not found in traditional Japanese music.

There are several ways to classify Japanese percussion instruments, but percussionists are reluctant to adopt the academic systems of classification. For the purposes of this book, I have classified percussion instruments according to the materials used as the principal sounding medium: instruments using leather or plastic, played with sticks or hands, are classified as **Membrane Percussion**; those made from wood or bamboo and played with sticks are classified as **Wood and Bamboo Percussion**; and instruments with metal or stone as the principal sounding medium are classified as **Metal and Stone Percussion**.

4–1: Membrane Percussion

Two families of drums fall into the membrane percussion category: *taiko* and *tsuzumi*. Academic theories claim that the *taiko* came from China and the *tsuzumi* from India and Tibet. Percussion instruments belonging to the *tsuzumi* family are characterized by a cylindrical wooden body shaped like an hourglass. All that remains of the once-large *tsuzumi* family are the *ko-tsuzumi*, the *ō-tsuzumi*,[2] and the *ikko* used in *gagaku*. I will begin my discussion with the *ko-tsuzumi* since it uses many performance techniques specific to Japanese percussion instruments, many of which are unique.

(1) *Ko-tsuzumi*

In the seventh century, the *yōko* or *kure-no-tsuzumi* were brought to Japan from southern China as part of the *gigaku* (*kuregaku*) ensemble.[3] There were four types of *yōko*: the *ikko* or (*ichi-no-tsuzumi*), *ni-ko*, *san-ko*, and *yon-ko*; the *ni-ko* and *yon-ko* no longer exist. The membrane used on both heads of these *tsuzumi* was fastened with a cord called the *shirabeo*, similar to modern *tsuzumi*. The *yōko*, however, were suspended from the neck of the performer and struck with a mallet in the right hand and the palm of the left hand. In the twelfth century CE, the performance practice for the smallest of the *yōko*, the *ikko*, changed, and it began to be played by striking one face with the right hand while the left hand manipulated the pitch. It was then that the name of this instrument changed to *ko-tsuzumi*: it is also called *tsuzumi*. First used by *Shirabyōshi*,[4] the *tsuzumi* became the primary instrument of the *hayashi* ensemble in the *nō* theater, a role it continued to play in the *hayashi* of the *kabuki* theater. The *tsuzumi* remains the center of both *hayashi* ensembles (figure 4.1). As the representative Japanese percussion instrument, it is of course present in other genres as well.

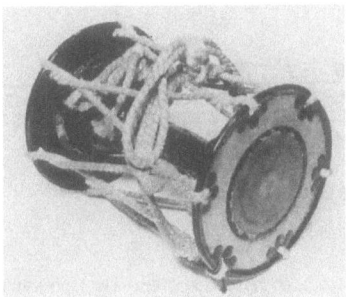

Fig. 4.1. The *ko-tsuzumi*

Tsuzumi bodies are made from cherry and are twenty-five centimeters in length. The circular membranes are fixed to both sides of the body with a hemp cord called the *shirabeo*. All drums belonging to the *tsuzumi* family use similarly shaped membranes that are created by stretching a skin over an iron ring. The two *ko-tsuzumi* membranes are made from tanned horse leather and have a diameter of 20 centimeters, the back membrane being thinner than the front. Recently, the sound quality of plastic membranes has developed to the point that it approaches that of horse leather membranes; the synthetic skins are often used because of the ease of sound production. The leather membrane should not become overly dry, which is why it common to see performers breathing on their instruments during performances. The performers place finely cut Japanese paper called *chōshi-gami*[5] on the front membrane in order to adjust the sound balance.

a) Performance technique

The performer holds a *ko-tsuzumi* in the left hand with all of the fingers gripping the *shirabeo* and places it on the right shoulder with the left elbow held high and the arm level. The balance of the tightened hemp *shirabeo* cord wrapped around the body vertically and horizontally directly influences the nuance of resulting sound. There are schools of *ko-tsuzumi* performance in which the second finger, third finger, and sometimes the first and fourth fingers of the right hand are used to strike the drum. *Ko-tsuzumi* performance technique is more than a simple strike with the fingertips through wrist action, but requires a vigorous stroke from a full extension of the arm.

Several different ways of striking the instrument exist, defined by the performer's manipulation of the *shirabeo* and the location and degree of strength by which the front membrane of the instrument is struck. Each way of striking the instrument has its own mnemonic, mnemonics being a useful method for practicing through recitation, as well as for communicating with other members of the ensemble.

Fig. 4.2. Ways of striking the *ko-tsuzumi*

1) *Po:* also referred to as *otsu*, represented by the symbol ○ in tablature notation, and pronounced "pon" within a pattern of consecutive quarter notes. *Po* is the most representative technique of the *ko-tsuzumi*. The front membrane is struck close to the center. The left hand grip on the *shirabeo* is relatively loose. The instant the front membrane is struck, the tension in the left hand is slightly reduced and then immediately returns to the original tension. This dynamic range is between the *mf* and *f*.

2) *Pu:* also referred to as *hodo*, expressed by the graphic symbol ⊖ or ⬤. *Pu* is similar to *po*, but sounds muffled or muted as the tension of the *shirabeo* is not

released after the front membrane is struck. This technique is performed between *p* and **mp**.

3) *Ta*: also referred to as *kashira*, expressed by the symbol △ or ﹀. The *shirabeo* are squeezed firmly and the membrane is struck near the rim at *ff*.

4) *Chi*: also referred to as *kan*, expressed by the symbol ●. This technique is the same as *ta*, but it is executed at a *p* dynamic level.

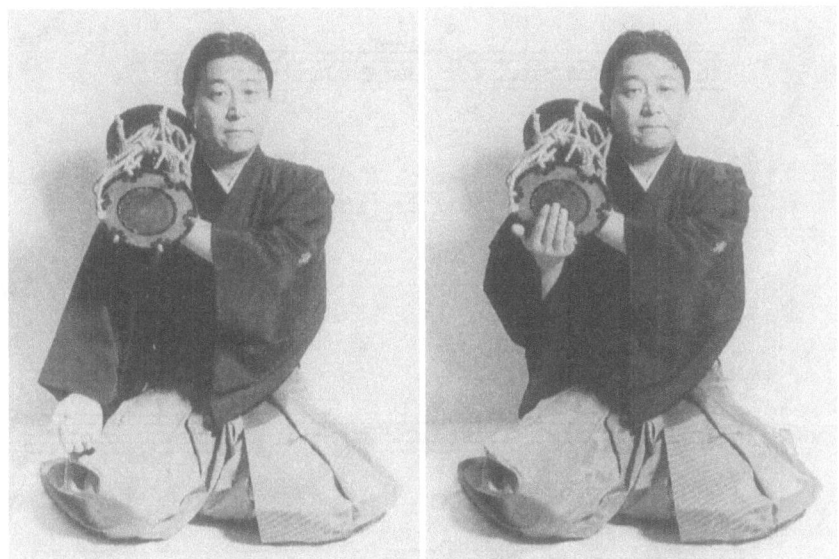

Fig. 4.3. Striking technique of the *ko-tsuzumi*

Because the playing position for *po* and *pu* differs from *ta* and *chi*, the sound quality of *ta* and *chi* is sharp. In figure 4.2, *ta* and *chi* are placed on the top line of the staff, while *po* and *pu* are placed in the middle of the staff. *Po* and *ta* are shown as *f*, while *pu* and *chi* are indicated as *p*, which allows the four distinct sounds of the *ko-tsuzumi* to be distinguished in Western staff notation. In performance, each one of these techniques can be performed consecutively, each distinguished by its unique timbre. As in figure 4.4, an ascending-descending glissando-like effect can be created by performing a series of *po* strikes, and can also be performed in numerous combinations. In traditional *hayashi*, the *ko-tsuzumi* often performs these fascinating patterns in combination with the *ō-tsuzumi*, *taiko* (or *shimedaiko*), and *nōkan*. In figure 4.5, I have introduced several representative *hayashi* patterns where the *ko-tsuzumi* plays with the *ō-tsuzumi*, *taiko*, and *nōkan*. The characters beneath the score are the corresponding mnemonics.[6]

As discussed in the introduction, the concept of *ma* is very important in Japanese traditional music. In the musical examples, the symbol ᴍ (e.g., α) is used to connote a rest of unmeasured length. Crescendo markings placed in the middle of these rests can be used to help the performer focus on heightening the energy and tension towards the next note. Due to the changing tension of the *shirabeo*, the *ko-tsuzumi* creaks during these moments of rest. These creaks, however, should be accepted as a unique characteristic of the instrument. These "noises" are especially prominent in figure 4.5,[7] measures a[8] and c.

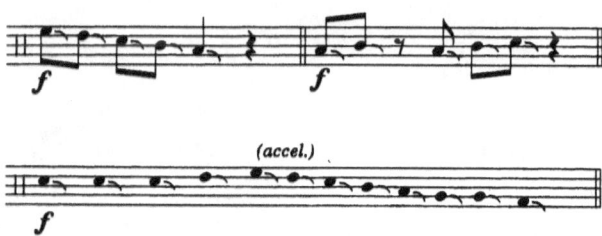

Fig. 4.4. A glissando effect

Fig. 4.5. Examples from *ko-tsuzumi* excerpts. (a) Examples in *Ranbyōshi*

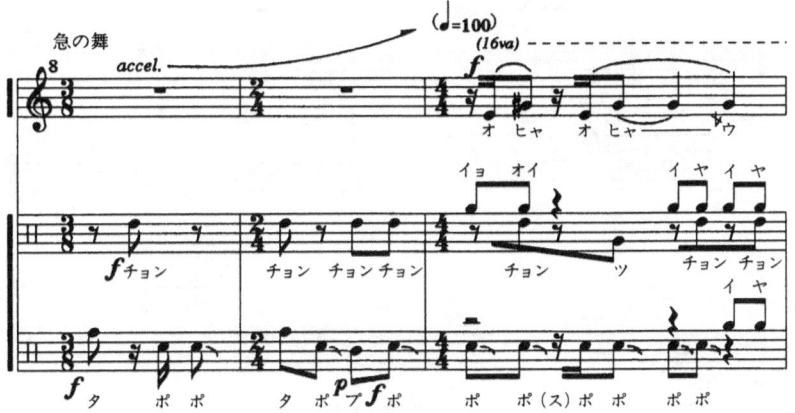

Fig. 4.5. Examples from *ko-tsuzumi* excerpts. (b) Examples in *Kyū no Mai*

Fig. 4.5. Examples from *ko-tsuzumi* excerpts. (c) Examples in *Chū no Mai*

Fig. 4.5. Examples from *ko-tsuzumi* excerpts. (d) Examples in an excerpt of an arrangement from *Shin-Yachiyojishi* (Part I), arranged by Naritoshi Tōsha

Fig. 4.5. Examples from *ko-tsuzumi* excerpts. (e) Examples in an excerpt of an arrangement from *Shin-Yachiyojishi* (Part II), arranged by Naritoshi Tōsha

(2) *Ō-tsuzumi*

The second drum of the four *yōko*, the *ni-ko*, is said to have developed into the *ō-tsuzumi*, also commonly referred to as the *ō-kawa*. The membranes for both sides of the *ō-tsuzumi* are made from cowhide, and, as with the *ko-tsuzumi*, the back membrane is thinner. The diameter of the membrane is larger than the *ko-tsuzumi* at twenty-three centimeters. The body is also made from cherry and is twenty-eight centimeters in length. Despite being larger than the *ko-tsuzumi*, the membranes are lashed more tightly to the instrument, creating a markedly higher pitch. Unlike the the *ko-tsuzumi*, which requires some humidity to produce the correct sound, the *ō-tsuzumi* membranes are dried over a fire before a performance. The continual drying of the skin considerably shortens their life span, and they are only usable a few times. Because of this, the *mokushō*[9] or another instrument is substituted for the *ō-tsuzumi* during rehearsal. High-quality plastic membranes are now being produced with considerably longer lifespans. The small thimbles placed on the fingers of the right hand are made from several layers of Mino paper that have been glued together.[10] Some performers also use a deerskin covering to protect the palm of the hand.

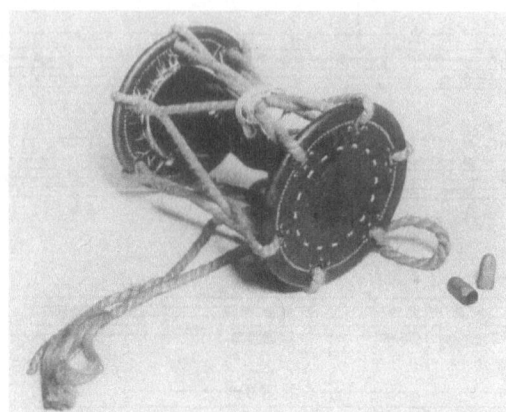

Fig. 4.6. The ō-tsuzumi

a) **Performance technique**

Rather than being placed on the shoulder, the ō-tsuzumi is placed above the left knee with the front membrane facing forward. The left hand grasps the hemp *shirabeo* from above and the right hand strikes the front membrane with the thimbles attached to the first, second, and sometimes third fingers (figure 4.7).

Fig. 4.7. Striking technique of the ō-tsuzumi

Depending on the force and the position of the strike on the membrane, there are three different sounds that can be produced from the *ō-tsuzumi*, Difference in pitch, however, is indiscernible (figure 4.8).

Fig. 4.8. Ways of striking the *ō-tsuzumi*

1. **Chon**: also referred to as *kashira*, indicated in tablature notation with the symbol △. The membrane is forcibly struck close to the center at *f*.
2. **Tsu**: also referred to as *kan* or *kone*, indicated with the symbol ● or ▲. The membrane is struck delicately at *p*.
3. **Don**: also referred to as *otsu*, indicated with the symbol ○. The original technique is the same position and the same dynamic level as *tsu*; however, after the right hand strikes the membrane, the hand and the thimbles remain on the membrane; today, however, performers now tend to execute this technique in the same way as *tsu*.

See figure 4.5a–d in the previous section for performance examples. As the membranes of the *ō-tsuzumi* are fastened tightly on the body of the instrument, there is no clear difference of timbre between different striking positions. In staff notation, it suffices to indicate different dynamics from *p* to *f* and leave the rest to the performer.

(3) *Ikko* and *San-no-tsuzumi*

Of the four *yōko*, the *ikko* and *san-no-tsuzumi* only survive as part of *gagaku* and *bugaku*. The *ikko* is suspended from the neck and struck with mallets held in both hands while dancing. The diameter of the membranes is approximately 24 centimeters, while the length of the body is approximately 26 centimeters.

The *san-no-tsuzumi* leads the ensemble in performances of *komagaku*, or "music of the right" *gagaku* music (figure 4.9). As mentioned above, in the past, all *yōko* were suspended from the neck of the performer; however, in current performance practice, the instrument is placed on the floor and struck with a stick held in the right hand. The diameter of the membranes is 43 centimeters, while the length of the body is 46 centimeters.

168 PERCUSSION INSTRUMENTS

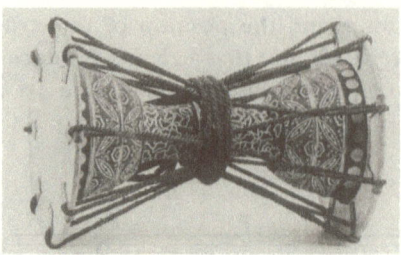

Fig. 4.9. The *san-no-tsuzumi*

These percussion instruments are no longer in common use, so I shall limit my discussion of them to the above.

(4) *Kakko*

From this point, I shall discuss the *taiko* family. Similar to *san-no-tsuzumi* in "right-side" style *gagaku* music, the *kakko* leads the ensemble in performances of Chinese-origin "music of the left" (*tōgaku*) *gagaku*. The body of the instrument, however, does not have an hourglass shape, but instead bulges. There is nothing to indicate that the *kakko* originated in India; instead, it is thought to have originated in Central Asia and was then imported as one of the instruments of the *tōgaku* ensemble. I think it should be considered as belonging in the *taiko* family. The *kakko* is the most frequently used *gagaku* percussion instrument in folk ensembles.

The length of the barrel-shaped body is 35 centimeters and it is made from oak, cherry, or mountain mulberry. The right and left membranes are both made from cowhide with a diameter of 23 centimeters. In performance, the *kakko* is set on a stand (figure 4.10). The two mallets, made from Chinese wood, are 36.5 centimeters in length.

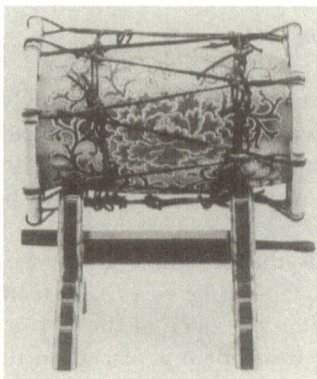

Fig. 4.10. The *kakko* on a stand

a) Performance technique

The mallet held in the right is called the "male," while the mallet held in the left hand is the "female." In classical *gagaku* performance there are three ways of playing, all of which can be combined (figure 4.11).

Fig. 4.11. Characteristic *kakko* playing techniques

1. ***Sei***: strike with the right hand on the first downbeat.
2. ***Katarai***: a pattern consisting of a right-hand stroke on the first downbeat followed by a *nagashi* from beat two, as shown in figure 4.11.
3. ***Mororai*** (also called *torotoro*): continue to strike the right and left mallets in alternation.

The gentle timbre of the *kakko* has a distinct freshness; it also has the advantage of not being easily masked in performance with other instruments. The sound itself evokes a classical elegance, and effective in creating a *gagaku*-like atmosphere.

(5) Gaku-daiko (for Gagaku)

The generic name for the *da-daiko*, *tsuri-daiko*, and *ninai-daiko* used in *gagaku* is the *gaku-daiko* (*gagaku-daiko*).

The *da-daiko* is also called the *kaen-daiko*. As illustrated in figure 4.12, *kaen-daiko* are adorned with a decorative object, bringing the total height to 364 centimeters. The tanned cowhide is 127 centimeters in diameter, while the body is 152 centimeters in depth. The pedestal on which the instrument is placed is 91 centimeters tall, and the performer stands on this to strike the instrument. Two mallets are used to play the *gaku-daiko*, each 91 centimeters in length and 4 centimeters thick. The head attached to the tip of the mallets is 9 centimeters in diameter. The performance technique is extremely simple, and limited to an occasional stroke on the downbeat.

Fig. 4.12. The *da-daiko*

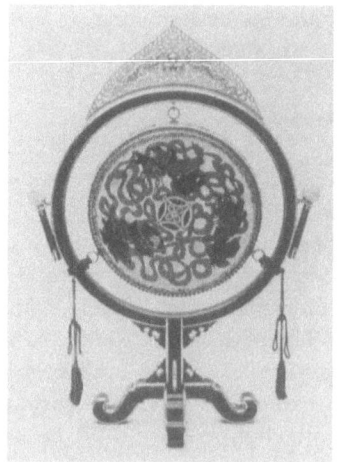

Fig. 4.13. The *tsuri-daiko*

As illustrated in figure 4.13, the diameter of the membrane of the *tsuri-daiko* is 54.5 centimeters, while the thickness of the body is 21 centimeters. Two mallets are used to play the *tsuri-daiko*, each 26 centimeters in length and 2.7 centimeters thick, and the diameter of the heads is 6 centimeters. In *gagaku*, the performer sits to play the *tsuri-daiko*. Like the *ō-daiko*, the performance technique is simple, and produces a low sound.

The *ninai-daiko* is used in processional-type *gagaku*. The diameter of the membrane is 82 centimeters making it a large instrument. Today, however, the likelihood of it being used is almost nonexistent, so I shall not discuss it here.

(6) *Ō-daiko*

Ō-daiko are also referred to as "festival drums," *yagura taiko*, or "Japanese drums." While the *ō-daiko* originally came from China, it is, in many ways, the representative instrument of Japan. Of course, the *ō-daiko* is found in festivals; it was also used as a means of communication,[11] and to create different moods in *kabuki* and other theater genres. It can be placed on a stand (similar to the *gagaku gaku-daiko*), played suspended, or placed on a float during a festival. Over the last two or three decades, the *taiko* has become increasingly popular among non-professionals, and there are many *taiko* teams active in Japan and abroad that have created ensembles with this instrument, the *shimedaiko*, and other percussion instruments. Some of the more popular *taiko* groups perform wearing nothing but a loincloth as they energetically strike immense mounted drums with thick, heavy sticks, which has introduced a visual aesthetic into the tradition. Even in more conservative performance groups like the Pro Musica Nipponia, the *ō-daiko* has a formidable presence on stage. I had many years of experience in conducting ensembles of Japanese instruments and composed several pieces where, among the percussion, the *ō-daiko* functions as the leader of the ensemble. Fortunately, I was able to bring these pieces to realization with the generous cooperation of the percussionist Takuo Tamura and his interest and expertise in directing and conducting. Despite each of these pieces incorporating folk and non-Western musical elements, they were well received internationally.

Ō-daiko come in many sizes. As illustrated in figure 4.14, they are shaped like a beer barrel. The body of the instrument is made from zelkova bark (for high quality *ō-daiko*) or *sennoki*[12] (for less expensive instruments). Cowhide is stretched across both membranes and the diameter ranges from 30 centimeters to over 1 meter. During the ō-daiko craze, the diameter of the instrument seemed to grow exponentially.

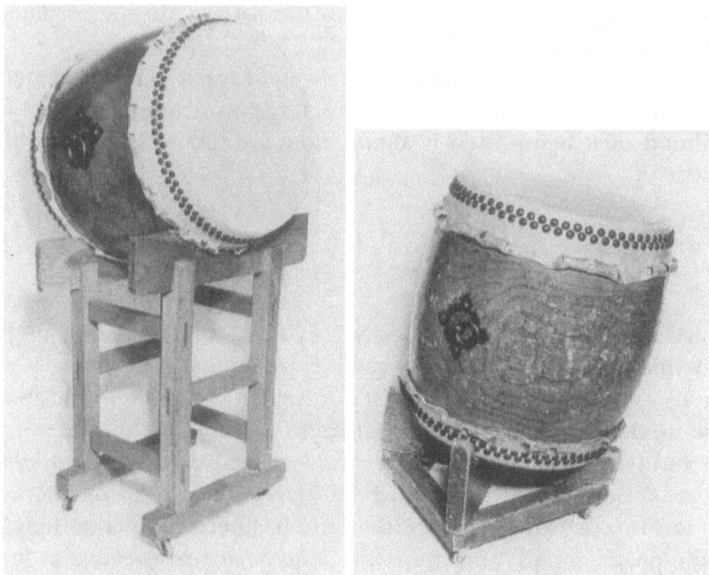

Fig. 4.14. The ō-daiko

a) The mallets

As illustrated in figure 4.15, there are many kinds of ō-daiko mallets. The commonly used *kashibachi* are 33 centimeters long and 2 centimeters thick. There are also mallets with balls of yarn attached to the ends called *yukibai*, which are used in *kabuki* to create the effect of snow. *Chōbachi* mallets, which are hard and long, beat the membrane slowly to create a deep vibrating sound imitating the sound of a storm. Thin *takebachi* mallets are used to deliver high-pitched sounds. When playing gigantic ō-daiko, there are many varieties of long and thick mallets used to introduce a visual element to a performance. Today, any object can be used as a substitute for traditional *taiko* mallets. When choosing to use an object other than a standard mallet, I recommend that the composer strike the membrane of the *taiko* and test the sound. Afterwards, the composer should accordingly note the appropriate mallet or implement to be used in order to achieve the desired timbre, artistic, or entertainment goal.

PERCUSSION INSTRUMENTS ☙ 173

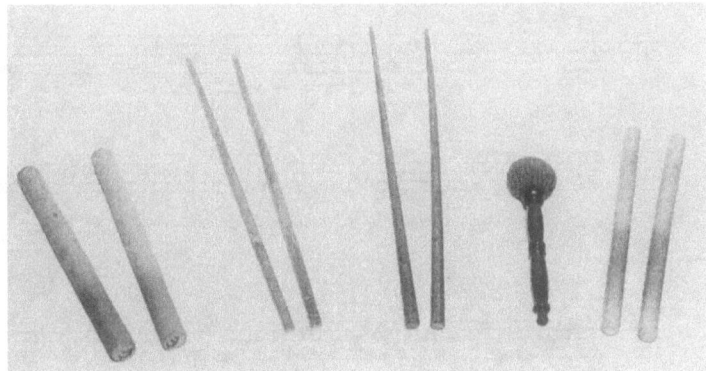

Fig. 4.15. Various kinds of *ō-daiko* mallets. From the left: *kashibachi*, *takebachi*, *chōbachi*, *yukibai*, and *hosobachi*.

b) Performance technique

Ō-daiko family playing techniques initially appear to be simple: the membrane of the instrument is struck with either a wooden mallet or the hands. The basic technique is to strike with a mallet, and striking the instruments with the hands should be designated with the instruction "by hands." Reverting to mallets should then be indicated with the instruction "with stick(s)." For other percussion techniques, the notation used for Western bass drums or bass tom-toms will convey the composer's intention. The *taiko*, however, embodies a certain spirit by its ability to express states of nature, for example, the musical effects for *kabuki*. I consider the *taiko* to be an instrument capable of great expression. Figure 4.16 shows the different scenes that can be portrayed with the *taiko*. The symbol △ indicates that the performer should hold the mallet in his or her left hand and lightly place the mallet on the membrane of the instrument. When the membrane meets the mallet, a buzzing sound is produced.

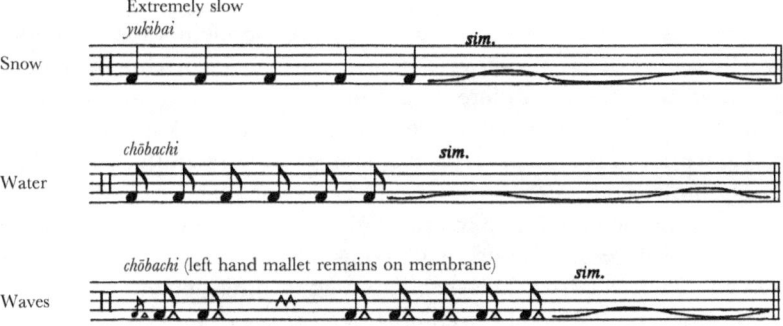

Fig. 4.16. Atmospheric musical effects of the *taiko*

The same pitch is obtained regardless of where the membrane of the drum is struck. The timbre of striking close to the rim and that of striking the membrane in the center, however, are different, and the pitch seems to rise the closer one strikes to the rim. This impression is very effective when striking the *taiko* continuously. Figure 4.17 presents excerpts that exhaustively adopt this particular technique. An audible difference in pitch will be heard when the left hand mallet presses down on the membrane of the drum and exerts pressure while the right hand continuously strikes the drum. Of course, if the stress on the membrane is released, the pitch will drop. This technique can be indicated in the score by writing "gliss," but it should also be accompanied with a written explanation.

Fig. 4.17. Rim technique of the *taiko* in an excerpt from Minoru Miki's *Totsu*

Striking the *taiko* on the rim or the side of the body is indicated with the symbol ↑. All Japanese drums use this symbol. The timbre and result, however, will differ according to the particular area struck, so it is best to explain in an annotation exactly where one should strike with the mallets.

In the last few decades, many new techniques and rhythmic patterns have been developed. Even though these rhythmic patterns appear or sound traditional, there are many cases where the patterns are known to be the creations of specific composers. If these patterns are imitated or borrowed, there may be plagiarism problems, and I would like composers to be cautious when making use of "traditional" rhythms. When devising new patterns, composers should imagine they themselves are holding the mallets, consider the degree of energy and passion with which a *taiko* performer will strike the instrument, and imagine how the mallets should be coordinated between the hands.

(7) *Gaku-daiko* (Used in Folk Music)

As can be seen in figure 4.18, the area between the membranes of the folk *gaku-daiko* is not as deep as on the *gaku-daiko* used in *gagaku*. In the shape of a simple basin, the drum is normally placed on a stand. This *taiko* comes in many sizes, and is pitched lower than the *ō-daiko*. Since it consumes very little space, the *gaku-daiko* is a very useful instrument in the percussion section. The *gaku-daiko* can use all of the mallets discussed in the previous section of this chapter.

176 · PERCUSSION INSTRUMENTS

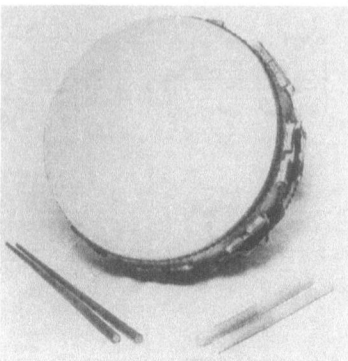

Fig. 4.18. The *gaku-daiko*

(8) *Shime-daiko* (Also Simply Called *Taiko*)

This *taiko* is also one of the distinctive percussion instruments of Japan, and has been documented since the *dengaku* of the Middle Ages.[13] Today, the *shime-daiko* appears in nearly all Japanese folk rituals. Figure 4.5 illustrates *shi-byōshi*, a particularly fascinating rhythmic pattern performed by the *shime-daiko* in the *hayashi* for both the *nō* and the *kabuki* theaters. In these performance traditions, the instrument is referred to as *taiko*, rather than *shime-daiko*.

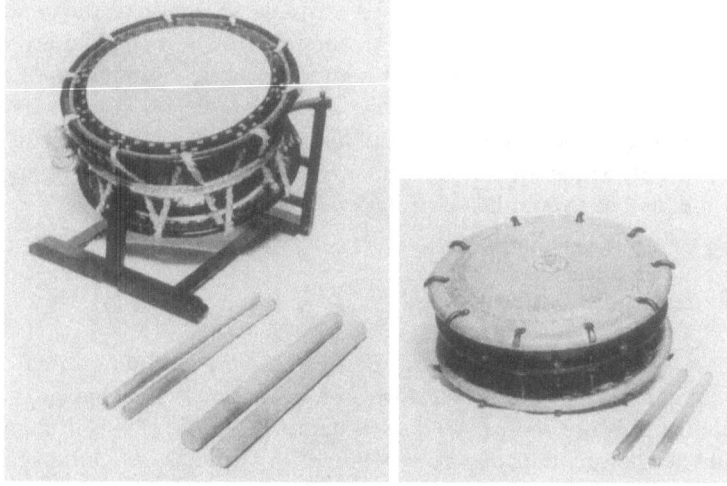

Fig. 4.19. The *Shime-daiko* and the *Shime-daiko* designed for outdoor use

As illustrated in figure 4.19, the body of the *shime-daiko* is made from zelkova, pine, Japanese bead, or chinaberry wood. The diameter of the protruding area in the center of the skin is 27 centimeters, and the height of the instrument is 15 centimeters. The top and bottom membranes, both of tanned cowhide, are wrapped around iron frames, which are then fastened to the body of the instrument by hemp *shirabeo* (or *tateshirabe*). The *shirabeo* is strung in alternation through holes that line the perimeter of the drum skins. A second cord, the *yokoshirabe*, is wrapped over the *shirabeo* around the perimeter of the body and tightened. Since the tension of these cords determines the pitch, the instrument is referred to as a *shime-daiko*.[14] These same principles apply to the *tsuzumi*. The membranes are 35 centimeters in diameter, and a small leather patch of deerskin 4 centimeters in diameter, the *bachi-kawa*, is pasted to the center of the top membrane. This patch represents the area where the *shime-daiko* is usually struck. There is also a very large patch called the *chōshi-gawa* pasted on the bottom membrane. When performing in a sitting position, a stand is used that allows the front of the *shime-daiko* to lie low.

There are two types of mallets. The thicker of the two is 33 centimeters in length and 2.5 centimeters in diameter. The thinner mallets are a few centimeters shorter with a diameter of 1.5 centimeters. Both thick and thin mallets are used in *nagauta*; however, for the *hayashi* for the *nō* theater, only the thicker mallets are used.

During the height of *taiko* popularity, many different kinds of *shime-daiko* were made, most of them removing the delicate lacquerwork and *shirabeo* cord in favor of a strong, solid body with the membranes fastened by iron clasps rather than the *shirabeo*.

a) Performance technique

In both the *nō* and the *nagauta hayashi*, the movements of the performer, such as the raising of the mallets and the striking gesture, are an established tradition with variations according to school. With the popular *taiko* groups, these performance techniques have been rendered even flashier. Of course, the *shime-daiko* is capable of executing Western percussion music, but in this section—as in the *ko-tsuzumi* and *taiko* sections—I will introduce traditional performance techniques accompanied with *shōga*, the corresponding mnemonic syllables (see figure 4.20).

Fig.4.20. Traditional *shime-daiko* performance techniques accompanied with mnemonics

1. *ten:* The distinction between large, medium, and small mallets changes the distance that the hands are raised in preparation to strike the *shime-daiko*. In tablature notation, symbols such as ◎, ⦿, ○, and ● can be used to indicate *ten*. Regardless of their size, the mallets are raised high and dropped while the arm remains extended. Both the left and right hands are used. In Western staff notation, *ten* strokes are always indicated as *f*, using either quarter notes or eighth notes, which means that the vibration is not be stopped.

2. *te:* This technique is indicated by the symbol ○. When the right hand strikes a *ten* and is immediately followed by a left hand stroke on the upbeat, the *ten* on the downbeat becomes *te*. It is indicated with eighth or sixteenth notes marked as *f*.

3. *ke:* This technique is indicated by the symbol ⦿. *Ke* is the mnemonic syllable used for the left-hand upbeat stroke that follows a downbeat *te* stroke. It is indicated with eighth or sixteenth notes with the dynamic marking of *f*.

4. *re:* This technique is indicated by the symbol ●. This stroke is also executed by the left hand, but in contrast to *ke* is a more delicate stroke. It is indicated with eighth notes with the dynamic marking of *mf*.

5. *tsu:* This technique is indicated by the symbol ⦁. Unlike the strokes described above, after a right-hand stroke, the mallet remains on the membrane, suppressing the reverberation. It is indicated with eighth notes or sixteenth notes marked as *p*.

6. *ku:* There is no symbol used to indicate this technique. It is the same stroke as *tsu*, but executed with the left hand. It is indicated with eighth notes or sixteenth notes with the dynamic marking of *p*.

The alternation of consecutive left and right hand sixteenth-note strokes at a fast tempo is called *kizamu*. Leaving the mallets on the membrane is known as *tsuke-bachi*, and is an effective technique unique to the *shime-daiko*. If this technique is combined with other techniques, to avoid an overcrowded score showing the frequent alternation of *p* and *f* dynamic markings, it is easier to mark the entire passage *p* and indicate dynamic expressions in the form of accents above the *ten* and *te* strokes, as illustrated in figure 4.21.

注） 符尾はかならずしも左右を分けなくてもよい。

Fig. 4.21. *Shime-daiko* dynamic expressions in the form of accents

With several *shime-daiko*, it is possible to change the tension of each, and create recognizable differences in pitch, which results in a unique effect depending on the compositional approach. Figure 4.22 is an excerpt from my composition for Japanese instruments and orchestra entitled *Kyū-no-Kyoku* ("Symphony for

Two Worlds"), where some of the string instruments and percussion compete against each other while the woodwinds provide a sustained background at a *p* dynamic level.

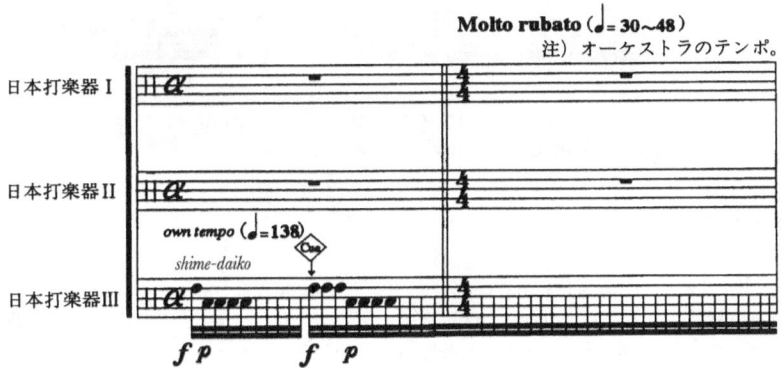

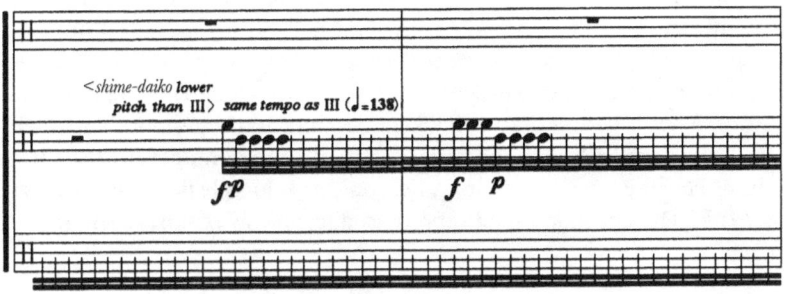

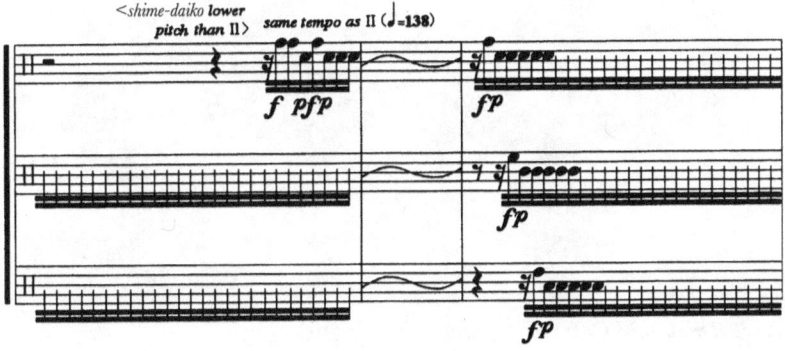

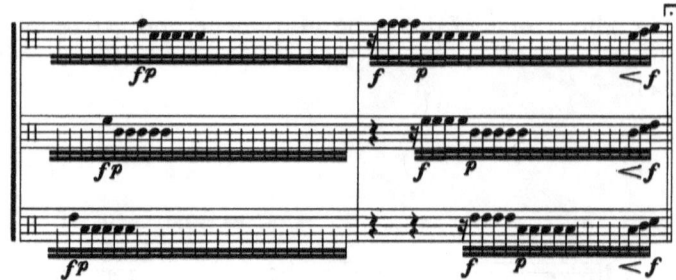

Fig. 4.22 Differences in pitch creating unique effects in an excerpt from Minoru Miki's *Kyū-no-Kyoku* ("Symphony for Two Worlds")

(9) *Dai-byōshi*

Originally, the *dai-byōshi* was used in *kagura*.[15] It is now a fixture of backstage music for *kabuki* and is used to portray lively city and festival scenes. As illustrated in the figure 4.23, the *dai-byōshi* resembles a *shime-daiko* with a long body. Like the *shime-daiko*, the membranes are stretched over iron rings at the top and bottom of the tub-shaped body, and fastened with a hemp *shirabeo* cord. Unlike the *shime-daiko*, however, the *dai-byōshi* lacks the small circle of deerskin (*bachi-kawa*) pasted in the center of the membrane, as well as the *chōshigawa*. Normally struck with two thin, long mallets, it is pitched higher than the *shime-daiko* and produces a loud and lively sound. The diameter of the head is between 26 and 33 centimeters. The length of the body for most *dai-byōshi* is between 27 and 38 centimeters. In the Aomori Nebuta festival, there is a large *dai-byōshi* called the *nagadō-daiko*, the membranes for which are made from either cowhide or horse hide. A *dai-byōshi* with loosely tied *shirabeo* is referred to as *do-byōshi*. The cowhide membrane is used to portray pastoral scenes.

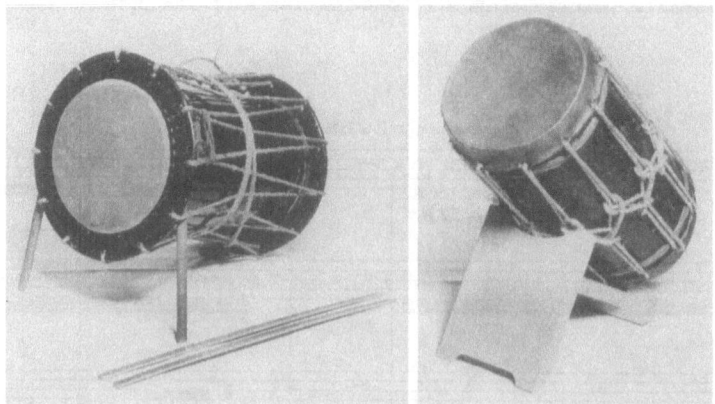

Fig. 4.23. *Dai-byōshi* (left) and *okedō-daiko* (right)

(10) Okedō-daiko

Normally called the *okedō*, this instrument was originally used in the Lion Dance. Also a fixture in the *geza hayashi* ensemble, the instrument is used to represent the approaching New Year and celebratory Lion Dance. As illustrated in figure 4.23, cowhide membranes are mounted on the top and bottom of a long, thin, tub-shaped wooden frame and fastened with *shirebeo* cords. *Okedō-daiko* come in many sizes, and the tone and timbre are well balanced. When the Pro Musica Nipponia was first formed, a set of four drums, ordered from high to low—a *shime-daiko*, a small *okedō*, a large *okedō*, and an *ō-daiko*—were arranged as a set for one performer to play.

The mallets used to strike the *okedō* are the same as for the *shime-daiko*, but the *okedō* can also be played with the hands.

(11) Uchiwa-daiko (Fan Drums)

Also known as *etsuki-daiko*, fan drums are made from cowhide or horsehide stretched over a wooden or iron frame and attached to a stand by a wooden handle. Figure 4.24 shows an arrangement of fan drums of various sizes. Originally, fan drums were religious instruments used by Buddhist devotees, especially members of the Nichiren sect, as they walked, reciting sutras and other sacred texts. Documentation suggests fan drums originated in Tibet in the form of *damaru* drums used by Lama monks.

Fig. 4.24. *Uchiwa-daiko* (fan drums)

The one-sided fan drums used in processionals are usually struck with thin wooden mallets 20 centimeters in length. As shown in figure 4.24, fan drums of various sizes can be arranged as a set, a concept developed by Hiromitsu Nishikawa in 1970. Many popular groups have started using fan drums, striking them with heavier mallets, and like the *shime-daiko* and other instruments that have been made into sets, the fan drum has become a percussion instrument with a distinct power and fascinating timbre.

(12) Other Percussion Instruments

In addition to the instruments discussed above, the names of many drums no longer performed have been preserved in Japan's millennia-long music history. There are also numerous other drums that have been continuously played for centuries, yet are not discussed in this chapter. Dancers from the Japanese court tradition still use the *keirōko* and *furi-tsuzumi*. More recent examples include the *hirazuri-daiko, jin-daiko, zeni-daiko, denden-daiko,* and *mame-daiko*. I think it would be fascinating to use wooden barrels as percussion instruments, as in *yagi-bushi*,[16] which uses upturned sake barrels, although these should probably be classified as wooden percussion instruments rather than as membrane percussion instruments. Any object in Japan that produces sound when its membrane is struck should be welcomed into the circle of *taiko*.

4–2: Wood and Bamboo Percussion

(1) *Sasara*

An instrument referred to as the *sasara* is mentioned in many texts; this term, however, normally refers to the *surizasara*. Widely used in folk music dances, it is mentioned in Heian-period (794–1185) literary documents at which time the *surizasara* was closely associated with *dengaku*.[17]

Crude saw-toothed nicks are carved into a wooden stick 30 to 40 centimeters long (documents refer to this as a *sasarako*), which is held in the left hand. In the right hand, a piece of bamboo (called the *sasara-take*), resembling a tea whisk, is scraped lengthwise along the *sasarako*, from the base to the tip (figure 4.25).

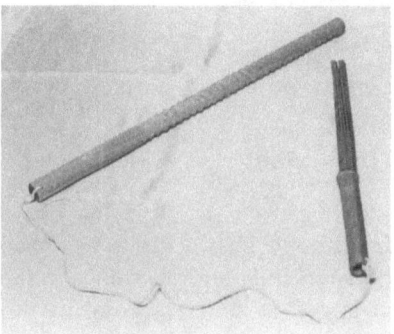

Fig. 4.25. The *sasara*

Effective rhythmic patterns can be constructed by combining hitting techniques with the scraping mentioned above. While the timbre is different, the performance technique of this instrument is similar to the guiro. *Sasara* are easily made, and even someone with no musical training can play one. In my operas and musical theater works, I write the *sasara* part (figure 4.26) so that it is in unison with the singer or actor.

Fig. 4.26. *Sasara* playing techniques, (a) *Sasara* example from Minoru Miki's opera *Wakahime* ("The Young Princess")

Fig. 4.26. *Sasara* playing techniques, (b) *Sasara* example from Minoru Miki's folk opera *Utayomizaru* ("The Monkey Poet")

(2) *Binzasara*

The *binzasara* is a percussion instrument widely used in *dengaku*. Even now, it is used in folk dances such as *kokiriko-bushi*. As shown in figure 4.27, the *binzasara* is constructed of twenty to thirty wooden (or bamboo) slabs tied with a long string. The performer holds each end and strikes the slabs together, or shakes them from side to side. *Binzasara* come in large and small sizes, the large versions having more than 100 slabs. With something this large, it is effective even if one section of the *binzasara* is used.

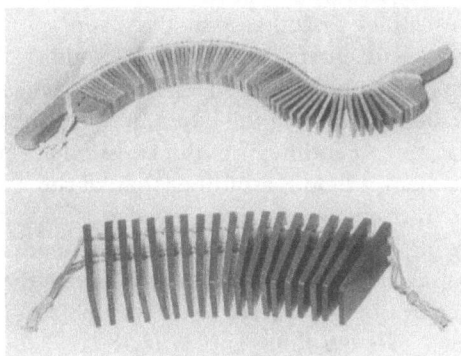

Fig. 4.27. The *binzasara*: upper diagram (a), lower diagram (b)

184 ❧ PERCUSSION INSTRUMENTS

Either ⌈ or ⌈̇ may be used for notation. As shown in figure 4.28, it can be used in different ways.

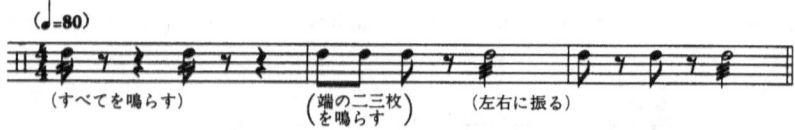

Sound all slabs   Sound two or three   Shake from side to side slabs at each end

Fig. 4.28. *Binzasara* playing techniques

As shown in figure 4.27b, there is a heavy *binzasara* with about twenty oak slabs. When a strong accent is needed, this is better to use. For notation, ⌈ is sufficient; however, ⌈̇ corresponds more closely to the image of the sound. While the size of the instrument is not fixed, the heavy *binzasara* slabs are 16 centimeters in length, 6 centimeters in width, and 1 centimeter thick; and the light *binzasara* slabs are roughly 6 centimeters in length, 2.3 centimeters in width, and 0.4 centimeters thick.

(3) *Shakubyōshi*

The *shakubyōshi* is the oldest Japanese percussion instrument. According to documents, it has been used to keep time in genres such as *kagura*, *yamatomai*, *azuma-asobi*, *kumeuta*, and *saibara*, all ancient genres closely tied to *gagaku*. The word *hyōshi* also refers to the *shakubyōshi*.

This instrument comprises two wooden slabs that are struck together (figure 4.29). The shape resembles a scepter that has been split vertically into two pieces. Made from boxwood, cherry, and plum, the wood easily splits lengthwise, which requires caution during performance. The *shakubyōshi* is 36 centimeters in length, 2.4 centimeters in width at the base where the instrument is held, 3.9 centimeters at the tip, and 1 centimeter in thickness on average. The size of the area where the instrument is held is a thinner than at the tip.

When playing this instrument, each wooden slab is held at the narrow end. Then, without separating either of the wrists, the thicker ends are opened and the slabs then struck together. The wide face of the slab held in the left hand is turned to the right and struck by the thin surface of the slab held in the right hand. The *shakubyōshi* is designed to keep time, and is unsuitable for rapid techniques. Additionally, in many cases the sound of the *shakubyōshi* does not fit well with other instruments. For notation, either ſ or ᛏ will suffice. In tablature, it is indicated with ..

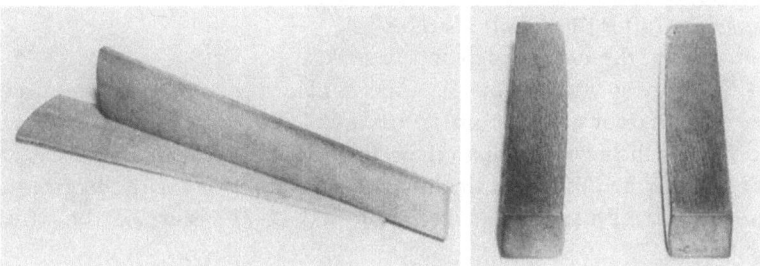

Fig. 4.29. The *shakubyōshi* (left) and the *hyōshigi* (right)

(4) *Hyōshigi*

Appearing during the Edo period, the *hyōshigi* was made for the various signals and calls in the *ningyō jōruri* puppet and *kabuki* theaters. It is also called *kigashira* (wooden head) or *ki* (wood). As indicated in figure 4.29, this instrument is made from two wooden blocks of oak. Some *hyōshigi* are squared, but the proper shape is with rounded striking surfaces. The most common *hyōshigi* are 20 centimeters in length; however there are various sizes depending on their use. For example, the *hyōshigi* in *sumo* and *hyōshigi* for neighborhood watches are different sizes. Like claves, it is possible to use *hyōshigi* as a rhythmic instrument.

The proper way of playing *hyōshigi* is to hold one of the sticks at a slight diagonal and strike them together. A location is needed where one can feel the clarity of the sound. Also, one must skillfully adjust the striking force to vary dynamics. While simple to play, it is rare to find an instrument where the quality of the performer is immediately apparent. Correctly played, this instrument can damage the eardrums, and people who use the instrument regularly, callers at *sumo* rings being the classic example, often have damaged hearing. The instrument must not be played close to someone's ears. For notation, either ſ or ᛏ will suffice.

In *kabuki*, a tense sound called *tsuke* is used to cut off a *mie*,[18] for fight scenes, and in scenes where an actor suddenly breaks into a run. The *hyōshigi* performer silently enters stage right and strikes the *hyōshigi* violently on a wooden board. Even though the *hyōshigi* is used in *kabuki* as a signal tool, it is nonetheless musical and its application is rigidly prescribed. There are, however, differences between Kantō and Kansai in how the *hyōshigi* is used. I have provided an example of how the *hyōshigi* is used in Edo (Kantō area) *kabuki* according to literary documents. Some of these musical gestures are now performed on other instruments, such as bells.

> Signals of the hyōshigi:
> *chakutōdome* (after the *taiko*): 2 strikes
> *shagiridome* (at the end of each act): 2 strikes
> *nichō* (after most of the props have been placed, played at the entrance to the second-floor green room): 2 strikes
> *mawari* (after the actor is prepared, performed in different locations): 3 strikes
> *naosu* (performed after confirming the preparations for the beginning of the act): 2 continuous strikes, followed by the start of the off-stage music
> *makuaki*: acceleration immediately after naosu, and continuing to beat at a fast, fixed tempo until the large stage props are ready, at which point the act begins.
> *tomegi*: at the beginning of an act, a continuous beat at a fast tempo, which is followed by one loud, final strike
> *makugire*: one strike of the *hyōshigi* signals the beginning of the last section of the act. Repeated strikes accelerate to a fixed tempo. When the curtain is completely closed, there is one final strike the *tomegi*.

Fig. 4.30. *Hyōshigi* used in Edo *kabuki*

(5) *Mokushō*

Mokushō were originally Buddhist instruments used in the Nichiren sect where they were struck to the rhythm of recitations. I bought many different-sized *mokushō* at a second-hand shop in Kyoto and used them for movie music, but when I started to use them in the early years of the Pro Musica Nipponia, other composers were delighted and they became a popular percussion instrument. In the early 1960s, even though *mokushō* were in *nō*, *kabuki hayashi*, and off-stage *kabuki* music, it was extremely rare to find them in concert settings with other Japanese percussion instruments. The appearance of *mokushō* on stage with instruments such as the *shime-daiko*, *okedaiko*, and sets of *taiko*—all discussed in the previous chapter—instantly transformed the percussion space of the Pro Musica Nipponia into the front of an antique store.

As illustrated in figure 4.31, *mokushō* are the same shape as *kinshō*, which will be discussed below. The diameter varies from 10 to 30 centimeters. *Mokushō* that produce a good sound are made from quince and the body sits atop three short legs. The mallets are wooden, originally shaped like a hammer. Since *mokushō* are often played with other percussion instruments, one can also use a hard *taiko* mallet.

Fig. 4.31. *Mokushō*

There is no traditional way of playing the *mokushō*. Figure 4.32 presents music for a set of four *mokushō;* they can be thought of as a poorly tuned xylophone. Soft tremolos are very effective. If the *mokushō* are overplayed, like the *hyōshigi*, it is hard on the ears; they also mask other instruments in an ensemble setting, and thus require caution. Using soft mallets designed for the marimba and xylophone is another way to strike *mokushō*.

Fig. 4.32. A set of four *mokushō* in an excerpt from Minoru Miki's *Tō*

(6) *Mokugyō*

Mokugyō have been used for more than a millennium in China. They have also become an integral part of the percussion section in Western orchestras, and are called Chinese blocks or temple blocks. *Mokugyō* were imported to Japan in the twelfth and thirteenth centuries CE with Zen Buddhism and, in other Buddhist sects, they are often struck in rhythm to sutra recitations. The fish design of *mokugyō* is said to come from the idea that humans should be like fish, never closing their eyes. In contrast to normal wood blocks, *mokugyō* produce a surprisingly humorous sound.

Most *mokugyō* are made from camphor or mulberry wood, and the inside is hollow, shaped like a bell. There are far more sizes of *mokugyō* than *mokushō*, ranging in diameter from a miniature size of 5–6 centimeters to nearly 1 meter; however, the extremes cannot be found everywhere. As illustrated in figure 4.33, *mokugyō* sold as instruments range from 10 centimeters to 30 centimeters. Authentic *mokugyō* mallets are wooden sticks, the ends of which are wrapped in leather or cloth to make a round division that produces a distinctive hollow sound. It is possible to have *mokugyō* struck "with ordinary stick(s)," but since the timbre is very different, I recommend taking a pair of percussion sticks and testing the sound to determine the most appropriate mallets for the composition. *Mokugyō* can only be played between *pp* and *mp*, but in rapid passages, rather than playing with mallets, interesting effects can also be produced by playing with the hands. The composer should indicate "with the hands" in the score.

Fig. 4.33. *Mokugyō*

Since *mokugyō* are international, it is unnecessary to give musical examples. The *mokushō* in figure 4.32 can be performed on *mokugyō* without making any changes. If a performer uses a set of *mokushō* and *mokugyō* at the same time without switching, I use the notation shown in figure 4.34. The *mokushō* are assigned to lines on the staff while *mokugyō* are assigned to spaces.

Fig. 4.34. A musical example using *mokushō* and *mokugyō*

(7) Yotsudake

Yotsudake are Japanese castanets used in folk dances. Two rectangular bamboo slabs are held in each hand, and since one set is comprised of four slabs in total, this instrument is called *yotsudake*.[19] While *yotsudake* are used to represent the lower classes in *kabuki*, they are also used in the elegant music and dances of Okinawa. As with castanets, the two slabs are struck against one another. Some *yotsudake* open with the hand; others, however, consist of bamboo slabs with no device to combine them into pairs. With this type of *yotsutake*, it is impossible to articulate complex rhythms, and they can only be used to maintain a basic pulse (figure 4.35).

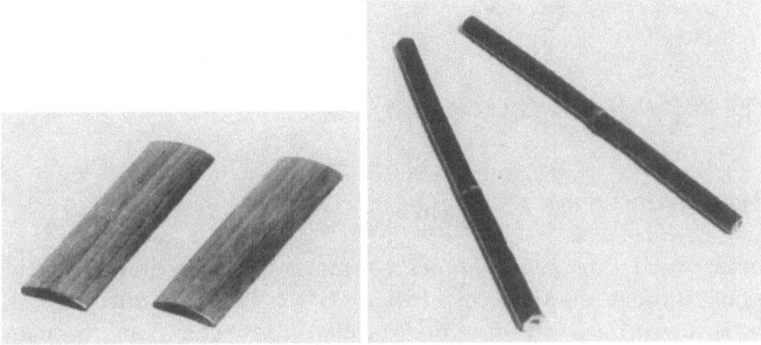

Fig. 4.35. *Yotsudake* (left) *and kokiriko* (right)

(8) Kokiriko

Kokiriko are used in folk dances, the *kokiriko-bushi* of Toyama Prefecture being the representative example. Consisting of two bamboo sticks between 20 and 30 centimeters long and a diameter between 1.5 and 2 centimeters, *kokiriko* are struck while dancing (see figure 4.35).

(9) Naruko

Naruko were originally noisemakers used to scare birds from the fields. There are many sizes and shapes; however, ten or so small-sized *naruko* can be cut, combined, and suspended as shown in figure 4.36. They sound when blown by the wind, but when brushed with both hands, the sound creates a lively accent.

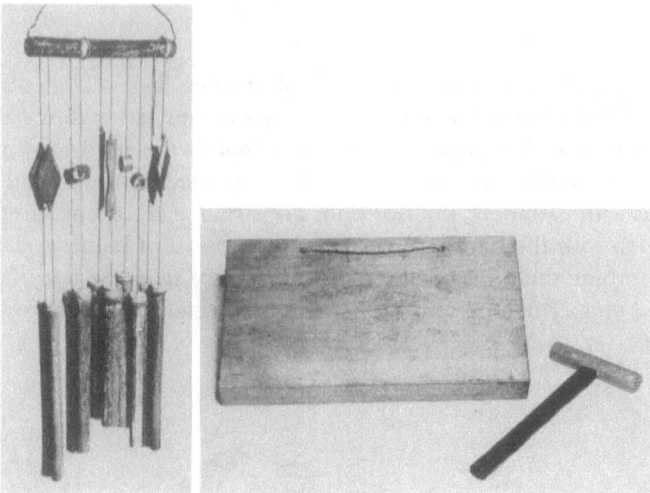

Fig. 4.36. *Naruko* (left) and *banki* (right)

(10) *Mokuban* and *Banki*

Mokuban are used to signal meal times in temples and the arrival of guests. Made from wood, those in the shape of a fish are called *mokuban*, while the rectangular boards shown in the illustration are called *banki*. They come in many sizes and are struck with a wooden hammer.

4–3: Metal and Stone Percussion

(1) *Dora* (Temple Bells)

Two representative Japanese bells are the *bonshō*,[20] shown in figure 4.37, used to mark time in Buddhist temples, and the *hanshō*,[21] used for warnings and in off-stage *kabuki* music. The appearance, the casting, and sound quality differ from Western bells. Given that they are Buddhist implements, these bells naturally originated in South Asia (India); nonetheless, *bonshō* have become more representative of East Asia—China, the Korean Peninsula, and Japan. In these countries, the bells are cast from the same materials and have the same shape; there are, nonetheless, differences in their construction. *Bonshō* temple bells range in height from 1.5 meters to 4 meters, making it impossible to move them for a performance. The height of most *hanshō* temple bells is 30 centimeters. While not impossible to borrow for stage use, it is necessary to realize that using *hanshō* as instruments requires considerable forethought.

Fig. 4.37. *Bonshō*

Temple bells are tolled with *shumoku* mallets,[22] the size of which differs according to the size of the bell. *Bonshō* are built to sound at one of five pitches: *banshiki* (B), *ichikotsu* (D), *hyōshō* (E), *sōjō* (G), and *ōshiki* (A).

(2) *Kin*

The *kin* is a Buddhist implement that originated in China. Their primary purpose is to provide signals during sutra incantations by Buddhist monks.

The timbre and long resonance are so liked that they are often used in concerts. As shown in figure 4.38, their shape resembles copper *hibachi* or the tea bowls used in the tea ceremony. *Kin* are made from copper or bronze. To produce a good sound, they are placed on top of small cushions. In spite of being cast in various sizes, with bores ranging from 15 to 45 centimeters, *kin* are not made according to pitch. For their use in performance, it is thus important to choose *kin* carefully so they do not clash with other instruments. This is a problem common with many percussion instruments, and as composers are not always available to observe performances of their works, they must entrust the piece to the performers' and conductor's sensibilities. As *kin* reverberate for such a long period of time, this is especially important. If several *kin* are to be used, it is necessary to know which will be the most appropriate for the music; otherwise the sound of the *kin* will annoy and confuse the listener. If this is a concern, indicate in the score or part that a *kin* with unclear pitches should be used.

192 ❧ PERCUSSION INSTRUMENTS

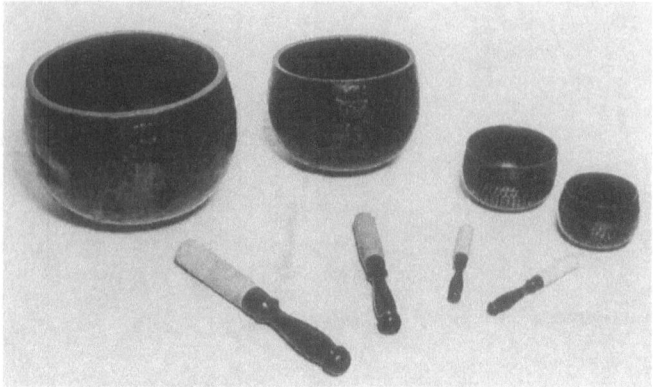

Fig. 4.38. *Kin*

When chanting sutra incantations, the rim is struck with a *bai*, a thick stick, the end of which is covered with leather or cloth. When using *kin* as musical instruments, the performance method remains the same, and is notated as shown in figure 4.39. The inside space of this instrument is an outstanding resonance chamber, and, since the 1960s, *kin* have often been played with a contrabass bow, as shown in figure 4.39b.

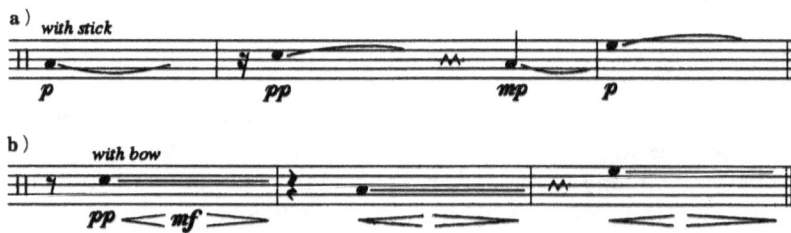

Fig. 4.39. *Kin* playing techniques

(3) *Shōko*

Similar to the different drums related to the *gaku-daiko*, the *daishōko*, *tsurishōko*, and *ninaishōko* used in *gagaku* all fall under the generic name of *shōko*. The *daishōko* is paired with the *da-daiko* drum. The shape and ornaments are similar to the *da-daiko*. The height is 152 centimeters and the base is 61 centimeters. The diameter of the section that produces sound is 36 centimeters. The two mallets are 52 centimeters long and 1 centimeter thick. The diameter of the beads made from water buffalo horn attached to the tips is 3 centimeters, smaller than *dadaiko* (figure 4.40). The performance techinique is simple, and limited to playing the downbeat of each measure. Occasionally, however, an ornamental stroke precedes the other instruments.

The *tsurishōko* is used with the *tsuridaiko*. The size, however, is smaller, being 17 centimeters in diameter, and the mallets are likewise shorter as well, only 33 centimeters in length. The performance technique is the same as the *daishōko*.

The diameter of the *ninaishōko* is 21 centimeters. This instrument is used solely for processionals.

Fig. 4.40. The *shōko*

(4) Kinshō

Similar to *mokushō*, *kinshō* are also made for use in *sutra* incantations. Their shape and performance technique—they are struck with a small mallet—is the same as *mokushō*. Made from bronze, *kinshō* come in various sizes, but they are used with less frequency than *mokushō*.

(5) Shō

There are four types of *shō* commonly used by the general public. The *shō* illustrated in figure 4.41 are arranged in order from the largest to smallest, and are called *sōgen*, *konchiki*, *chanchiki*, and *matsumushi*. All are struck with a hammer, also shown in the figure.

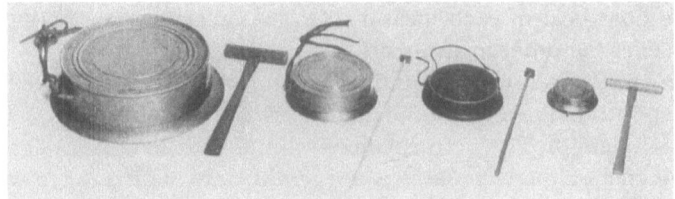

Fig. 4.41. Various kinds of *shō* (From the right: *sōgen, konchiki, chanchiki, and mutsumushi*)

Matsumushi is also the name for two small *kinshō* used in off-stage *kabuki* music that are used to create the effect of insects (figure 4.42), as is the *orugoru*.

Fig. 4.42. *Matsumushi*

(6) *Kane (Atarigane)*

This instrument also is called *atarigane, changiri,* and *chanchiki,* and is used in folk dances such as the *Awa* dance and in *hayashi* festival music. The tip of the wooden mallet is affixed with a small cylindrical hammer made from metal or deer horn, as in figure 4.43.

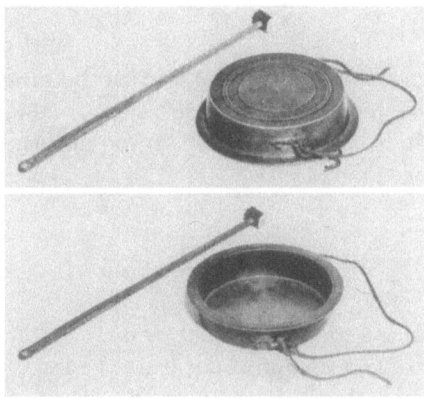

Fig. 4.43. *Kane (atarigane)*

There are two ways to play this instrument. One consists of suspending a legless *kinshō* by a string from a frame or handle, which is then held in the left hand, and striking it with a metal mallet held in the right hand. The second way is more complicated, as the timbre and resonance are modified when striking. For the second method, the *kane* must fit into the palm of the left hand. The thumb and fourth finger are placed on the metal lip of the instrument for support (figure 4.44). Please refer to musical figures 4.45 and 4.46 as I explain the playing method.

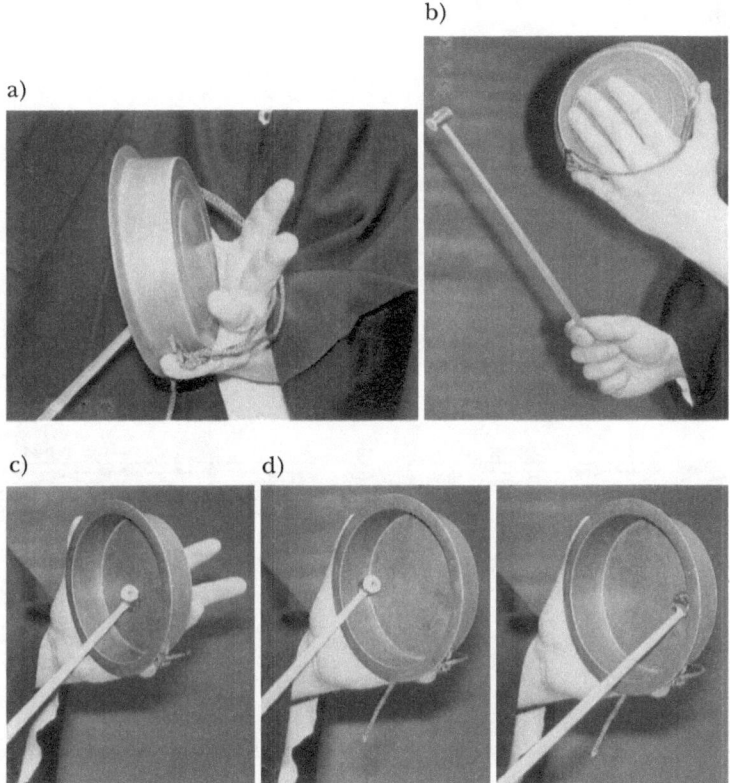

Fig. 4.44. Left- and right-hand techniques for playing the *kane:* (a) Left-hand technique (open), (b) Left-hand technique (closed), (c) Right-hand technique (open), (d) Right-hand technique (closed)

a) Left-hand technique:
Open (o): Bend the wrist of the left hand back and remove the index, middle, and ring finger from the instruments. See figure 4.44a.

Close (+): Cup the wrist of the right hand while resting the index, middle, and ring fingers on the back of the instrument. See figure 4.44b.

b) Right-hand technique:

Open (o): Strike the middle of the *kane* with the circular side of the mallet. See figure 4.44c.

Close (+): Move the mallet either up and down or left and right and strike the inside wall of the instrument. After striking the left (or bottom), strike the opposite part to the right (or top). See figure 4.44d.

In actual performance, the rhythm more closely resembles the score on the right in figure 4.46.

Fig. 4.45. *Kane* (*atarigane*) left-hand playing techniques

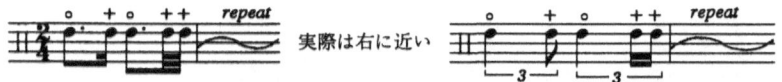

Fig. 4.46. *Awa* dance *kane* playing technique

(7) Dora

This instrument is normally called the *wadora*.[23] The gongs found in large numbers throughout China and Southeast Asia normally do not have protruding bosses in the center; only the *bao lue* has a round boss. As in figure 4.47, the gongs that came into Japan all have a high protrusion in the center and the sound quality is clearly different. Among various types of gongs, only the *wadora* can reproduce the atmosphere of a Japanese temple. They are made from copper, ranging in diameter from 30 centimeters to over 45 centimeters. A string passes through a small hole and is held with the left hand, or the *wadora* is suspended from a frame or hung on a wall. The mallets are normally wooden sticks with a bulb wrapped in cloth attached to the end. Similar to *kin*, *wadora* can also be played with a contrabass bow.

Fig. 4.47. The *wadora*

(8) *Nyōbatsu*

Nyōbatsu are also called *myōbachi* or *myōhachi*. As shown in figure 4.48, they are cymbals made from copper or bronze, ranging from 30 to 45 centimeters in diameter. One performance method is to fix one *nyōbatsu* on a stand and strike it with a mallet. *Nyōbatsu* can also be performed like cymbals. The timbre of *nyōbatsu* reflects the materials from which they are made, and it is therefore necessary to presume that timbre differs from instrument to instrument.

Fig. 4.48. *Nyōbatsu*

When *nyōbatsu* are used to accompany *shōmyō*,[24] the edges are lightly brushed together after they have been struck to produce a noisy rattling that resembles the sounds of the intense processionals in Tibetan Buddhist chant rituals. To damp the sound, the edges of both *nyōbatsu* are pressed against the abdomen.

(9) *Chappa* (*Dobyōshi*)

As shown in figure 4.49, *dobyōshi* are small *nyōbatsu* used in *kagura*, and are also used as part of the off-stage *kabuki* music when portraying China. They are also called *dōbatsu* or *dōbachi*. Originating in West Asia and India, *dobyōshi* entered Japan through China in the eighth century CE. The off-stage *kabuki* musicians refer to *dobyōshi* as *chappa*. They are always played by striking the two faces. Like the Balinese *ceng-ceng*, *dobyōshi* can also be mounted on a fixed surface with the striking side face up and performed with a second set held in the hand. Rather than copper, they are occasionally made from steel; for example, the *chappa* used in the Iwate Prefecture *yamabushi*[25] *kagura*, where they are known as *tebiragane*.

Fig. 4.49. *Chappa* (*dobyōshi*)

(10) *Suzu*

Suzu are also called *rei* and *rin*, and when used as pilgrim bells (figure 4.50a), they are called *shinrei*, and resemble Western bells. Shaped like an extremely small *bonshō*, small rods called *shita*[26] hang inside the sound chamber. In Japanese, the word *suzu* generally indicates a round, bell-shaped object with a long, thin opening at the bottom that contains a hard, small ball inside as shown in figure 4.50b. *Suzu* are classified into two types: a single *suzu*, called *tanrei*, and multiple *suzu*, called *fukurei* (or *tarei*). As seen in figure 4.50c, there are many kinds of *fukurei*.

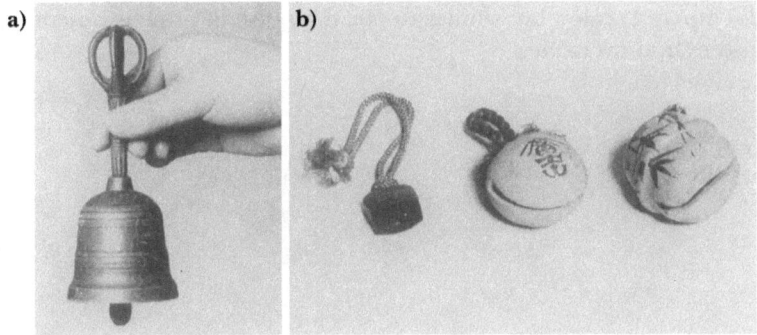

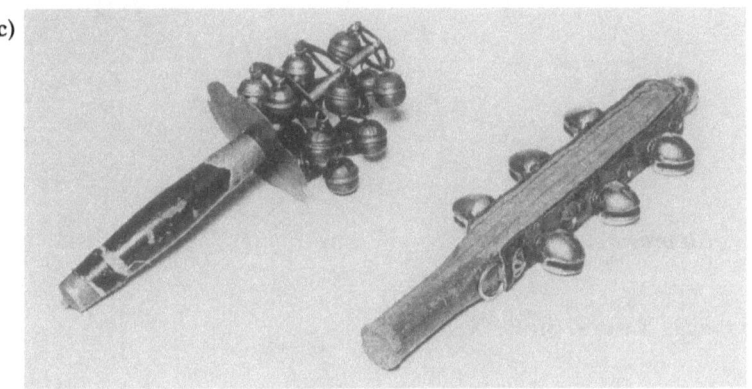

Fig. 4.50. Types of *suzu*: (a) *shinrei*, (b) *tanrei*, and (c) *fukurei*

Tanrei range from 1 centimeter to 10 centimeters. In ancient times, there were earthen *suzu* called *dorei*. This is one of the few indigenous Japanese instruments.

The *fukurei* include *mikorei*[27] and *suzu* struck or shaken in the hands while dancing. Tremolo is naturally very effective.

(11) *Orugoru*

An *orugoru* is constructed by attaching several *rin* (bells shaped like extremely small *bonshō* without the inside ball) of different sizes to a wooden board (figure 4.51). Lined on their side, they are rung with a hammer or metal mallet: the sound has a long decay time. During the Meiji period (1868–1912), the *kabuki geza* musicians came to call this instrument the *orugoru* as the sound resembles music boxes imported from the West. It is possible to arrange *orugoru* in equal-tempered scales, but similar to *kin*, the sense of pitch is obscure since they are so rich in overtones.

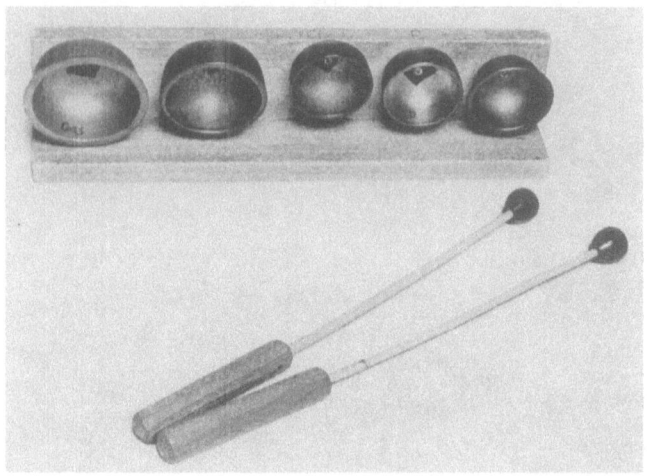

Fig. 4.51. An *orugoru*

(12) *Sanukite* (Natural Stone Xylophone)

In early Chinese history, there was a stone instrument tuned to twelve pitches known as the *kei*; there was even an instrument tuned to eighteen pitches. A single-tone metal *kei* was imported to Japan along with Buddhism and has been preserved as a national treasure, but an instrument that could play a melody never appeared.

In 1891 a German scholar, a Dr. Weinschenk, named a specimen of stone that a Dr. E. Naumann had brought from Kagawa Prefecture "sanukite." With the volcanic activity in the Seto-Uchi area during the Miocene[28] era, magma flows cooled and hardened into distinctive formations with the crystals aligned in the same direction. These formations became "the stone that emits sound." Takeshi Nagao collected stones of different sizes and arranged them by pitch, after which he presented them to the Emperor Taishō as a stone *koto*. I believe the *sanukite* is an invaluable Japanese melodic percussion instrument, and wish to classify and document this stone instrument as such in this book.

Following her father's dying wish, Nagao's daughter, Keiko Miyawaki, deepened our consciousness of *sanukite* as an instrument. Collecting rod-shaped sanukite stone deposits from the mountain recesses, she selected stones by the clarity of their timbre and lack of overtones, adjusted the thickness and length with machinery, and arranged them in scales. One can also admire the grain of the worked stones, which resembles wood grain and is capable of withstanding strong blows. It is possible to machine cut the stones, arrange them according to pitch and timbre, and polish them beautifully; however, stones treated this way are easy to break during a performance, as the grain has been ignored.

Sanukite can be used in two ways. The stones can be arranged in a keyboard formation, or they can be suspended (figure 4.52). The suspended stones are larger and thicker, and have a much better resonance.

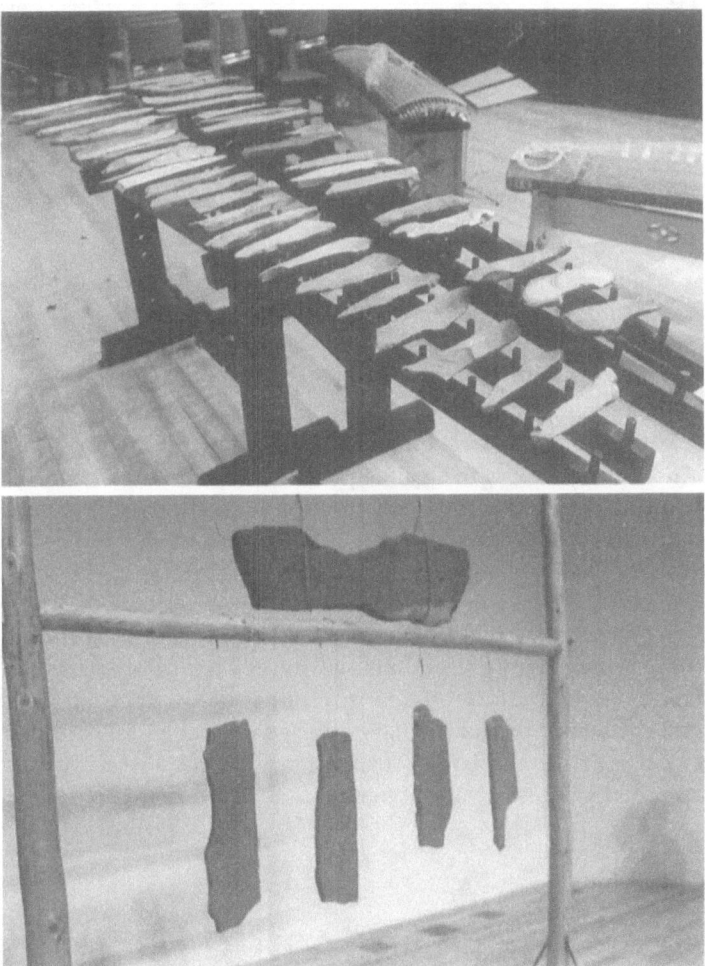

Fig. 4.52. *Sanukite* positioned on a keyboard stand (top) and suspended *sanukite* (bottom)

The range of the *sanukite* is shown in figure 4.53. All chromatic pitches within this range are available. A number of slabs fall outside equal temperament. By choosing these slabs, this eloquent, transparent instrument is capable of expressing the deeply mysterious to the horrifying. The *sanukite* slabs may be played with any kind of percussion mallet.

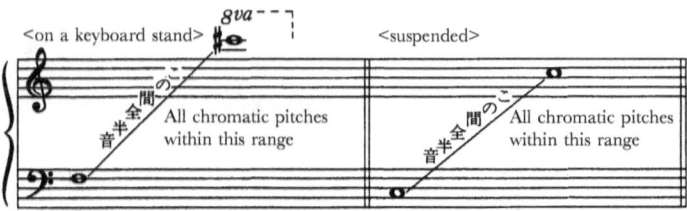

Fig. 4.53. Range of the *sanukite*

In 1969, when only half of the current range was available, I wrote music for commercials using only the *sanukite*. I also composed a work for *sanukite* and cello. As an instrument, the *sanukite* usually can only be used as a rental, but I am expecting the appearance of works which identify this instrument as both an ancient and contemporary Japanese melodic percussion instrument.

Stones exist all over the world, but my birthplace, the island of Shikoku, is known for the production of many fine quality stones, not only *sanukite*. In 1981, when I composed *Concerto Requiem* for 21-string koto and Japanese instrumental ensemble, in the lengthy introduction and ending of the work, half of the ensemble switch from playing their instruments to striking stones together to a simple beat, an important motif in the work. I drew inspiration for this from the Eastern and Western idea that humans return to the earth after they die, and I felt I should use stones from my hometown to represent the earth.

This work has been performed dozens of times all over the world. Audience reaction and the work's reputation have clearly shown that the rhythmic beating and the sound of the stones have a strong impact. I find this to be an excellent example of the attributes of natural materials as instruments.

Afterword

Over twenty years ago, I was told it was necessary for me to write this book. As time passed, I began to feel guilty about my lack of motivation. This is a feeble excuse, but while I was involved with the Pro Musica Nipponia after its establishment in 1964, I was completely absorbed in expanding the repertory, finding performance opportunities, and I had neither the time nor the energy to write. After composing *Shunkinshō* in 1975, the composition of operas came to occupy half of my output, and the writing of a book on the theoretical use of Japanese instruments seemed even more remote.

At the same time, the number of compositions for Japanese instruments was rapidly increasing. I came to believe that somebody would compile a book on Japanese instrumentation that included a discussion of classic techniques and a discussion of newly developed techniques commonly found in contemporary works. It had to happen: it was my only salvation! After all, several introductory guides had been published, and I had released a two-record set, *Introduction to Japanese Instruments*, through Columbia in 1972 (in 1987, this was expanded to a four-record set). With the record set, I felt, more or less, that I had acquitted myself of this onerous responsibility.

From 1985, I distanced myself from the Pro Musica Nipponia for a period of ten years. During this time, I had the leisure to objectively view Japanese instruments. I also had numerous opportunities to work with Chinese and Korean instruments. I also expanded the range of my opera work to include computer-generated music with regular Western instruments. In distancing myself from the music of my own culture, I saw it in a new light, and came to appreciate anew the allure of Japanese instruments. With this experience, I realized that it was necessary for me to reconsider some of the perceptions of contemporary music and traditional instruments that I had had when I was so engrossed in promoting this music.

In 1994, thirty years after the founding of the Pro Musica Nipponia, Orchestra Asia—an ensemble of ethnic instruments from Japan, China, and Korea—was established in Seoul. I was given responsibility for its artistic progress. More necessary than anything else was the contribution of works by composers from all over the world. For this purpose, instrumentation texts for the instruments of each of these countries had to be published in Japanese,

Korean, Chinese, and English. I had no time to ask myself who would write such a book. In the fall of 1994, I stopped composing and producing, and devoted myself to the writing of this book, *Composing for Japanese Instruments*. In late 1995, I finished the writing, but data entry and proofreading took over half a year.

When I finished the book, I felt the person to whom I should first express my gratitude was Mr. Ponfun Park, the Artistic Director of the Korean National Wind Ensemble. As an esteemed Korean colleague, it was difficult to refuse his eager requests for this book. Also, as I look back to my twenties, I must next acknowledge my venerable teacher, the great Akira Ifukubue, to whom I entirely entrusted my studies. How beneficial has his book *Kan-gen-gaku-hō*[1] been for Japanese composers! With my modest contribution of *Composing for Japanese Instruments* to the world, as his pupil, it is my deepest wish to extend the path of my teacher's music into the future. It is with this intention that I wrote this book.

I also wish to thank my former colleagues of the Pro Musica Nipponia, who provided me with a practical knowledge of Japanese instruments, and supported me by their passion. They are my collaborative authors in spirit. I also wish to thank the current members of the Pro Musica Nipponia, who, with warm help, provided me with ideas and recordings of musical examples, as well as modeling for the photographs and supplying instruments (representative: Takuo Tamuro). Among these people, there are performers who gave their time to gather necessary data and researchers who supplemented my memos with what was lacking; I wish to take this opportunity to express my sincere gratitude to the following people: wind instruments: Kōhei Nishikawa, Shigeyasu Fujisaki, Makoto Takei, Hiroshi Yonezawa, Hiroshi Soekawa, Takako Nishihara, and Yūji Nishihara; string instruments: Junkō Handa, Junkō Tahara, Yumiko Tanaka, Mika Sakaguchi, Tetsuko Kudō, Kiyoko Motegi, Haiko Otsuka, and Azechi Keiji; percussion: Hiromitsu Nishikawa, Taichi Ozaki, and Michio Usuki; copyist Mika Kobayashi, and *koto* maker Takashi Nakajima. Thank you.

The theories and descriptions in this book are based on notes I have been taking for many years. I did my utmost to fill those gaps in my knowledge with the suggestions and the criticisms of other composers and performers. When my notes and memory were unclear as to the origins the different instruments, I turned to Hisao Tanabe's *Nihon-no-gakki*,[2] Eishi Kikkawa's *Nihon-no-ongaku*[3] and the theories of the many contributors to the *Ongaku-jiten* published by Heibonsha.[4] In doing so, I have attempted to avoid any preconceptions I may have had.

I wish to thank Jun Asaka, the President of Ongaku-no-Tomosha, who recognized the significance of this book and pushed the publication forward regardless of any hopes for profit. Sparing no pains for over half a year on the troublesome work of publishing this book, even foregoing holidays to wholeheartedly take up the task of editing, I would also like to thank Yasuaki Hayashi. Words cannot express my gratitude. The completion of this book is due to him.

In bringing the English translation of this book to fruition, I express my gratitude to several people. First, to the young American composer Marty Regan, who came to Japan to study with me for two years at Tokyo College of Music, became a member of AURA-J (an ensemble I co-founded in 1998) and has composed many works for traditional Japanese instruments that have been commissioned, performed, and commercially recorded. He undertook the English translation of this work while pursuing his doctoral studies in composition at the University of Hawai'i, Manoa. Second, Philip Flavin, a flawlessly bilingual scholar and superb performer of Japanese music (specifically the *shamisen* and *koto*) from the University of California, Berkeley, who undertook the editorial oversight for the English translation of this work. Third, Professor Ralph Locke, senior editor of the Eastman Studies in Music series, who kept alive the possibilities of publishing this work in English, and Tim Madigan and Suzanne Guiod at the University of Rochester Press, for their assistance through the years. Fourth, Marié Abe, Janice Kande, and Adam Steckler, all graduate students at the University of California, Berkeley, who, over several years, gathered a formidable amount of materials for the Appendix and distilled it to its current form under the supervision of Professor Bonnie C. Wade. Fifth, the Center for Japanese Studies at the University of California, Berkeley for contributions to the underwriting of this project. Finally, this translation and its publication surely would not have come to reality without the support and encouragement of my long-time friend and scholar of Japanese music, Professor Bonnie C. Wade of the University of California, Berkeley. She encouraged me to have the work translated, found a publisher, and has contributed in countless other ways to its appearance.

I bow my head entirely to all who have helped me. Above all, I thank the person who has continued to support me for many long years, tolerating my selfish devotion to writing and composition, my wife, Nanako Miki. I dedicate this first book to you with all my gratitude.

Minoru Miki
August 1, 1996/ August 1, 2006

Appendix I

Works for Japanese Instruments by Minoru Miki

Compositions

1962

***Title: *Sonnet*
Instrumentation: 3 *shakuhachi*
Duration: 6′
Publisher/Recordings/Commission/Other: published by Zen-on Music, recorded on Columbia JX-21 and RVC 6096

1963

***Title: *Kurudando*—Cantata for Japanese instruments and mixed chorus based on melodies from the Amami district
Instrumentation: Mixed chorus, *shinobue*, 3 *shakuhachi*, 3 *shamisen*, bass *koto*, 3 percussion
Duration: 15′
Publisher/Recordings/Commission/Other: published by Ongaku no Tomo Sha, recorded on Columbia SX-24, commissioned by Miniamihon Broadcasting, awarded a prize in a commercial broadcasting convention

1964

Title: *Concerto for Strings and Japanese Instruments*
Adagio in *Yo* mode
Allegro in *In* mode

Three asterisks (***) indicate that the composition was awarded the National Art Festival Grand Prize in 1970 for the Columbia Recording of "Music of Minoru Miki performed by Ensemble Nipponia." Three bullets (•••) indicate that the composition was awarded the National Art Festival Prize for Excellence in 1979 for the Camerata Recordings of "Minoru Miki and Keiko Nosaka: The World of the 21-String Koto."

Instrumentation: 3 *shakuhachi, hosozao shamisen, biwa,* 2 *koto,* bass *koto,* 2 percussion, string ensemble
Duration: 11', 8'
Publisher/Recordings/Commission/Other: performed at the first concert of the Pro Music Nipponia, pulled from subsequent works lists

1965
   Title: *Prelude for Japanese Instruments*
Instrumentation: *shinobue,* 2 *shakuhachi, hosozao* (and *futuzao*), 2 *koto,* bass *koto,* percussion
Duration: 8'
Publisher/Recordings/Commission/Other: this piece became the first movement of *Paraphrase after Ancient Japanese Music*

1966
   Title: *Two Pastorals*
Instrumentation: *shinobue,* 3 percussion
Duration: 5', 6'
Publisher/Recordings/Commission/Other after the premiere, this became a trial piece
   ***:Title: *Paraphrase after Ancient Japanese Music*
      I. Prelude
      II. Sohmon
      III. Tanomai
      IV. Ruika
      V. Kagai
Instrumentation: *shinobue,* 2 *shakuhachi, shamisen, biwa,* 2 *koto,* bass *koto,* 2 percussion, soprano vocalise
Duration: 28'
Publisher/Recordings/Commission/Other: recorded on Columbia JX-24 and Denon Coco-78461, commissioned by the Japan Broadcasting Corporation

1967
   ***:Title: *Figures for Four Groups* (*Aya, Iki, Kuse, To*)
Instrumentation:
Aya: 2 *koto* and bass *koto*
Iki: shinobue, ryūtūteki, and 2 *shakuhachi*
Kuse: 2 *shamisen* (*hosozao* and *futuzao*), *biwa*
To: 2 percussion
Duration: 24' (6' each)
Publisher/Recordings/Commission/Other: published by Zen-on-Music, recorded on Columbia JX-23, *Kuse* commissioned by Japan Broadcasting Corporation, one of these pieces was composed in 1969

1968
   Title: *Ballades for Winging*

Instrumentation: *shinobue*, 3 *shakuhachi*, *hichiriki*, 3 *shamisen*, 3 *koto*, bass *koto*, 2 percussion, mixed chorus, tenor solo
Duration: 22′
Publisher/Recordings/Commission/Other: recorded on Columbia JX-22, poem in the second half of the piece by Satoshi Akiyama

1969
   ***Title: *Ballades for Koto Solo: Vol. 1—Winter*
     I. *Little Overture*
     II. *The Longing*
     III. *A Winter Nigh*
     IV. *Lullaby for my Doll*
     V. *The Coming of Spring*
Instrumentation: *koto* solo (13-string)
Duration: 16′
Publisher/Recordings/Commission/Other: published by Zen-on-Music, recorded on Columbia JX-23 and Victor-VX10
   ***Title: *Jō no Kyoku* ("Prelude for Shakuhachi, Koto, and Strings")
Instrumentation: *shakuhachi*, 21-string *koto*, *shamisen*, and strings
Duration: 16′
Publisher/Recordings/Commission/Other: published by Zen-on-Music, recorded on Columbia JX-21 and Camerata 30 CM-22
N.B. This piece marks the first time the 20-string *koto* appeared on stage (October 24, 1969). It is the first piece of "Eurasian Trilogy."
   ***Title: *Tennyō*
Instrumentation: *koto* solo (20-string)
Duration: 16′
Publisher/Recordings/Commission/Other: published by Zen-on-Music, recorded on Columbia JX-21, Camerata CMT-1018, commissioned by Keiko Nosaka
N.B. This is the first piece composed for 20-string *koto* solo. Premiered on November 7, 1969 by Keiko Nosaka.

1970
   ***Title: *Kokyō*
Instrumentation: *shakuhachi* solo
Duration: 12′
Publisher/Recordings/Commission/Other: published by Zen-on-Music, recorded on Columbia JX-22
***Title: *Convexity: Concerto for Three Groups of Sankyoku and a Japanese Drum*
Instrumentation: *shinobue*, 2 *shakuhachi*, 2 *shamisen*, *biwa*, *koto*, 20-string *koto*, bass *koto*, Japanese drum
Duration: 23′
Publisher/Recordings/Commission/Other: recorded on Columbia JX-22 and Denon Coco-78461, commissioned by Nihon Columbia

1971

•••Title: *Sao no Kyoku* (*"Venus in Spring"*) and *Tatsuta no Kyoku* (*"Venus in Autumn"*)
Instrumentation: *koto* solo (21-string)
Duration: 9' each
Publisher/Recordings/Commission/Other: published by Zen-on-Music, recorded on Camerata 32CM-55, commissioned by Keiko Nosaka
N.B. Starting with these pieces, the 20-string *koto* became the 21-string *koto*.
Title: *Tanu Tanu Ballade*
Instrumentation: children's chorus, baritone, *shinobue*, *hichiriki*, 3 *shakuhachi*, *shamisen*, *biwa*, 2 *koto*, 21-string *koto*, bass *koto*, 3 percussion
Duration: 24'
Publisher/Recordings/Commission/Other: recorded on Columbia YS-10141, commissioned by Shikoku Broadcasting, poetry by Masaharu Fuji
Title: *Miyabi no Uta* and *Hinaburi no Odori*
Instrumentation: *shakuhachi*, bass *koto*
Duration: 6', 9'
Publisher/Recordings/Commission/Other: published by Zen-on-Music, recorded on Columbia GZ-7005

1972

Title: *Warabeuta ni Yosete*
Instrumentation: *koto* solo (13-string)
Duration: 4'
Publisher/Recordings/Commission/Other: recorded on Columbia EX-7005
Title: *Participation I, II, III*
Instrumentation: duet for any combination of Japanese instruments (or trio if percussion is added)
Duration: 3' each
Publisher/Recordings/Commission/Other: composed as an ensemble textbook
Title: *Ne, Ushi, Tora, U/Yok Kon Kon*
Instrumentation: song and Japanese instruments (or piano)
Duration: 2'
Publisher/Recordings/Commission/Other: published by Hoso Shupann Kyokai (version with piano accompaniment), commissioned by Japan Broadcasting Company, poetry by Hiroo Sakata
Title: *Sohmon II*
Instrumentation: mixed chorus (vocalise), 21-string *koto*
Duration: 15'
Publisher/Recordings/Commission/Other:

1973

Title: *Ne, Tori* ("Opening for a Ceremony")
Instrumentation: *nōkan*, 2 *shakuhachi*, 2 *shamisen*, 2 *biwa*, 21-string *koto*, 2 *koto*, bass *koto*, 2 percussion

Duration: 16'
Publisher/Recordings/Commission/Other:
   Title: *Hatsu ne Shū* (contains five pieces)
Instrumentation: *koto* solo
Duration: 2'–3' each
Publisher/Recordings/Commission/Other: for beginning *koto* students, continues in 1978
   •••Title: *Hakuyō*
Instrumentation: violin, 21-string *koto*
Duration: 27'
Publisher/Recordings/Commission/Other: recorded on Camerata CMT-1016
   Title: *Poem in the Evening*
Instrumentation: *shakuhachi, koto, shamisen*
Duration: 7'
Publisher/Recordings/Commission/Other: published by Zen-on-Music, recorded on Camerata CMT-1001
   Title: *Participation IV, V, VI*
Instrumentation: duet for any combination of Japanese instruments (or trio if percussion is added)
Duration: 3'
Publisher/Recordings/Commission/Other: continuation of ensemble textbook
   Title: *Danses Concertantes I: Four Seasons*
   I. Spring is Dancing
   II. Whirling Water
   III. Autumn and Harvest Dance
   IV. Flower of Wind
   V. Epilogue
Instrumentation: *shinobue, shakuhachi, shamisen, biwa,* 2 *koto,* bass *koto,* 2 percussion
Duration: 20'
Publisher/Recordings/Commission/Other: recorded on Camerata 32CM-54
   Title: *Koto Futae*
Instrumentation: 2 *koto*
Duration: 11'
Publisher/Recordings/Commission/Other: published by Zen-on-Music

1974
   Title: *Koei*
Instrumentation: *shakuhachi* (*koto* and *ko-tsuzumi* in one part)
Duration: 21'
Publisher/Recordings/Commission/Other: composed for a film by Claude Gagnon

1974
Title: *Ha no Kyoku* ("*Koto Concerto No. 1*")
Instrumentation: *koto* solo (21-string), orchestra (2.2.2.2–4.3.2.1perc/str)
Duration: 24′
Publisher/Recordings/Commission/Other: rental from Ongaku-no-Tomosha, recorded on Camerata 30C-223 and King KICC2019
N.B. This is the second piece of the "Eurasian Trilogy."
Title: *Honjū*
Instrumentation: *shamisen* (*hosozao*) solo
Duration: 9′
Publisher/Recordings/Commission/Other: published by TA Photo and Sound Office, recorded on Camerata CMT-1001, commissioned by Hirokazu Sugiura
Title: *Aya II*
Instrumentation: 2 *koto*, bass *koto*
Duration: 7′
Publisher/Recordings/Commission/Other: commissioned by Sawarabi Kai
Title: *Muma no Shirabe*
I. Boat Song
II. Beggar's Song
III. Lullaby
Instrumentation: *koto* solo, voice, contrabass
Duration: 2′, 2′, 6′
Publisher/Recordings: commissioned by Michi Ozawa, poem by Satoshi Akihama
Title: *Matsu no Kyoku*
Instrumentation: *shakuhachi*, *shamisen*, 21-string *koto*, 2 *koto*, bass *koto*, women's chorus
Duration: 16′
Publisher/Recordings/Commission/Other: commissioned by Matsunomi Kai, from the *Kinkaiwakashū*
Title: *Ki-Do-Ai-Raku*
Instrumentation: male chorus (or mixed chorus), *biwa*, *shakuhachi*, *koto*
Duration: 5′, 3′, 6′, 7′
Publisher/Recordings/Commission/Other: poem by Satoshi Akiyama

1975
Title: *Shunkinshō*. An opera in three acts
Instrumentation: *koto* solo (21-string and 13-string), *jiuta shamisen*, *shakuhachi* (optional), orchestra (2.1.1.1–2.2.2.0–3perc/str)
Duration: 120′
Publisher/Recordings/Commission/Other: published by Zen-on-Music, commissioned by Nihon Opera Kyokai, libretto by Jun Maeda based on an original story by Jun-ichiro Tanizaki
•••Title: *Hinaburi*
Instrumentation: 21-string *koto*, flute or *shakuhachi*

Duration: 10'
Publisher/Recordings/Commission/Other: recorded on Camerata CMT-1016

1976
Title: *Wa*
Instrumentation: *shakuhachi, shamisen, biwa,* 21-string *koto,* bass *koto,* percussion
Duration: 15'
Publisher/Recordings/Commission/Other: published by the Japan Federation of Composers, recorded on Camerata 32CM-54
Title: *Sinfonia Concertante per Wasan*
Instrumentation: bass solo, female chorus, *Nōkan,* 21-string *koto,* orchestra (2.2.2.2–2.2.2.0–3 perc/str)
Duration: 22'
Publisher/Recordings/Commission/Other: commissioned by Nagoya College of Music
Title: *Wasan Concerto*
Instrumentation: *Nōkan,* 2 *shakuhachi, biwa, shamisen,* 21-string *koto,* bass *koto,* orchestra (2.2.2.2–2.2.2.0–3perc/str)
Duration: 22'
Publisher/Recordings/Commission/Other: commissioned by Nagoya College of Music, in commemoration of the 800th anniversary of Shinran's birth; seven of Shinran's sutras used
Title: *Sabaku no Hana*
Instrumentation: *koto* solo (21-string)
Duration: 15'
Publisher/Recordings/Commission/Other:
Title: *Ballades for Koto Solo: Vol. 2—Spring*
  I. The Young Sprout
  II. March
  III. Skylark
  IV. Around my Country
  V. The Greening
Instrumentation: *koto* solo (21-string)
Duration: 18'
Publisher/Recordings/Commission/Other: recorded on Camerata CMT-1017 and Camerata 32CM-55 ("The Greening" only)
Title: *Urakagura ("Sekai no Hōkok")*. An improvisational theater piece
Instrumentation: singers, actors, shinobue, 3 *shakuhachi, shamisen, biwa, kokyū,* 21-string *koto, koto,* bass *koto,* 2 percussion
Duration: 60'
Publisher/Recordings/Commission/Other: libretto by Satoshi Akihayama
Title: *Tsuki Uta*
Instrumentation: various Japanese instruments and song
Duration: 11'
Publisher/Recordings/Commission/Other

Title: *Hote*
Instrumentation: 2 *shinobue*, 3–6 *shakuhachi*, *kokyū*, 2 *shamisen*, 2 *biwa*, 2 21-string *koto*, 2 *koto*, 2 bass *koto*, 4 percussion
Duration: 30'
Publisher/Recordings/Commission/Other: recorded on Camerata 32CM-54

1977
Title: *Taro* (cantata for 5 voices, children's voices, and 17 Japanese instruments)
Instrumentation: childrens' chorus, soprano, boy soprano, mezzo-soprano, alto, bass, shinobue, 3 *shakuhachi*, *kokyū*, 2 *shamisen*, *biwa* (and tambura), 2 21-string *koto*, 2 13-string *koto*, 2 bass *koto*, 3 percussion
Duration: 57'
Publisher/Recordings/Commission/Other: poetry by Taizo Horai, commissioned by Japan Broadcasting Company
Title: *Rubi*
Instrumentation: *biwa* solo
Duration: 9'
Publisher/Recordings/Commission/Other: commissioned by Mikiko Yamada
Title: *Tsuki Uta*
Instrumentation: various Japanese instruments, voice
Duration: 11'
Publisher/Recordings/Commission/Other:
Title: *Danses Concertantes No. 2—Naruto Hicho* (Prologue, Chie no Kyoku, Promenade A, Okashina Akunin Tachi, Promenade B, Otsuna Rhapsody, Yamachidori, Tsukiyo no Kenshi)
Instrumentation: *shinobue*, 2 *shakuhachi*, *kokyū*, 2 *shamisen*, *biwa*, 21-string *koto*, *koto*, bass *koto*, 2 percussion
Duration: 15'
Publisher/Recordings/Commission/Other: from the NHK drama series *Naruto Hicho*, recorded by Toshiba
•••Title: *Visions of Rice*
Instrumentation: narration, 21-string *koto*
Duration: 18'
Publisher/Recordings/Commission/Other: published by Ongaku-no-Tomosha, recorded on Camerata CMT-1017, words by Satoshi Akiyama, commissioned by Keiko Nosaka, English and German versions also available
•••Title: "Overture and Shunnoden" from the opera *Shunkinshō*
Instrumentation: *koto* solo (21-string), orchestra (2.1.1.1–2.2.2.0.3.perc/str)
Duration: 18'
Publisher/Recordings/Commission/Other: recorded on Camerata CMT-1015

1978
Title: *Hatsu ne Shū* (cont. from 1973) (Koto no ha, Osanai inori, Nagori, Tanjōbi no Okurimono, Tsugi Naani, Tsukumaeta, Uta I, Uta II, Otedama, Ne, Ushi, Tora, U, Yane no ue no toritachi, Mizube no Akebono, Ame no mizumi no yacht no kamemotachi)

Instrumentation: *koto* solo (13-string)
Duration: 2′–3′ each
Publisher/Recordings/Commission/Other: for beginning *koto* students
   Title: *Ai for Shakuhachi and Strings*
Instrumentation: *shakuhachi* solo, strings
Duration: 6′–9′
Publisher/Recordings/Commission/Other:
   Title: Dance Tragedy *Tsuru*
Instrumentation: soprano, *shakuhachi, kokyū, biwa*, 2 21-string *koto*, percussion
Duration: 57′
Publisher/Recordings/Commission/Other: libretto by Taizo Horai, commissioned by Midori Nishizaki the Second
   Title: *Tsuru—Karaku* in one act
Instrumentation: soprano or tenor (narration), *shakuhachi*, 2 21-string *koto*
Duration: 30′
Publisher/Recordings/Commission/Other: libretto by Taizo Horai

1979
   Title: *An Actor's Revenge*—An opera in two acts
Instrumentation: 21-string *koto, shamisen, ko-tsuzumi*, 8 singers, male or mixed chorus, orchestra (2.0.2.0–1.0.1.0–2–3.perc/vln.va.vc)
Duration: 140′
Publisher/Recordings/Commission/Other: published by Faber Music, London, libretto by James Kirkup, based on an original story by Otokichi Mikami, commissioned by the English Music Theater
   Title: *Mitsuyama Bansho*. A dance drama
Instrumentation: *shamisen* solo, mixed chorus, soprano, orchestra (2.0.2.0.-1.0.1.0.203.perc/vln.vla.vc)
Duration: 70′
Publisher/Recordings/Commission/Other: commissioned by The Japanese Classical Dance Association
   •••Title: *From the East*
Instrumentation: *koto* solo (21-string)
Duration: 13′
Publisher/Recordings/Commission/Other: recorded on Camerata CMT-1017
N.B. The second part may be played as *Godan no Shirabe* separately.
   Title: *Matsu Yo*
Instrumentation: *shinobue, shakuhachi*, 21-string *koto, koto* ensemble
Duration: 15′
Publisher/Recordings/Commission/Other: published by Mikinen Collection, poetry by Minoru Miki, commissioned by Matsunomi Kai
   Title: *Murasaki no Fu*
Instrumentation: *shamisen* solo (w/ singing in one place)
Duration: 12′
Publisher/Recordings/Commission/Other: poetry adapted from the Kokuinshū, commissioned by Akiko Yazaki

Title: *New Kagurauta* and *Onitte Ittai Nandarō*
Instrumentation: song, *shinobue, shakuhachi, shamisen, biwa*, 21-string *koto*, bass *koto*, 2 percussion
Duration: 5', 3'
Publisher/Recordings/Commission/Other: for *Kagura* 1979

1980
Title: *Danses Concértantes No. 3—A Tale of Hachiro*
Instrumentation: *shinobue, shakuhachi, shamisen, biwa*, 21-string *koto*, bass *koto*, percussion, song and narration
Duration: 21'
Publisher/Recordings/Commission/Other: recorded on Camerata CMT-4003, constructed from the music for Kakashiza shadow theater
Title: *Shiosai*
Instrumentation: 21-string *koto*, cello
Duration: 8'
Publisher/Recordings/Commission/Other: recorded on Camerata 30CM-208
Title: *Little Suite*
    I. Hoshi no Matsuri
    II. Tsuki no De
    III. Nagisa to Taiyō
Instrumentation: *shinobue, shakuhachi, kokyū, biwa, shamisen*, 2 *koto*, bass *koto*, percussion
Duration: 5', 5', 4'
Publisher/Recordings/Commission/Other: this piece was composed as educational material for the Pro Musica Nipponia Summer Ensemble Workshop; parts can be chosen freely
Title: *Rondo for Tanomai*
Instrumentation: *shinobue*, 3 *shamisen* (*hosozao, chūzao, futozao*), 8 percussion
Duration: 8'
Publisher/Recordings/Commission/Other:
Title: *Awa no Tanuki Bayashi*
    I. Ukibyōshi
    II. Bakashuchi
    III. Tanikubushi
    IV. Mochitsuki Daiko
    V. Abare Dabuki
Instrumentation: *shinobue, shamisen*, song, Japanese percussion (*oodanuko, mamedanuko, mokugyō*)
Duration: 7'
Publisher/Recordings/Commission/Other:
Title: *Autumn Fantasy*
Instrumentation: *shakuhachi*, 21-string *koto*
Duration: 14'

Publisher/Recordings/Commission/Other: published by Ongaku-no-Tomosha, recorded on Camerata 32CM-55, commissioned by Sakata Seizan
Title: *Berodashi Chonma*—Karaku in one act
Instrumentation: 21-string *koto*, song and narration
Duration: 28'
Publisher/Recordings/Commission/Other: published by Zen-on-Music, recorded on Camerata 32CM-14

1981
Title: *Concerto Requiem ("Koto Concerto No. 3")*
Instrumentation: *koto* solo (21-string), 2 *shinobue*, 6 *shakuhachi*, *kokyū*, *biwa*, *futozao shamisen*, 2 21-string *koto*, bass *koto*, 4 percussion
Duration: 23'
Publisher/Recordings/Commission/Other: recorded on Camerata 32CM-55, commissioned by Fuji Television Network
Title: *Requiem Lontano*
Instrumentation: 21-string *koto*, synthesizer
Duration: 23'
Publisher/Recordings/Commission/Other: revised in 1987 as an alternate version of *Concerto Requiem*
Title: *Iwaki Dance*
I. Tōcha
II. Iwakibushi
III. Wazei
Instrumentation: voice, *shamisen*, *shakuhachi*, *hayashi*
Duration: 10'
Publisher/Recordings/Commission/Other:
Title: *Kyū no Kyoku* ("Symphony for Two Worlds")
Instrumentation: *shinobue*, 4–6 *shakuhachi*, 2 *shamisen* (*hosozao* and *futozao*), *biwa*, 2–3 21-string *koto*, 2–3 bass *koto*, 4 percussion, orchestra (3.3.3.3–4.3.3.1–3.perc/str)
Duration: 36'
Publisher/Recordings/Commission/Other: published by Zen-on-Music, recorded on Camerata 30CM-223, Eterna827901, commissioned by the Gewandhaus Orchestra for their 200th anniversary
N.B. Along with *Jō no Kyoku* (1969) and *Ha no Kyoku* (1974), *Kyū no Kyoku* completes the "Eurasian Trilogy."

1982
Title: *Sonnet II, III, IV, V*
Instrumentation:
II. Tanabata no Kyoku for 2 *shakuhachi*
III. Yamachidori for *shakuhachi* solo
IV. Untitled for 3 *shakuhachi*
V. Kinkakufu for *shakuhachi* solo
Duration: 3', 3', 6', 6'

Publisher/Recordings/Commission/Other: published by Seiwa Ongei
Title: *Hatsu ne Shū* (cont. from 1973 and 1978) (Kanashikeredo, Genbakusho no Hitachi ni, Hirajōshi wo Tsukurō, Hatsune I, Hatsune II)
Instrumentation: *koto* solo
Duration: 2'–3' each
Publisher/Recordings/Commission/Other:
Title: *Hatsu ne Shū* (Futatsu no Kaidan de, Ironaoshi, Doran, Uta)
Instrumentation: *koto* solo (21-string)
Duration: 2'–3' each
Publisher/Recordings/Commission/Other:
Title: *Touge no mukou ni nani ga aru*, a choral opera
Instrumentation: *shinobue, shakuhachi, hosozao shamisen, futozao shamisen, biwa,* 21-string *koto*, bass *koto*, percussion, six singers, mixed chorus
Duration: 105'
Publisher/Recordings/Commission/Other: original story and libretto by Masakazu Yamazakai
Title: *Shamisen Kijūsō*
Instrumentation: 2 *shamisen*
Duration: 2'
Publisher/Recordings/Commission/Other: part of *Touge no mukou ni nani ga aru*
Title: *Tsuki no Usagi*—Karaku for Children
Instrumentation: *shamisen* and narrator, *shinobue*, percussion
Duration: 17'
Publisher/Recordings/Commission/Other: original story by Ichiro Wakabayashi, *futozao* version made in 1991
Title: *Cassiopeia 21*
Instrumentation: 5 21-string *koto* (including soprano and bass 21-string *koto*)
Duration: 15'
Publisher/Recordings/Commission/Other: commissioned by Keiko Nosaka and the 20-String Koto Ecole
Title: *Yui* I
Instrumentation: 2 *shō*, piano
Duration: 14'
Publisher/Recordings/Commission/Other: commissioned by Yaeko Okudaira

1983

Title: *Rainbow Overture*
Instrumentation: *shinobue*, 2 *shakuhachi, biwa, hosozao shamisen, futozao shamisen,* 21-string *koto*, koto, bass *koto*, 2 percussion, and Chinese orchestra
Duration: 8'40"
Publisher/Recordings/Commission/Other: this piece marks the beginning of a collaboration with an ethnic instrumental orchestra (March 3, 1983 at Red Tower Auditorium in Beijing)
Title: *Kaiware no Uta*
Instrumentation: 2 21-string *koto*

Duration: 6'
Publisher/Recordings/Commission/Other: commissioned by Yoko Naito and Hisako Naito
Title: *Ballades for Koto Solo, Vol III: Summer*
  I. A Dewdrop
  II. To the South
  III. Dancing Girls
  IV. Under the White Wind
  V. A Squall
Instrumentation: *koto* solo (21-string)
Duration: 18'
Publisher/Recordings/Commission/Other: commissioned by Michiko Takita
Title: *Utayomizaru* ("The Monkey Poet"), a musical-opera in two acts
Instrumentation: 21-string *koto*, *shinobue* and *shakuhachi*, gamelan percussion, conductor (who also plays percussion), 12 singers
Duration: 113'
Publisher/Recordings/Commission/Other: published by Zen-on-Music, original story and libretto by Mitsuo Kawamura, English version by Colin Graham, commissioned by Geidankyo
Title: *August, 1945*
Instrumentation: 21-string *koto*, orchestra (3.3.3.3–4.3.3.1–3.perc/str)
Duration: 5'
Publisher/Recordings/Commission/Other: composed as "Orchestral Message 1983 of the Japanese Musicians Against Nuclear Weapons"
Title: *Ode to Forest* (second part of *Yui II*)
Instrumentation: 21-string *koto*, cello
Duration: 11'
Publisher/Recordings/Commission/Other: recorded on Camerata 30CM208

1984
Title: *Matsu no Kyōsōkyoku* (*Koto Concerto No. 4*)
Instrumentation: 21-string *koto* solo, *shakuhachi*, *shamisen*, 2 *koto*
Duration: 20'
Publisher/Recordings/Commission/Other: commissioned by Matsunomi Kai
Title: *Rhapsody*
Instrumentation: *koto* solo (21-string)
Duration: 15'
Publisher/Recordings/Commission/Other: material derived from the solo part of *Koto Concerto No. 4*
Title: *Danses Concértantes IV—Kita no Uta*
  I. Yoake
  II. Yuri no Odori
  III. Mushitachi no Odori
  IV. Seirei no Odori
  V. Odoke

VI. Daichi ni Mau
Instrumentation: *shinobue*, 2 *shakuhachi*, *kokyū*, *shamisen*, *biwa*, 21-string *koto*, *koto*, bass *koto*, 2 percussion
Duration: 23'
Publisher/Recordings/Commission/Other: new version of *Shiki-emaki Hokkaido Ten to Chi to Hito* ("*Four Season Picture Scrolls: Hokkaido, Heaven, Earth, and People*") composed in 1981

1985
   Title: *Yui III—Flowers and Water*
Instrumentation: *shakuhachi*, 21-string *koto*, *futozao shamisen*, string quartet, harp
Duration: 13'
Publisher/Recordings/Commission/Other: composed with the assumption that it would be used as theater music for *Suishoku-Hanamai*, by Iwanami Movies
   Title: *Jōruri*. An opera in three acts
Instrumentation: *shakuhachi*, 21-string *koto*, *futozao shamisen*, orchestra, seven singers
Duration: 160'
Publisher/Recordings/Commission/Other: published by Zen-on-Music, commissioned by the Opera Theater of St. Louis, original story and libretto by Colin Graham
   Title: *Koto Concerto No. 5*
Instrumentation: 21-string *koto* solo, orchestra
Duration: 15'
Publisher/Recordings/Commission/Other: material taken from the overture, prelude of act II, scene 1, and the interlude of act III of *Jōruri*
   Title: *At the Flower Garden*. A mini opera
Instrumentation: *shinobue*, *kayagum*, vibraphone and drums, tambura (who also conducts), four singers
Duration: 20'
Publisher/Recordings/Commission/Other: composed as one piece for the "1985 Omnibus Opera Message of the Japanese Musicians Against Nuclear Weapons"
   Title: *Rurui Hikyoku*
Instrumentation: *shakuhachi* solo
Duration: 10'
Publisher/Recordings/Commission/Other: material taken the *shakuhachi* parts of *Jōruri*

1986
   Title: *Poemusica: Frog Fantasy*
Instrumentation: *shinobue* (and *shakuhachi*), synthesizer, percussion, twelve singers
Duration: 45'
Publisher/Recordings/Commission/Other: revised into *Yomigaeru* in 1992

1989

Title: *Soul*—for Japanese and Korean Ethnic Orchestra
  I. *Chinkon* or *Tamashizume* ("Ritual")
  II. *Shinkon* or *Tamafuri* ("Festival")
Instrumentation: *shinobue*, 3 *shakuhachi*, *kokyū*, *hosozao shamisen*, *futozao shamisen*, 2 *biwa*, 21-string *koto*, *koto*, bass *koto*, 4 percussion, Korean ethnic instrument orchestra
Duration: 24′
Publisher/Recordings/Commission/Other: movement II adopted from *Hote*

1990

  Title: *Kaminoyama Kakashi Bayashi* (Kakashi Tōjō Bayashi, Kakashirabe, Karakoronba, Kotobayashi, Pugaro Daiko, Chūgoku fu Kaoren Gaku)
Instrumentation: *shinobue*, 21-string *koto*, marimba, percussion
Duration: 20′
Publisher/Recordings/Commission/Other: commissioned by Kaminoyama Kanko Kyokai
  Title: *Ballades for Koto Solo, Vol IV: Autumn*
  I. A West Wind Brings
  II. Tower on the Lake
  III. Migrating Birds
  IV. Scarecrows
  V. Moonlight on the Journey
Instrumentation: *koto* solo (21-string)
Duration: 21′
Publisher/Recordings/Commission/Other: commissioned by Reiko Kimura
N.B. This piece marks the completion of the Ballades for koto.

1991

  Title: *Yoshitsune Daiko*
Instrumentation: percussion ensemble
Duration: 4′
Publisher/Recordings/Commission/Other: commissioned by Komatsujima City
  Title: *Kincho Daiko*
Instrumentation: *shinobue*, percussion ensemble
Duration: 4′–6′
Publisher/Recordings/Commission/Other: commissioned by Komatsujima City

1992

  Title: *Yomigaeru*. A folk opera in two acts
Instrumentation: *shinobue* (and *shakuhachi*), percussion, synthesizer, drum machine, sampler, mixed chorus and fourteen singers
Duration: 144′

Publisher/Recordings/Commission/Other: commissioned by Okayama City Hall, original story and libretto by Ray Nakanishi, material adopted from *Poemusica: Frog Fantasy* (1986), orchestral version completed in 1994
Title: *Orochi Den*. A folk opera in one act
Instrumentation: *shakuhachi, percussion,* piano, trombone, dancers and eleven singers
Duration: 40'
Publisher/Recordings/Commission/Other: original story and libretto by Asaya Fujita, *kagura* part added to *Tennohan and Yamatano Orochi* (1990) to create a new piece
Title: *Ki no Kane*
Instrumentation: 2 *shinobue, nōkan, ryūteki,* 3 *shō, hichiriki,* 2 *shakuhachi, kokyū,* 3 *shamisen* (*hosozao, chūzao,* and *futozao*), *biwa,* 2 21-string *koto,* bass *koto,* 3 percussion, soprano, women's chorus
Duration: 33'
Publisher/Recordings/Commission/Other: commissioned by the Pro Musica Nipponia

1993
Title: *Shizuka and Yoshitsune*. A grand opera in three acts
Instrumentation: 21-string *koto, ko-tsuzumi,* orchestra (3.3.3.3–4.3.3.1–3.perc/str), 16 singers and mixed chorus
Duration: 117'
Publisher/Recordings/Commission/Other: original story and libretto by Ray Nakanishi, commissioned by the Kamakura Performing Arts Center in commemoration of their founding
Title: *Terute and Oguri*. A musical drama in two parts
Instrumentation: *shakuhachi,* 21-string *koto,* violin, cello, 2 percussion, 2 horns, 2 trumpets, 2 trombones, 7 singers and mixed chorus, actors and many dancers
Duration: 118'
Publisher/Recordings/Commission/Other: libretto by Asaya Fujita, commissioned by the Nagoya Art Creation Center for their 10th anniversary

1994
Title: *Folk Symphony* ("*Den Den Den*")
Instrumentation: *shinobue,* 4 *shakuhachi,* 2 *shō, biwa, hosozao shamisen, futozao shamisen,* 3 21-string *koto,* 3 bass *koto,* 2 percussion, 23 Chinese ethnic instruments, 20 Korean ethnic instruments
Duration: 120'
Publisher/Recordings/Commission/Other: composed for Orchestra Asia, premiered by Orchestra Asia for its debut concerts in Seoul, Tokushima, and Okayama in June 1994, recorded on Shinnara and Raon
Title: *Lotus Poem*

Instrumentation: *shakuhachi* solo, *shinobue, shakuhachi, biwa, shamisen, futozao shamisen*, 2 21-string *koto*, bass *koto*, 2 percussion
Duration: 17'
Publisher/Recordings/Commission/Other: joint commission from Iowa University and the Pro Musica Nipponia

1995

Title: *Ito no Haru Aki*
Instrumentation: *koto, shamisen*
Duration: 11'
Publisher/Recordings/Commission/Other:
Title: *Sumidagawa* ("*The River Sumida*"). An opera in one act
Instrumentation: 21-string *koto*, violin, *rin*, cello, clarinet (doubling bass clarinet), percussion, soprano, tenor, bass, mixed chorus
Duration: 56'
Publisher/Recordings/Commission/Other: original libretto by Motomasa Kanze, libretto by Asaya Fujita
Title: *Kusabira*. An opera in one act
Instrumentation: 21-string *koto*, violin, cello, bass clarinet, percussion, tenor, baritone, mixed chorus
Duration: 28'
Publisher/Recordings/Commission/Other: original libretto from the *kyōgen Kusabira*, libretto by Asaya Fujita, commissioned by Geidankyo (Japan Council of Performers' Organizations) to commemorate the 30th anniversary of their founding
N.B. These two operas may be performed together.

1996

Title: *Loulan as a Dream*—for Orchestra Asia
Instrumentation: "Orchestra Asia" [*dizi*, 2 *shinobue*, 4 *shakuhachi*, 2 *taegum*, 2 *shō*, 2 *sheng, suena*, 4 *piri, liuchin, pipa, biwa*, 2 *shamisen, yangqin*, 4 *kayagum*, 3 21-string *koto*, 3 bass *koto*, 5 percussion, 4 *gaofu*, 6 *erfu*, 4 *haegum*, 2 *gjunfu*, 4 *ajeng*, 2 *dagefu, didagefu*]
Duration: 13'
Publisher/Recordings/Commission/Other:

1997

Title: *Pipa Concerto* (version for Orchestra Asia)
Instrumentation: pipa solo, "Orchestra Asia" [*dizi, shinobue*, 4 *shakuhachi*, 2 *taegum*, 2 *shō*, 2 *sheng, suena*, 4 *piri, liuchin, biwa*, 2 *shamisen, yangqin*, 4 *kayagum*, 3 21-string *koto*, 3 bass *koto*, 5 percussion, 4 *gaofu*, 6 *erfu*, 4 *haegum*, 2 *gjunfu*, 4 *ajeng*, 2 *dagefu, didagefu*]
Duration: 29'–32' (with cadenza)
Publisher/Recordings/Commission/Other:

1998

Title: *Requiem 99—Concerto for Marimba and Japanese Instruments* (1998)
Duration: 20′–23′ (with cadenza)
N.B. Marimba version of *Concerto Requiem* (1981). Solo part is alternative.

1999

Title: *The Tale of Genji.* An opera in three acts (1999)
Instrumentation: orchestra (2.2.2.2–2.2.2–3 perc/str), *pipa, qin,* 21-string *koto,* lyric soprano, lyric soprano, 2 spinto soprano, lyric mezzo-soprano, coro mezzo-soprano, contralto, tenor, 3 baritones, bass-baritone, mixed chorus
Duration: 180′ (Act I: 65′, Act II: 63′, Act III: 29′)
Publisher/Recordings/Commission/Other: original story by Lady Murasaki Shikibu, libretto by Colin Graham

2000

Title: *Trio Concerto—Music from the Tale of Genji*
1) Prologue—At Seiryo-Den
2) Fujitsubo
3) Rokujo no Miyasudokoro
4) To No Chujo
5) Genji, waiting for Murasaki "It's always the one I see"
6) Autumn Festival and Kokiden
7) Murasaki and Aoi
8) Aoi's Death and Rokujo
9) Kokiden and Suzaku
10) Pipa Interlude—Akashi
11) Epilogue—Forever

Instrumentation: solo shakuhachi, solo *pipa,* solo 21-string koto, Japanese instruments (*shinobue, hichiriki,* 2 *shakuhachi, hosozoa shamisen, futozoa shamisen, biwa,* 2 21-string *koto,* bass *koto,* 2 percussion
Duration: 44′
Publisher/Recordings/Commission/Other:

2000

Title: *Memory of the Earth* (1st movement of "Symphony of the Earth")
Instrumentation: solo *shakuhachi,* solo *morin-khuur* (Mongolian spike fiddle), solo *pipa,* solo 21-string *koto,* soli Balinese gamelan percussion (*trompong,* 2 *gangsa pomade* as *polos,* kendang) with solo *gangsa pomade* as *nyangsih*
Orchestra (3.3.3.3–4.4.4–5perc/str)
Duration: 25′
Publisher/Recordings/Commission/Other:

2001

Title: *Setouchi Nocturne*—for Japanese instruments
1) At an Ancient Port

  2) Golden Waves (with pipa solo) or Silver Waves (without pipa solo)
  N.B. *shakuhachi* parts are different
  3) At the Mercy of the Current
Instrumentation: 2 *shakuhachi*, 2 *koto*, bass *koto*
Duration: 17′
Publisher/Recordings/Commission/Other:
  Title: *Lotus Concerto*—for solo *shakuhachi* & orchestra
Instrumentation: *shakuhachi* solo, orchestra (1.1.1.1–1.1.1–2 perc/hp/str)
Duration: 17′–18′
Publisher/Recordings/Commission/Other:

2002

  Title: *Heian Music Scope* (trio version)
  1) Introduction—Darkness and a Wraith
  2) A Forbidden Love
  3) A Passage of time
  4) Friends in Fun
  5) Longing for an Eternal Homage
  6) Pipa Interlude—Seaside Joy
Instrumentation: *shakuhachi*, 21-string *koto*, *pipa*
Duration: 21′30″
Publisher/Recordings/Commission/Other:
  Title: *Origin*—quintet for "Asia Ensemble" for their debut concert
Instrumentation: *shakuhachi*, *erhu* (or *morin-khuur*), *pipa*, 21-string *koto* (or guzhen), da-sanxian (or *futozao shamisen* or bass *koto*)
Duration: 16′20″
Publisher/Recordings/Commission/Other: recorded on Asia Ensemble. Yui Records YUCD0001, 2003

2003

  Title: *Koto Pieces for Peace*. 51 short pieces for beginning *koto* students
Instrumentation: *koto* solo & 2 *koto*, bass *koto*, *shakuhachi*, voice
Duration: 2′–4′ each
Publisher/Recordings/Commission/Other:
  Title: *Firefly Suite for Koto Ensemble*
  1) A Light Storm
  2) Living Eggs
  3) Flickering Toccata
  4) Song of Life
Instrumentation: 2 *koto*, bass *koto*
Duration: 14′–15′ (2′55″, 2′10″, 3′40″, 5′)
Publisher/Recordings/Commission/Other:

2005
> Title: *Hagoromo*. Music drama for soprano, baritone and traditional Japanese instruments
> Instrumentation: *shinobue*, 2 *shakuhachi*, *biwa*, *shamisen*, 2 21-string *koto*, bass *koto*, percussion
> Duration: 80' (Miki composed 18 out of 30 songs, approximately 40')
> Publisher/Recordings/Commission/Other: collaborative composition with composers from AURA-J, libretto by Toyoko Nishida

2006
> Folk Symphony (Op.120–1), poem by Nanako Miki, "Furusato no Kaze"
> Instrumentation: 2 *shakuhachi*, *shamisen*, 2 21-string *koto*, bass *koto*, orchestra (2.2.2.2–4.3.3.1.4 perc/str), and mixed-choir
> Duration: 25'
> Publisher/Recordings/Commission/Other: premiered November 4, 2007 at the Tokushima Kyōdo Bunka Kaikan, commissioned by Tokushima Prefecture for their 2nd National Cultural Festival.

2008
> Title: Shamisen Concerto
> Instrumentation: solo *shamisen*, *shinobue*, 2 *shakuhachi*, *shō*, 2 21-string *koto*, bass *koto*, 2 percussion
> Duration: 15' (includes a three-minute cadenza)
> Publisher/Recordings/Commission/Other: premiered March 11, 2008 at the Yotsuya Kumin-kaikan, Tokyo at the 21st AURA-J concert, *shamisen* solo by Tetsuya Nozawa, conducted by Tōru Sakakibara
> Title: *Kirei*
> Subtitle: Duet for *Shakuhachi* and 21-string *koto*
> Instrumentation: *shakuhachi* and 21-string *koto*
> Duration: 8'
> Publisher/Recordings/Commission/Other: premiered in August 2008 in Tokyo, *shakuhachi* by Seizan Sakata, 21-string *koto* by Kaneri Kimoto

Arrangements

Year: 1965
> Title: *Three Awa Lullabies*
> Instrumentation: *shakuhachi*, *shamisen*, *koto*, bass *koto*, percussion
> Duration: 10'
> Publisher/Recordings/Commission/Other:

Year: 1975
> Title: *Three Festival Ballades*
> Instrumentation: 3 *koto*, bass *koto*
> Duration: 15'
> Publisher/Recordings/Commission/Other:

Year: 1979
　Title: *Natsu no Jōjoshi* ("Summer Poem")
Instrumentation: *shakuhachi, 3 koto,* bass *koto*
Duration: 13′
Publisher/Recordings/Commission/Other:
Originally distributed by Columbia Music Entertaiment, Inc. on a four LP set ("The Music") in 1970, released by Nihon Westminster Co.Ltd on a three CD set in 2006
Nihon Westminster Co. Ltd JXCC-1017
1) *Jō no Kyoku* (1969)
2) *Tennyo* (1970)
3) *Paraphrase after Japanese ancient music* (1966)
Nihon Westminster Co.Ltd JXCC-1018
4) *Sonnet* (No.1) (1962)
5) *Convexity* (1970)
6) *Kokyō* (1970)
7) *Figures for Four Groups* (1967–68)
Nihon Westminster Co.Ltd JXCC-1019
8) *Kurando* (1963)
9) *Ballades for Koto Solo: Vol. 1—Winter*
10) *Ballades for Winging* (1968)

Appendix II

Contemporary Works for Traditional Japanese Instruments by Composers Other than Minoru Miki, 1981–2015

Minoru Miki wrote in his Afterword that, as a result of his use of Japanese traditional instruments in his compositions and the rapidly increasing number of pieces being written for Japanese instruments, he decided to write this book. Due to the success of his and other major Japanese composers—those both preceding and following him—in promulgating such a compositional undertaking, Miki thought it important to bring to the reader's attention a sampling of such works written by others.

This appendix of composers and the works they have written for traditional Japanese instruments includes both Japanese and non-Japanese composers. Thousands of compositions for traditional Japanese instruments have been written, so this appendix is, by necessity, very selective. The choices have been made based on the availability of these works on CD or in published scores; even so, that body of compositions is also limited—by time-frame as well as by easy accessibility. It is now possible to have such a select appendix due to the ubiquitous World Wide Web through which the reader can add exponentially to it.

Bonnie C. Wade
Berkeley, California
May 2008

Keys to the Listing of Japanese Publishers, Recording Companies, Composers, Works, and of Instruments Used by Both Japanese and Non-Japanese Composers

Publishers

AM	Tokyo Art Center, Academia Music
Akane	Akane Foundation

FV   Feedback Verlag
JFC   Japan Federation of Composers: Scores: JFC-XXXX; Records: R-XXXX; CD
KO   Katei Ongakukai
MV   Merke Verlag/Editions
NSR   Japan Shakuhachi League
NPM   North Pacific Music
OGT   Ongaku no Tomo Sha
Shinten   Shinten Editions (Shinten Ongaku Kyokai)
SJ   Schott Japan
TUE   Toho University Editions
TA   TA Photo and Sound Office
ZG   Zen-On

Recording Companies

Information on recordings is given in the form of matrix number.

Composers

An asterisk (*) beside the name of a composer indicates an individual who has an appreciable number of works for traditional instruments that are not listed here. Composers of works for traditional instruments not included in this appendix can be found on the Web or through information from the JFC and other sources (see below).

Because most works for traditional instruments have not been published, composers are often willing to provide scores upon request. Some of them are listed below. Others can be found on the Web or through contact information from the JFC.

AIZAWA, Shirotomo (1962–)
IMAI, Shigeuyuki (1933–)
FUJIIE, Keiko (1963–)
FUJIEDA, Mamoru (1955–)
KAWASAKI, Etsuo (1959–)
MATSUO, Masataka (1959–)
MIYAGI, Jun–ichi (1952–)
ODAIRA, Koichi (1960–)
SANO, Yoshimitsu (1955–)

S(C) ENSHU, Jiro (1934–)
SHIBUYA, Takucho (1930–)
SHIMAZU, Takehito (1949–)
SUIGIURA, Masayoshi (1921–)
TAKAHASHI, Yuji (1938–)
TANAKA, Shuichi (1966–)
URATA, Kenjiro (1941–)
YAMAMOTO, Junnosuke (1958–)

Japanese Composers and Works

The selective list of works by Japanese composers on recordings or published in score is drawn primarily from one invaluable source: the annual editions of *Works by Japanese Composers*, published by the Suntory Music Foundation, whose basic aim is the development and diffusion of works by Japanese composers. The publication is made possible with the generous support and editorial work of the Japan Federation of Composers (above, JFC), a non-profit organization whose aim is to foster the creative work of Japanese composers in numerous ways, but most pertinently here, by publication of a selection of new pieces annually. To compile *Works by Japanese Composers*, the JFC asked each composer to select what they considered to be their major works. While most are not specialists in traditional music, the instrumentation of hundreds of works comprises or includes at least one traditional instrument. In the selective list provided here, only those which have been published either in score or recording are shown. The JFC will provide further information, including means of obtaining *Works by Japanese Composers* or their publication catalogue, and contacting a composer or publisher (fax 03-3589-5344).

Other Sources

Numerous books and articles have been written on Japanese composers who write for traditional Japanese instruments; space constraints cause only a few to be listed here. An invaluable source is *Change and Continuity in Contemporary Japanese Music: A Search for a National Identity* by Judith Ann Herd (Ann Arbor, Michigan: UMI Dissertation Services, 1987). In this work, Herd discusses the birth of a national compositional style, the neo-nationalist movement, the experimental movement, and the new Japanese avant-garde and provides information and insight on compositions utilizing traditional Japanese instruments. The most comprehensive study of Japanese composers and their music, including works for traditional Japanese instruments, is *Yōgaku: Japanese Music in the Twentieth Century* by Luciana Galliano (Lanham, MD: Scarecrow Press, 2002). Her extensive bibliography includes a section on writings about individual composers. More has been written about Toru Takemitsu than the many other famous and excellent Japanese composers, including *A Way a Lone. Writings on Tōru Takemitsu*, edited by Hugh de Ferranti and Yōko Narazaki (Tokyo: Academia Music Limited, 2002), *The Music of Toru Takemitsu* by Peter Burt (Cambridge: Cambridge University Press, 2001), and Takemitsu's own *Confronting Silence: Selected Writings*, translated by Yoshiko Kakudo and Glenn Glasow (Berkeley, CA: Fallen Leaf Press, 1995). In her *Music in Japan. Experiencing Music, Expressing Culture* (New York and London: Oxford University Press, 2005), Bonnie C. Wade discusses several major Japanese composers including Keiko Fujiie, Toshio Hosokawa, Toshihide Niimi, Akira Nishimura, Yuji Takahashi, and Joji Yuasa, as well as Minoru Miki.

Non-Japanese Composers and Works

A good source for works for *shakuhachi* by American composers is Ralph Samuelson's compilation in the *Contemporary Music Review*, vol. 8, part 2 (1993–94), pp. 89–93. Works listed there are not listed below. The selective list below—again, only works published in score or on recording—has been gleaned from various sources.

Japanese Composers

AIZAWA, Shirotomo (1962–)
"'*Suma*' from the Tale of Genji" for Japanese insts, vv (2001) RKC8001
ANDO, Yuki (1961–)
"Three Pieces from '*Kojiki*'" for *biwa, shino*, pf, *nōkan* (1999) JILA; JILA-1109
AOSHIMA, Hiroshi (1955–)
"'*Chu-shin-gura*'" for male vv, 2 *shami* (1985) ICR-1530
AZECHI, Keiji (1948–)
"*Ryōanji*" for *dai-kyoku* (1995) 25CM-447–448
"Harmony of Rainbow" for *koto* trio (1999) Katei Ongaku Shuppan
"*Kisaragi*" for *Kokyu* (2000) Azechi Kokyu Ongakuin
ENDŌ , Masao (1947–)
"Time's Puff" for 2 *shami* (1986) SJL-2398–2402 FUJII, Bondai (1931–94)
*FUJIIE, Keiko (1963–)
"DE TERRA CAELUM ET DE CAELO TERRAM" for *ryu, hichi, 3 shō, gakubiwa, gakuso* (1999) CD with *Music in Japan, Experiencing Music, Expressing Culture*, by Bonnie C. Wade (New York: Oxford University Press, 2005)
FUJITA, Masanori (1946–)
"Aurora II" for 2 *koto*, perc (1982) WB-7093-ND
FUJIWARA, Yutaka (1960–)
"*Usubeni-zome no Yoru ni Yosete*" for 13-str *koto* (1992) Shinten Ed.
"*Moegi no Oto no Mori de*" for *shami*, 13-str *koto* (1992) Shinten Ed.
"*Uguisu ni Yō-nashi*" for 2 *shaku* (1992) Shinten Ed.
GONDAI, Atsuhiko (1965–)
"Ritual of Love" for *shō*, Orch (2002) WPCS-11503
"Infinite Light/Boundless Life" for *shomyo, gagaku*, sop, org (2002) Fontec
HAYAKAWA, Masaaki (1934–)
"*Gen-ei*" for *shaku*, vn, perc, Strs (9–50 players) (1998) JFC-9803
HAYASHI, Yoshiteru (1934–)

"Rhapsody" for *koto*, orch (1983) FO-1995
*HIGO, Ichiro (1940)
"*Yanagawa-shikyoku*" for *koto* (1997) CRCM-60035
HIRAI, Kozaburo (1910–2002)
"A Mask Fantasy" for m-sop, *koto*, 17-str *koto* (1985) OGT
"Flower Robber" for sop, *shaku*, *koto* (1988) ONT
"Praise to '*Sakura*'" for sop, ten, *shaku*, pf (1995) ONT
"Song of a Poor Wife Whose Husband is Sent to Remote Battle-field 'Azumakoiuta'" for sop, ten, *shaku*, pf (1996) ONT
HONMA, Masao (1930–)
"*Sokyo II*" for 20-string *koto* and 17-string *koto* (1984) JFC-8402; R-8502 vol. 10
*HOSOKAWA, Toshio (1955)
"*UTSUROI*" for *shō*, hp (1986) OGT
"Birds Fragments IV" for *shō*, vc, perc (1991) SJ
"Landscape V" for *shō*, str quartet (1993) SJ
"Wie ein Atmen im Lichte" for *shō* (2002) SJ
"In *Ajimono—Somon-ka I*" for v, *koto*, vc, ens (2002) SJ
"*Toku tomo—Somon-ka II*" for v, *koto*, vc, ens (2002) SJ
"Garden at First Light" for *gagaku* (2002) SJ
*ICHIYANAGI, Toshi (1933–)
"Luminous Space" for *shō*, ondes Martenot, orch (1991) SJ
"Encounter" for *shomyo*, *gagaku*, *shaku*, perc, vc (2002) FOCD-9183
*IFUKUBE, Akira (1914–2005)
"5 Poems after Man-yō-Inaba" for sop, alt fl, *koto* (25 Corde) (1994) 25CM391-2
"*Pipa Xing*—d'après poème de Bo Ju-yi" for 25-string *koto* (1999) 28CM-558
*IKEBE, Shinichiro (1943–)
"*Echigo-Jishi*" for *shami*, orch (1983) TCM-1003
"*Rin-Rin Fu*" for 1 *shaku*, 1 *sangen*, 1 *koto*, 2 *shaku*, 2 *sangen*, 2 *kotos*, 17-str *koto*, 2 perc (1988) Shinten
"Pansy Etude" for *sangen*, *koto*, 17-str *koto* (1993) TA
"*Retsu-Retsu-fu*" for *sangen*, cb, perc (1993) Victor/VICG-8079
"On a Treetop" for 20-str *koto* (1995) Camerata/30CM426
"Poppy Etude" for *shaku*, 2 *sangen*, 2 *koto*, 17-str *koto* (1997) ALM/ALDC-9028
"*Tsuchi no Katachi*" for Japanese drum ens (1998) ZG
IMAI, Shiguéyuki (1933–)
"*Han Geinou Mandala*" for *tegun*, *chango*, 20-str *koto*, Japanese perc, orch (1995) TYCY-5473
"2 Framménti Poetici '*Nambu*'" for 17-str *koto*, 4–13-str *koto* (2002) JFC-0202; R-2003, CD vol. 31
*ISHII, Maki (1936–2003)
"*HAKUDAKU MU for yoninno kai* (op. 51)" for *shaku*, 213-str *koto*, 17-str *koto* (1983) OGT
"*KAGUYA-HIME*—Sinfonische Suite für Schlagzeuggruppen (op.56)" for Japanese perc, perc (1984) Moeck-Ed

"Symphonic Poem 'GIOH' (op. 60)" for *ryu, shino,* nōkan, v, orch (1984) MV [Moeck-Ed]
"*Haku* (Op. 62)" for *shaku, shami,* 2 *koto* (1985) OGT
"*Gedatsu* (Op. 63)" for *yokobue,* orch (1985) Moeck-Ed
"Monoprism II (Op. 65)" for Japanese perc, perc (1985) Moeck-Ed
"*Kaguyahime*—Ballet Version (Op. 56-b)" for Japanese perc, perc (1985) Moeck-Ed
"*Gioh-Gedatsu* (Op. 60 + 63)" for *yokobue,* orch (1986) Moeck-Ed
"Musik für *Shō* und Violoncello (Op. 77) for *shō*, vc (1988) Moeck-Verlag
"*Shō myō Kō kyō I* (Op. 105)" for *ryu,* orch (1995) FOCD-2523
"'*Jinkan Yume no Gotoshi* (Life is Like a Dream)'—Based on Poetry of Luo Guangzhou, Cao Cao, Cao Zhi and Su Shi (Op. 110)" for narrator, *ryu,* 20-str *koto,* marimba, cb, 4 perc (1997) CD: ROI; Ra-981005C
*KANETA, Choji (1948–)
"Tranfigurations II" for fl, 20-str *koto* (1988) JFC-8809
*KANNO, Yoshihiro (1953–)
"Tapestry I with Voices of *Shōmyō* (Revision) for Tape (1990) FOCD-3128
"Undulating Water" for *koto*, 17-str *koto* (1992) Shinten Ed.
"Winter Lull" for 2 *koto* (1992) Shinten Ed.
"Water Mirror" for *shaku, koto* (1992) Shinten Ed.
"Les Temps des Miroirs—L'Horizontale du Vent (Revision)" for *ryu, shō,* tape (1993) FOCD-3184
"*Kumo* (Spider)" for orch, *gagaku, nōkan, shō, futozao* (1998) FOCD-3449
KAWASAKI, Etsuo (1959–)
"*Fū-rai*" for 3 *shaku,* 3 *koto,* 17-str *koto,* Japanese perc (1990) Shinten Ed.
"*Yukiai*" for 2 *biwa* (1991) Shinten Ed.
"*Haru Urara*" for *koto, shaku* (1991) Shinten Ed.
"*Aki no Mai*" for *koto, shaku, shami* (1991) Shinten Ed.
"*Tangetsu-fu*" for *koto*-ens (1991) Katei Ongakukai
"*Shirei no Fu*" for Japanese ens (1992) Katei Ongakukai
"*Sōgetsu-fu*" for *koto, shaku* (1992) Katei Ongakukai
"The Stone Monument of Dreams" for str quartet, shino, koto (1994) Bamboo BCD-009
"*Koto Futatsu*" for 2 *koto* (1999) Bamboo BCD-031
"Suite *Sakabayashi* (Revision)" for vn, vc, *shaku, shami,* 20-str *koto* (1999) Bamboo BCD-031
"*Aoba no Fu*" for 2 *shaku, koto, shami* (1999) Bamboo BCD-038
"Suite *Kyoto*" for *shaku, shino, koto, shami,* Japanese perc, synth (2000) SF-170
KIYOSE, Yasuji (1900–1981)
"Quintets" for 2 *shaku,* 2 *koto,* 217-str *koto* (1973) ZG
"*Shakuhachi* trio" for 3 *shaku* (1973) ZG
KOBAYASHI, Arata (1929–)
"The Figure of Sound by *Shō* and Marimba" for *shō,* marimba (2004) JFC-0309; R-2005, CD vol. 33

KOJIMA, Yuriko Hase (1962–)
"Water-Moon" for 20-str *koto* (2002) JFC-0206
KOMORI, Akihiro (1931–)
"*San guo zhi*" for orch, *biwa*, *shō*, *koto*, Chinese perc, *erhu* (1990) GES-9507
KONDOH, Harue (1957–)
"Music for *shakuhachi* solo" for *shaku* (1992) JFC-9306
KONKOH, Iwao (1933–)
"An Impression—Three Movements for One 17-string and Two 13-string *Kotos*" for two 13-str *koto*, 17-str *koto* (1995) TLV-9.703.26
KOUDA, Jun (1957–) "Rapsodia" for fl, 25-string *koto*, marimba (1997) JFC-9705
KOYAMA, Kaoru (1955–2006)
"*Kira Kira*" for *ryu*, orch (1991) S-JFC-9202
KOYAMA, Kiyoshige (1914–2009)
"Quartet, *shakuhachi*, *kotos* (3) no.1" for *shaku*, 3 *kotos* (1966) OGT
"Quartet for *shakuhachi*, 2 *kotos* and *jushichigen*; Trio for 2 *kotos* and *jushichigen*" for *shaku*, 13-str *koto*, 17-str *koto* (1973) ZG
KUSANO, Jiro (1955–)
"*Fūen*" for 2 *shaku*, *koto*, 17-str *koto* (1989) Shinten Ed.
KUSUNOKI, Tomoko (1949–)
"The prelude for a fictitious opera '*Ren*'" for *shaku*, vc (1980) JFC-8310
MAEDA, Satoko (1956–)
"Stella of Akane, M. Angel" for *shaku*, gtr, cb (2002) Akane Foundation
MAKINO, Yutaka (1930–2005)
"*Nami no uta* (double concerto)" for Japanese ens (1981) WB-7094
MAMIYA, Michio (1929–)
"*Kio*" for *shaku* and vc (1989) ZG
"Quartet for *shakuhachi*, *sangen*, and 2 *kotos*" for *shaku*, *sangen*, 2 *kotos* (1963) OGT
"*Nonouta*, no.1 for *koto* solo" for 1 *koto* (1986) ZG
*MASUMOTO, Kikuko (1937–)
"Reflections" for Japanese ens (1995) JFC-9309
MATSUDAIRA, Yori-aki (1931–)
"To the Victims of Cain" for *shami* (. . .) VZCG 508, VXCG-65
MATSUMOTO, Hinoharu (1945–)
"*HANA-TSUTAE-NO-TABI*" for 4 *kotos* or 4 hp (1986) JFC-8615
"variation after the Theme of 'Etenraku-Imayō' for the Children Ensemble" for Japanese ens, children's vv, 2 perc (1997) Katei Ongaku Kai Ed
MATSUNAGA, Michiharu (1927–)
"Time of Winds, the Interval of Strings" for *shaku*, 20-str *koto* (2005) JFC-0409
MATSUO, Masataka (1959–)
"Phonosphere I (Revision)" for *shaku*, orch (1995) WWCC-7262
"Phonosphere I (Revision)" for *shaku*, orch (1997) ANTES EDITION BM-CD 31. 9112 "Sound. Sound III" for *shō*, cb (2000) ALCD-9023 "Sound. Sound III (Revision)" for *shō*, cb (2001) ALCD-9023 "Symphonietta (Revision)" for *shaku*, 2 *shami*, 213-str *koto*, 17-str *koto* (2002) ALCD-9028

MATSUSHITA, Isao (1951–) "*Azusa Yumi*" for *koto, koto* ens (1987) ONT "*Ao no Rōshō*" for 3 vv, male chorus, Japanese ens (1987) ONT "*Hingashi no*" for *shaku, shami, koto* (1987) ONT "*Kaze no Rōshō*" for *nōkan* (1988) ONT "Sea Space" for vn, 13-str *koto*, pf (1990) ONT

MINAMI, Satoshi (1955–)
"Coloration Project IX, Op. 17–9" for 2 *shaku*, 220-str *koto*, perc (1997) JFC-9707

MIWA, Masahiro (1958–)
"Spiritus Domini" for 20-str *koto*, portable cassette recorder (1993) AO Shuppan
"*Akebono*-inheritance" 13-str *koto*, computer (1994) Feedback Verlag

MIYAGI, Jun-ichi (1952–)
"Dorian Dance" for *shaku, shami*, 13-str *koto* (1990) Shinten
"Travels in Savanna" for *shaku*, 13-str *koto* (1990) Shinten
"Durga" for 2 *shaku* (1990) Shinten

MOCHIZUKI, Misato (1969–)
"Intermezzi II" for *koto* (2002) Breitkopf & Härtel

MORI, Kurodo (1950–97)
"*Ten*" for *shami* (1993) Shinten Ongaku Kyōkai

MORI, Yoshiko (1962–)
"*Ra-sen*" for 213-str *koto*, 17-str *koto* Tōhō University Edition

MOROI, Makoto (1930–2013)
"*Chikurinkitan-shō 'Hidairoha'*" for 4 *shaku*, 19 *naruko* (1991) SRCR-8605
"A Contradiction within a Contradiction—Contradiction IV" for perc, 230-string *koto*, 4 *shaku* (1992) KICC-80

MUNAKATA, Kazu (1928–)
"Mono Opera 'Ah Money' based on a Japanese Folk Story" for baritone, *Chikuzen-biwa*, pf (1991) JFC-9103; R-9201 CD vol. 20; FPCD-1571

*MURAO, Sachie (1945–)
"3993 *Koto, Nara no Shiki* (Frühling)" for 2 *shaku*, 2 20-str *koto*, 17-str *koto* (1991) JFC-3991
"The four seasons of ancient capital Nara (Spring)" for 2 *shaku*, two 20-string *koto*, 17-string *koto* (1992) JFC-9216
"6094 The Four Seasons of an Ancient Capital Nara . . . (Winter)" for 2 *shaku*, 3 *koto, tsuzumi*, sop (1995) JFC-9516
"1001 Ein Gedicht von Flöten II" for *iwabue, nōkan, shino*, ocarina, zampona, quena (2005) JFC-0414

NAGASAWA, Katsutoshi (1923–2008)
"Two Dances" for Japanese ens (199_) WWCC-7389
"Three Ballads to '*Hida*'" for Japanese ens (199_) WWCC-7389
"*Hoshun*" for *shaku* (199_) WWCC-7389

NAKAJIMA, Haru (1942–)
"*Shiroi Manjushage*" for mez-sop, *koto, shaku* (1991) ZG
"*Jagatara-bumi*" for sop, 17-str *koto, shaku* (1991) ZG
"Baby Spider" for sop (or mez-sop), *koto* (1994) ZG

"Chisel and Cherry Blossoms" for tenor, *koto, shaku* (1994) ZG
"Fantasy of '*Oku no Hosomichi*'" for baritone, *koto, shaku* (1994) ZG
"*Man-yo* Songs '*Tabanare Oshimi* '" for female vv, pf, *koto, shaku* (2002) ZG
NAKAMURA, Akikazu (1954–)
"Dorian in Blue Sea" for *koto, shaku*, gtr, elec bass, perc (1995) PWS-9601
"Close Your Eyes" for vn, *koto*, 17-str *koto* (2001) MQCP-1
"Paraselene" for vn, *koto*, 17-str *koto* (2001) MQCP-1
NAKAMURA, Noriko (1965–)
"*Kurita*" for 13-str *koto* (2001) JFC-0014
NAKAMURA, Yōko (1957–)
"Fantasy variation on a Theme of '*Hietsukibushi*'" for 2 *koto*, 17-str *koto* (2002) YRCD-004/AY
"A grieving crane deep in the forest" for *nōhkan* (2005) JFC-0416
NAKAMURA, Yukitake (1944–)
"*Komabue*" for mez-sop, *komabue* (1986) OGT
NAKAO, Tozan (1876–1955)
"*Tozan-ryu Shakuhachi Onpu*" for *shaku* (1948–51) ZG
NARITA, Kazuko (1957–)
"Konzert Op. 39" for vn, pf, *shaku, koto*, orch (1992) Ed. Jobert en Laye
NIIMI, Tokuhide (1947–)
"Trois Élégies pour *koto*: prelude for 20-string koto and 17-string *koto*" for 20-str *koto*, 17-str *koto* (1982) JFC-8222
"Altyere" for 20-str *koto*, vc (1995) 30CM-426
"The Cosmic Tree" for 20-str *koto*, orch (1996) ZG; WWCC-7284
"*Fujin Raijin*" for Japanese big drum, org, orch (1997) CMCD-28051
"TROIS ÉLÉGIES" for *koto* (1979) JFC
"PRELUDE" for 20-string *koto* and 17-string *koto* (1980) JFC
NISHIMURA, Akira (1953–)
"*Taqsim*" for 20-str *koto* (1982) JFC-8218
"The Navel of the Sun" for *hichi*, orch (1989) ZG; 32CM-110
"*Fugenraku*" for *gagaku*, Japanese ens (1990) FOCD
"Serpent in the Sky" for *yokobue*, orch (1994) ZG
"*Jukai*—Concerto for 20-stringed *Koto* and Orch" for 20-str *koto*, orch (2002) ZG
OKABE, Fujio (1947–)
"The Dance" for *shaku*, pf (1983) T 840787
OMURA, Tetsuya (1951–)
"*Soh-oh-ka*" for *shaku* and 20-str *koto* (1993) JFC-9219
OZAKI, Toshiyuki (1946–)
"Dialog" for *shaku*, pf, perc (1980) JFC-8005
"*Mizore Furu* . . . (Falling Sleet)" for *shaku, shami*, wind chime JFC-9318
*SAEGUSA, Shigeaki (1942–)
"Cosmos IV: *Ugetsumonogatari Asajigayado*" for vv, 3 *shami, suzu*, synth (1981) KVX-1102

"Suite '*Hannyaharamitta*'" for *fue* (*shino, ryu, nōkan*), synth, vocorder, gtr, elec bass, perc, Latin perc (1983) TP-80162
"Suite '*Take no Sonofu*'" for *fue* (*shino, ryu, nōkan*) (1983) TP-80162
"*Sangen* Concerto '1 December 1993 Sangen'" for *shami*, Chinese ens (1993) ESCK8033
"Four Concertos" for vn, vc, pf, sangen (March 6, 1994)
"Oratorio '*Yamato Takeru*' (Revision)" for sop, alto, 2 ten, 2 bar, bass, mixed vv, children's vv, *fue, hichi, shō, kokyu,* orch (1994) TOCZ9047–48
"Opera '*Chūshingura*'" for orch, 12 vv, mixed vv, *sangen*, 3 timp, perc ens (1997) SRCR 1969–71
SATOH, Somei (1947–)
"*Kaze no Kyoko*" ("Music for the Wind") for *shaku* (1980) Selling Agent: Academia Music
*SATO, Yoko (1971–)
Wind Path for *shak*, 13-str *koto, shami* (2012) on Kokoro Records KKR-004
Inner Tide for 21-str *koto* (2010) on Ring Records 0001
Shadows for *shaku* and *sham* (2010) on 24 Records TFRC-1001 and Sion Records SCD-009
The Road for *shami* (2007) on Sion Records SCD-013
Fuka Nisetsu for 21-str *koto* (2007) on Tokyo CMC TCMC-061105
Snow Falling on the Heart for *shami*, 13-str *koto*, and 17-str *koto* (2004) on Sion Records SCD-007
A Poem of the Rain for 21-str *koto* (2001) on Celestial Harmonies 13191-2
*SHIBATA, Minao (1916–96)
"*Fuchū Sankei*" for mixed vv, Fuchubayashi, Ishibue (1995) ZG
SHIDA, Shoko (1942–)
"Chutney sweet" for *shō* (1976) JFC-7605
"*Fukura semê*" for *nōkan*, fl (2000) JFC-0016
SHIMIZU, Kensaku (1961–)
"I Just Wanna Be Loved" for 213-str *koto*, 217-str *koto* (1995) KVOR-002
SHIMOYAMA, Hifumi (1930–)
"Transmigration no.2" for *shaku*, vc, hp (1985) JFC-8514
"*Ichigo no Tsukikage*" for 17-str *koto*, vc, tape (1998) SDL-JP 30.001–96CD
"*Kaze no Toh*" for *shaku*, 20-str *koto*, perc (2000) LMCD-1586
SHINOHARA, Makoto (1931–)
"*Nagare for shamisen*" for *shami, kane, kin* (1981) ZG
"*Tayutai*" for *koto* (1975) ZG
"Ways of Dreams" for Japanese ens, Chinese orch, mixed vv (1992) ZG
SUGIURA, Masayoshi (1921–)
"*Manusa Marga*" (1970) JFC-7005
"*Shigon'bo* (A Collection of Songs for Voice and ko-tsuzumi)" for mixed vv, ko-tsuzumi (1991) JFC-9110
SUMI, Atsuki (1948–)

"*Chi no Sakana*" ("Fish on horizon") for *shaku, shami* (1997) JFC-9714; R-2002, CD vol. 30; ALCD-9014
"*Toh-fu-sho*" for *shō, shaku*, perc (1995) JFC-9419; R-9801, CD vol. 26
"Two songs on the poem 'Magic Lantern'" for baritone, *shami* (2002) JFC-0115
"Lotus Fish" for *shaku, go* stones (2004) JFC-0316
TAKAHASHI, Masamitsu (1949–)
"Homages to the Harvest Moon" for *shino*, 13-str *koto* (1981) JFC-8221
TAKAHARA, Hirofumi (1934–)
"Communion IV" for sop, *shō* (2004) JFC-0318
TAKEMITSU, Toru (1930–96) "Autumn" for *biwa, shaku*, orch (1990) Paris: Editions Salabert
"Eclipse" for *biwa, shaku* (1981) Paris: Editions Salabert
"Ceremonial—An Autumn Ode—" for *shō*, orch (1992) SJ
TAMBA, Akira (1932–)
"Interference I" for *shami, shaku, koto* (1980) JASRAC
"Interference II" for sop, *shami*, 2 *koto, shaku* (1981) JASRAC
"Interference III" for 2 *koto, shaku* (1987) JASRAC
"Interference IV" for *koto, shaku* (1990) JASRAC
TANAKA, Masaru (1946–)
"Acala II" for *shaku*, perc (2002) KICC383
TSUBONOH, Katsuhiro (1947–)
"Conjunction" for *shami*, v (1987) JFC-8702
UCHIKAWA, Hiroyuki (1947–)
"*Yobukoe ari*" for *shō, ryū, hichi, koto, biwa, taiko, kakko, shōko* (1985) JFC-8813
"Order and Truth" for *shaku* (1990) JFC-9009
URATA, Kenjiro (1941–)
"*Hekitan* No. 4" for *shaku, shami, koto* (1991) ONT
YAMAMOTO, Junnosuke (1958–)
"*Mao Kūkai*" for *shaku*, computer, 5 synth, 3 sampling machines, hp, sutras, wind orch (1989) VDR-28073
"Future Echo" for *shaku*, computer, synth, effect (1990) APCE-5079
YANAGIDA, Takayoshi (1948–)
"*Jōhi-haku-un*" for *shaku* (1992) North Pacific Music
YOSHIMATSU, Takashi (1953–)
"The Age for Birds Op. 26" for *shaku*, 20-str *koto* (1986) CMT-1100
"*Suigenfu*" for *shaku, koto* (1989) Shinten Ongaku Kyōkai
YOSHIZAKI, Kiyotomi (1940–)
"*Junkansuru Kisetsu*" for *shami, koto*, elec org (1997) in *Works for Electone: '97 Zen Nihon Denshi gakki Kyuiku Kenkyukai Erekuton No Tame No Sakuhin Shu*. Zen Nihon Denshi Gakki Kyoiku Kenkyukai

Non-Japanese Composers

BENNETT, Gerald
"*Kyōtaku*" for *shaku*, tape (1987) Wergo, vol. 9 in *Computer Music Currents*

"Dances of the Angel" for *shaku*, perc (1994) Edition Modern
*BLASDEL, Christopher Yohmei
On Voice from Afar, Voices from Within CD: Tecy-28001:
    "Yearnings" for *shaku* (1987)
    "Dorian Dance" for *shaku*, 20-str *koto* (1987)
    "The gates of Heaven and Earth" for *shaku*, cb (1988) "The Tears of Heaven" for *shaku*, pf (1988)
    "Storytelling on a Winter's Night" for *shaku*, sop (1989)
    "The Shadow of the Rose" for *shaku*, oud (1989)
    "Worthless *Shakuhachi*: Fived Songs from the *Kangishu*" for *shaku*, sop, *shami* (1989)
*BROWN, Chris
"Waves" for *shaku*, interactive computer system (1999) *Between/Waves* Sparkling Beatnik Recordings CD0006
BROWN, Elizabeth
"Migration" for *shaku*, vn, va, vc (1990) Quetzal Music; *Bang on a can LIVE*, vol. 2, Composer Recordings CD 646
"Orrery" for *shaku*, viola d'amore, perc (1992) Quetzal Music
"The Secret Life of Birds" for fl, *koto* (1992) Questzal Music
CAGE, John
"Two 3" for *shō*, 5 conch shells (1991) Henmar Press
"One 9" for *shō* (1991) Henmar Press
COWELL, Henry
"Concerto II" for *koto*, orch (1983) C. F. Peters
DENYER, Frank
"A monkey's paw" for *shaku*, va, bass recorder, vn, 2 ocarinas, perc, mixed vv (1991) Continuum
DICK, Robert
"Venturi Shadows" selections, one for *shaku* (1991) O. O. Discs
DIMOV, Bojidar
"Hauch der Nymphe" for *shaku* (1995) Dohr
GELB, Philip
"Purple Wind" for *shaku*, *koto*, perc, elec (1996) on: "Purple Wind" CD, Ryokan Recording. With Miya MASAOKA (*koto*), Gino Robair (perc).
HOVHANESS, Alan
"Sonatas for *Ryūteki* and *Shō*" (1962) C. F. Peters Corp.
"Sonatas for *Hichiriki* and *Shō*" (1962) C. F. Peters Corp.
"Sonatas for *Koto*" (1963) C. F. Peters Corp.
LITTLE, David
"*Shakuhachi*" for flute solo (1989) Donemus
*LOEB, David
"*Raisetsu*" for *koto* (1984) Accentuate Music
"*Shimobashira*" for *shami* (1984) Accentuate Music
"*Shumaku*" for *shino* (1984) Accentuate Music
"*Asakua*" for *biwa* (1985) Accentuate Music

"*Ieyosei*" for *shaku* (1985) Accentuate Music
"*Sammu*" for *shaku* (1985) Accentuate Music
"*Sankyoku no. 2*" for *shaku, shami, koto* (1985) Accentuate Music
"Three Ceremonial Dances" for *shino* (1987) Accentuate Music
"*Ginshi*" for *shaku* (1988) Accentuate Music "*Akiguno*" for *koto*, pf (1989) Accentuate Music
"*Fukyo*" for viola da gamba, *shaku* (1989) Accentuate Music
"*Kahyo*" for cl, 2 *koto* (1989) Accentuate Music
"*Namihibiki*" for vc, *shaku* (1989) Accentuate Music
"Spring Song" for *koto* (1989) Accentuate Music
"*Tsubo no Kyoku*" for *shino*, gtr (1989) Accentuate Music
"A Land of Remote valleys" for *shino*, gtr (1990) Accentuate Music
"Eagles Nest" for 13-str *koto*, 17-str *koto* (1990) Accentuate Music
"*Imariro*" for *koto*, VC (1990) Accentuate Music
"*Kukyo*" for *shino*, *koto*, vc (1990) Accentuate Music
"*Mujinkyo*" for *biwa*, *koto* (1990) Accentuate Music
"Rural Scenes No. 2" for *shino*, gtr (1990) Accentuate Music
"*Ryusho*" for *shino*, gtr (1990) Accentuate Music
"Soundprints" for cl, *koto* (1983) Rancorp
MICHAEL, Frank
"*Shakuhachi*: op. 38, nr. 5" for *shaku* (1990) Zimmermann
NEPTUNE, John Kaizan
On *West of Somewhere* for jazz ens, *shaku* (1981) Milestone CD M-9113 "Bamboo Blues" "Four Seater" "S. F." "*Shakuhachi* Dance" "*Shakuhachi* Shuffle" "South of Somewhere" "West of Somewhere"
OSBORNE, Thomas
"Tumbling from the Ninth Height of Heaven" for 13-str *koto*, vn (2007) on Duo Vio-LINK-oto: Taking the Scarlet, Centaur Records CRC 3056
REASON, Dana
On *Primal Identity* for pf and *shaku* (1996) Deep Listening CD "Neina" for pf, *shaku* "Infinite Worlds" for pf, *shaku*
*REGAN, Marty
"fastpass!" for *shami, ko-tsuzumi* (2012) Mother Earth Publishing R0001-1
"Song-Poem of the Eastern Clouds" for 21-str *koto*, shak (2001) Mother Earth Publishing No. R0002-1
"Evanescent Yearning . . ." for 13-str *koto*, sham (2008) Mother Earth Publishing No. R0003-1
"Light of the Rainbow" for *shami*, 17-str *koto* (2003) Mother Earth Publishing R0004-1
"Maqam" (2005) for solo shami (2005) Mother Earth Publishing No. R0005-1
"Shadows of the Moon" for *shak, shami* (2008) Mother Earth Publishing R0006-1
"Voyage" (2008) for *shaku*, string quartet (2008) Mother Earth Publishing No. R000-7

"dragoneyes" for *shak, shami*, 21-str *koto* (2004) Mother Earth Publishing R0008-1

On *Shamisen Works by Marty Regan: Performed by Tetsuya Nozawa* (2014) Kokoro Records KKR 006:
"Made of Mercury" for 2 *shami* (2013)
"Evanescent Yearning . . ." for 13-str *koto, sham* (2008)
"Shadows of the Moon" for *shak, shami* (2008)
"fastpass!" for *shami, ko-tsuzumi* (2007)
"Devil's Bridge" *for sham, biwa* (2010)
"Light of the Rainbow" for *shami*, 17-str *koto* (2003)
"phoenix" for flute, *shami* (2009)

On *Selected Works for Japanese Instruments, Vol. 3: Scattering Light, Scattering Flowers* (2014) Navona Records NV 5933:
"Beyond the Sky" for *shino*, 3 *shak, biwa, sham*, 2 21-str *koto*, 17-str *koto*, perc. (2005)
"Koto Concerto No. 1: Spirit of the Mountains" for solo 21-str *koto*, 2 13-str *koto*, 17-str *koto* (2008)
"Scattering Light, Scattering Flowers" for *soprano, shaku*, 25-str *koto* (2011)
"phoenix" for flute, *shami* (2009)
"Shakuhachi Concerto No. 1: Southern Wind" for *shak* solo, *shino*, 2 *shak, shami, biwa*, 2 13-str *koto*, 17-str *koto*, perc. (2008)

On *Works for Shakuhachi by Marty Regan: Voyage/Performed by Shōzan Tanabe* (2013) Bamboo Records BCD-082:
"Summer Dances" for *shaku, shami*, 17-str *koto* (2011)
"Voyage" (2008) for *shaku*, string quartet (2008)
"Hydrangea" (2012) for *shaku*, contrabass (2012)
"Two Moments for Solo Shakuhachi" for solo *shak* (2012)

On *Selected Works for Japanese Instruments, Vol. 2: Magic Mirror* (2012) Navona Records NV 5933:
"flamefox" for *shak* quartet (2007)
"dragoneyes" for *shak, shami*, 21-str *koto* (2004)
"In the Night Sky" for *shaku*, 21-str *koto*, percussion (2010)
"Magic Mirror" for *shami, hichiriki, ryūteki, shō, shinobue, shaku* (2008)
"Voyage" (2008) for *shaku*, string quartet (2008)
"Devil's Bridge" *for sham, biwa* (2010)

On *Selected Works for Japanese Instruments, Vol. 1: Magic Mirror* (2010) Navona Records NV 5831:
"Song-Poem of the Eastern Clouds" for 21-str *koto, shak* (2001)
"Evanescent Yearning . . ." for 13-str *koto, sham* (2008)
"In Remembrance . . ." for *shak*, piano trio (2006)
"fastpass!" for *shami, ko-tsuzumi* (2007)
"Forest Whispers . . ." for *shak*, vc (2008)

ROOSEVELT, J. Willard
"Flute and Fiddle" for bass, alto, standard 1.8, *shaku*, picc, 2 vn (1975) American Composers Alliance

ROTHENBURG, Ned
"*Yakuoji*" for *shaku* solo (1987) Thenro Music
Untitled for *shaku* (1990) Thenro Music
SCHELL, Michael
"Duets" for *koto*, hp (1990) Blank Media
SCOTT, Stuart
"*Shakuhachi* Suite: Op. 71" for *shaku* solo (n.s.) Sale, Cheshire
SINGER, John
On *Moonlit Castle* for *shaku*, hp (1990) CD Empty Bell Music JS-03 "Seascape" for *shaku*, hp "To Infinity" for *shaku*, hp
TEITELBAUM, Richard
"*Hi Kaeshi hachi Mi Fu*" for *shaku* solo (1974) published in *Pieces*, edited by Michael Byron, Aesthetic Research Center, Vancouver, BC, Canada
"Blends" for *shaku*, synthesizer, perc (1977) Lumina Records L005
VETTER, Michael
On *Memories into the Presence* for *Koto* (1990) Wergo Spectrum CD SM 1052-2:
  "Here" for *koto*
  "Now" for *koto*
  "Therefore" for *koto*
  "Where" for *koto*
  "You" for *koto*
WHITE, Frances
"Birdwing" for *shaku*, computer (1996) on CDCM *Computer Music Series* vol. 25 (1997) Centaur Records CRC-2347
*WOMACK, Donald Reid
On *Breaking Heaven* (2014) Albany Records TROY 1517:
  "Bend" for *shaku*, *shami*, 21-str *koto* (2006)
  "*Tachibana* (Sword Flower)" for 2 *shaku* (2009)
  "Off Balance" for *shami* (2008)
  "Three Trees" triple concerto for solo *shaku*, *biwa*, 21-str *koto*, with 3 *shaku*, *shami*, 2 perc., 3 21-str *koto*, 17-str *koto* (2013)
  "Breaking Heaven" for *shaku*, 13-str *koto*, vc (2011)
On *Walk Across the Surface of the Sun* (2010) Albany Records TROY 1175:
  "Walk Across the Surface of the Sun" for *shō*, *shino*, 2 *shaku*, *shami*, *biwa*, perc, 2 21-str *koto*, 17-str *koto* (2008)
  "strung out" for 13-str *koto*, vn (2007)
  "Koto Coloring Book" for 21-str *koto* (2008)
  "A Glinting Edge of Sky" for *shaku*, 21-str *koto* (2008)

Notes

Introduction

1. Translator's note: *Gagaku* is imperial court music.
2. There are numerous theories about Japanese scales and modes. In order to avoid confusion, however, I have limited my discussion of Japanese scales to the five listed in figure I.1.
3. The *yonanuki* scale is a diatonic scale with the fourth and seventh scale degrees removed, *yo* being four, *na* being seven, and *nuki* meaning "removed."
4. Translator's note: *Tatami* are traditional woven straw flooring mats. *Fusuma* are sliding doors covered with Japanese paper.
5. Translator's note: A Japanese aesthetic concept that suggests qualities such as impermanence, humility, simplicity, asymmetry, and rusticity, among others. See Andrew Jupiter, *Wabi-Sabi: The Japanese Art of Impermanence*. Boston, Tokyo: Tuttle Publishing, 2003.
6. Translator's note: "An unquantifiable metaphysical space (duration) of dynamically-tensed absence of sound." See Tōru Takemitsu, "One Sound," *Contemporary Music Review* 8, no. 2 (1994): 3.

Chapter One

1. Translator's note: *Yamato* is another name for Japan.
2. Translator's note: The *tempuku* and *hitoyogiri* are prototypes of the *shakuhachi*.
3. Translator's note: A trumpet shell or conch.
4. Translator's note: The botanical name for *medake* is *Pleioblastus simonii* or simply, Simon.
5. Translator's note: *Hayashi* are Japanese drums and transverse flutes; *nagauta* is a genre that developed in the *kabuki* theater.
6. Translator's note: A popular form of *kagura* that presents ritualized dance-dramas reenacting mythological themes.
7. Translator's note: Meaning three-length pipe and eight-length pipe, respectively.
8. Translator's note: In this system, the pitch a is assigned the numerical value of 1. Hence, the sanbon (三本) is named as such because the perfect fifth above the fundamental (e) on this length *shinobue* is a b, which is two half-steps above a (a = 1, b^b = 2, b = 3). See figure 1.5 for further clarification.

9. Traditionally, *go* is produced by completely opening holes five, six, and seven, resulting in a quarter-tone. The symbol ◒ in the fingering chart indicates the ¼ opening of a hole.

10. Translator's note: Heian period (794–1185) vocal music genres.

11. Translator's note: An on-stage ensemble consisting of the *nōkan, ko-tsuzumi, ō-tsuzumi*, and *shimedaiko*.

12. Translator's note: Japanese harvest celebration.

13. This chart illustrates fingerings in the dynamic range of *mp*. When performing *pp* or *ff*, the fingerings will change. ● indicates that the hole may be closed in order to stabilize the instrument. An open fingering is also acceptable.

14. Translator's note: A repository of ancient art treasures located in Nara.

15. With the *shinobue* and *ryūteki*, I distinguished parts of the range into A, B, and C based on performance effectiveness, but with the *shakuhachi* I distinguished parts of the range into *otsu* and *kan* based on the difference in overtones.

16. Translator's note: Although lost in translation, this expression references the difficulty of learning the *shakuhachi*, implying that it takes three years to learn the simple act of creating vibrato via head movement, which is one of the trademark techniques of the *shakuhachi*.

17. The symbol [m⎯⎯⎯] is used to indicate the *muraiki* technique and to show the strength of the breath.

18. Translator's note: *Honkyoku* is the repertoire of "original" pieces for the *shakuhachi*.

19. Translator's note: *Komagaku* is *gagaku* music considered to have originated from Korea.

Chapter Two

1. The use of the Chinese character 弦 or 絃, both of which mean "string," is confusing. Until 絃 was dropped as a Chinese character included in public education, it was used exclusively for all musical instruments. 弦, on the other hand, was used in textbooks for Western instruments, while 絃 is used exclusively for Japanese instruments. This book follows the same practice.

2. Translator's note: The characteristic buzz or drone of the *biwa*.

3. Even though composers should use an 8va bassa treble clef, most only write a treble clef when composing for the *biwa*. For the *biwa* and *shamisen* to be comprehended internationally, I recommend that composers always use an 8va bassa treble clef.

4. In Kansai *biwa* performance practice, the pitch d is referred to as *i-pon* (one), and as one ascends by half-steps, numbers follow in order (i.e., $e^b=2$, e=3, etc.).

5. Translator's note: In contrast to the English definition of "multiple stop," in traditional Japanese music, *jūon* may include dyads, triads, or even four- or five-note chords comprised of nothing but open strings.

6. Translator's note: A port in Osaka.

7. Translator's note: The area of Tokyo and the surrounding environs.

8. Translator's note: The area of Kyoto, Osaka, and the surrounding environs.

9. This diagram is from Kiyoko Motegi's book *Bunraku*. The characters beneath the staff are the names of the forty-seven positions used on the *Gidayū shamisen*. I

would like to add two points. First, to correspond more closely with the normal range of the *futozao shamisen*, the pitches have been transposed down a major third from the original diagram. Also, from attending a workshop on traditional *Gidayū* performance with Yumiko Tanaka, another researcher, I learned that the positions *e* and *te*, being a minor second apart, can be used interchangeably. In addition, individual discrepancies exist for positions in the high range such as *e, hi, mo, se, su,* and *kyo*. This is why these pitches are omitted in the diagram. Since composers inclined to use elements of traditional *Gidayū* music will be interested in this phenomenon, I have borrowed this explanation from Yumiko Tanaka. Whole notes in the diagram indicate frequently used pitches, while black notes indicate seldom-used pitches. The slurred arrows connecting two pitches indicate idiomatic and easy-to-execute movements, while the dotted lines with arrows attached to their ends indicate closely related positions on adjacent strings. Regardless of the string, the minor second above any open string has a strong tendency to resolve to the open string. Also, the positions for a perfect fourth, fifth, and the octave above each of the open strings can be considered nuclear pitches that create a sense of cadence or closure. Positions indicated with black notes tend to be used in the violent scenes in historical plays, but whether a historical play, or a play of everyday life (*sewamono*), these positions are also used in scenes in which the emotions and otherwise atypical conditions are emphasized.

10. Figure 2.41 includes several representative patterns taken from the *Gidayū shamisen* repertoire originally transcribed by Yumiko Tanaka. None of these transcriptions are examples of music used to accompany melancholy emotions. Figure 2.42 includes excerpts from several of my compositions.

11. Translator's note: Referred to in Japanese as *tataku*.

12. Figure 2.45a–c illustrates several characteristic patterns of the *Tsugaru shamisen*. Playing positions, however, are not indicated in these figures.

13. On the *sanshin*, the first string is called *ūjiru* (male string), the second string is called *naka-jiru* (middle string) and the third string is called *miijiru* (female string). The pitches *karō* and *hichi* are higher in *ni-agari* tuning. Depending on the piece and sometimes within one piece, the pitch *shaku* can be sharp or flat.

14. ♯ is pitched slightly higher than ♭. On the *sanshin*, the symbol T = ウチ (*uchi*), and is called *uchūtō*, while the symbol V = すくい (*sukui*) and is called *kakitō*. The actual sounding pitch of figure 2.48a–c is a fourth or fifth lower than written.

15. See Keiji Azechi, *Nihon no kokyū no chōgen ni okeru san-sagari no imi ni tsuite* (*The Significance of the Lowered-3rd Tuning in the Japanese Kokyū*) in *Tōyō Ongaku Kenkyū*, 57.

Chapter Three

1. In public broadcasting, this instrument is often called the "*sō*," using the Chinese-style reading. Most Japanese, however, use the Japanese reading "*koto*." Presently, in traditional Japanese music, especially in ensemble settings, the kin is rarely used. I make an effort to refer to this instrument as the "*koto*" as much as possible. The eleventh-century *The Tale of Genji* refers to the two instruments as the *sō no koto* and the *kin no koto*.

2. Translator's note: The terms *gakusō, chikusō,* and *zokusō* refer to historical instrument types. The *gakusō* refers to the *koto* used in *gagaku*. The *chikusō* refers to the *koto* used in *Tsukushigoto* (vocal works derived from court music) founded by the priest

Kenjun in the sixteenth century and named after Tsukushi, a province in northern Kyūshū. The *zokusō* refers to the modern *koto*. Kengyō Yatsuhashi (1614–85) invented *hirajōshi*, a tuning derived from the *in* scale, and reset the *Tsukushigoto* compositions using the new scale. This music became known as *zokusō* or as *zokugaku* ("common music"). These terms developed as a result of the instrument being used in new genres, not because of major structural differences between them. See Henry M. Johnson, "A 'Koto' by Any Other Name: Exploring Japanese Systems of Musical Instrument Classification." *Asian Music* 28, no. 1 (Autumn 1996–Winter 1997), 43–59.

3. Translator's note: a unit of weight, 3.75 grams.

4. With the *koto*, it is unusual to refer to pitches by the Japanese system of *ippon* or *ni-hon*. Performers accustomed to Western notation often refer to a scale deriving its name from the pitch of the first string. If the first string is tuned to D, it is called "D-one." The "one" refers to the first string.

5. 1) In the past, the tension of *koto* strings was looser, and it was possible to raise the pitch of a string a minor third by *oshide*. Looser strings, however, allow the bridges to move, and during the course of a performance, pitches would gradually rise. The tension is now considerably tighter, and raising a pitch a whole step is the limit. In the piece *Rokudan*, there is one passage where the pitch is to be raised a minor third, but faking this passage and playing a major second has become a habit among *koto* players.

2) When executing *oshide* in the lower range, the amount of string to the left of the bridge is very short. Moreover, the player must reach with the left arm, and sometimes stand. *Oshide* in the lower range are more problematic than in the middle range, and there are times when it is impossible to raise the pitch by a major second in the lower range.

3) This applies to all Japanese instruments, but symbols for various techniques often differ, depending on the playing school and composer. I am as rational as possible in my approach, and try to use symbols which are easier to understand and which are connected to other Japanese instruments and instruments from other countries. Many of these symbols have already become universal. In this book, I take the same position and try to use symbols that composers can easily understand.

6. With bowed string instruments, slur markings indicate bowings, but with plucked string instruments, it indicates one strike of the plectrum or pick, or a left-hand pizzicato. Slur markings are also used when playing, in one continuous gesture, all of the notes in between two pitches a few strings away, similar to a piano glissando.

7. Compared to a piano, the reverberation of the *koto* is short, but compared to a *biwa* or *shamisen*, it is long. In the lower range of the koto, the resonance is twice as long as notes in the upper range. Specifically, in the middle range notes reverberate for about 3 to 5 seconds. Even if there is no indication in the score in regards to when to stop the reverberation, competent performers use their own musical judgment and stop the reverberation in an appropriate way to improve the level of their performance. Average performers, however, almost always allow the strings to reverberate, so audiences think that this is an attribute of the *koto*. When composers do not want the sound to become muddy and want to cut off the reverberation, they must indicate this in the score. However, it is better not to restrain the freedom of the performer by overusing damping symbols.

8. Translator's note: A *kinuta* is a wooden block and mallet used to soften silk and bring out its luster. *Kinuta* compositions use this rhythm to evoke the image of autumn. Musically, they are characterized by a four-*dan* (section) structure with similar thematic material, and an ostinato, which represents the beating of the *kinuta*. The

end of each *dan* is marked by a cadential melody. Timbral and rhythmic changes to the basic pattern are interwoven, creating a melody replete with instrumental devices.

9. Translator's note: *Jiuta* literally means "songs of the Kansai region." In the Edo period (1603–1868), this term designated the musical genres for the *shamisen* transmitted by the blind musicians who also performed *koto* and *kokyū*.

10. Translator's note: A folk dance from Tokushima City, Shikoku that is performed annually in August during the O-bon season, an event for commemorating one's deceased ancestors. Japan is comprised of many islands, but there are four main ones and Shikoku is one of them—Honshu, Hokkaido, and Kyushu being the other three. Miki was born on Shikoku.

11. Translator's note: Otherwise known as the *zheng* or *guzheng*.

12. Although the soprano and bass 21-string *koto* have not become standard, I think they are ideal instruments. The soprano 13-string *koto* has existed for a while.

Chapter Four

1. It is unnecessary to use a five-line staff for percussion instruments with indefinite pitch. For percussion instruments that only play rhythms, a one-line staff is sufficient. For percussion instruments that produce two or three pitches, it is acceptable to use extra lines accordingly. Since most composers use commercially available staff paper without percussion staves, assign the lines and spaces to be used according to the range of the instrument in question. These should remain fixed for the duration of one piece. If a percussionist must switch between different instruments, even though the instruments may be clearly designated in the score, it is best to write the name of the instrument with each change. Instead of a treble or bass clef, using percussion clefs has become an international standard.

2. Translator's note: Meaning small *tsuzumi* and large *tsuzumi*, respectively.

3. Translator's note: An ancient Japanese mask play. According to the Chronicles of Japan, *gigaku* was brought to Japan from the Wu region (modern Zhejiang) in 612 CE. Evidently, after the masked actors had paraded in temple grounds, they would perform short dances accompanied by flutes and percussion.

4. Translator's note: Senjū Shirabyōshi was the most famous female court musician of the Heian period (794–1185). She began what became the tradition of female entertainers dancing in male attire This was later referred to as *shirabyōshi*-style dancing. The *shirabyōshi* dancers used *ko-tsuzumi* in their performances.

5. Translator's note: Literally meaning "tuning paper."

6. In the *hayashi* of *nō* theater and *kabuki hayashi*, the *nōkan*, *ko-tsuzumi*, *ō-tsuzumi*, and *taiko* (sometimes the *taiko* is absent) comprise a group called *shi-byōshi*, and occupy an important role in the development of a piece. The *shi-byōshi* can be seen in other genres of traditional Japanese music. This ensemble makes use of many fascinating melodic and interlocked rhythmic patterns. With song, narration, and drama, there is a system of combining various musical and rhythmic patterns, like the tiles of a mosaic, to provide accompaniment and interlude music. Whether this is a creative activity or the result of centuries of development is a topic for academic inquiry; nevertheless, the *shi-byōshi* is one of Japan's extraordinary arts.

7. The notes on the upper part of the staff in the *ko-tsuzumi* and *ō-tsuzumi* part are *kakegoe*, the rhythmic calls of the performers. α indicates a measure of undefined duration. ● indicates a note of undefined duration. ⋏ indicates a rest of undefined length.

8. The words written above the staff are the pattern names. In traditional music, the patterns differ subtly according to the time period and school. It is important for the reader to realize that these musical examples may sound different in an actual performance, according to the school and the particular function and situation of the *hayashi*.

9. Translator's note: Japanese woodblocks.

10. Translator's note: Mino refers to a rural town in Gifu Prefecture historically known for its handmade paper. Mino paper is thin and strong, and is also used for sliding translucent paper screens (*fusuma*) found in traditional Japanese houses.

11. Translator's note: In the Heian (794–1185) period, *taiko* were used in battles, functioning like bugles to issue commands to distant warriors.

12. Translator's note: a large deciduous tree with a blackish-brown fissured bark. Also known as *harigiri* and used for furniture, buildings, and veneer. The botanical name is *kalopanax septemlobus*.

13. Translator's note: *Dengaku* are Japanese harvest celebrations and consist of dances performed by villagers during the rice-planting celebrations at the New Year and during the planting season in early summer.

14. Translator's note: The verb *shimeru* means "to fasten," hence, the prefix *shime-* is derived from this verb.

15. Translator's note: Sacred shinto dances.

16. Translator's note: A *bon* dance folk song from Gunma Prefecture.

17. See note 13.

18. Translator's note: Climactic moments in *kabuki* where actors hold exaggerated, expressive poses in order to establish their character.

19. Translator's note: In Japanese, *yotsu* means "four "and *take* means "bamboo."

20. Translator's note: a large hanging temple bell suspended inside a wooden complex constructed specifically to house the bell. The Japanese character for *bon* means "purity."

21. Translator's note: literally meaning "half-size bell."

22. Translator's note: mallets with heads made from pieces of deer antler.

23. Translator's note: *Wadora* means Japanese gong.

24. Translator's note: Buddhist ritual chanting.

25. Translator's note: Yamabushi were Japanese mountain ascetics and warriors, mostly from the Shingon sect of Buddhism

26. Translator's note: Literally meaning, "tongue."

27. Translator's note: Literally, "shaman maiden bells."

28. Translator's note: A geological period from 23,000,000 to 10,000,000 years ago.

Afterword

1. Translator's note: Akira Ifukube's *Kan-gen-gaku-hō* is one of the most frequently used orchestration texts in Japan.

2. Translator's note: "Japanese instruments."

3. Translator's note: "Japanese music."

4. Translator's note: "Dictionary of Music."

Glossary

aitake 合竹: the eleven chord clusters of the *shō* used in *gagaku*

biwa 琵琶: Japanese short-necked fretted lute, closely related to the Chinese *pipa*. Originally used to accompany narratives and song. It has four or five strings and a pear-shaped body made from quince, red sandalwood, or mulberry

bugaku 舞楽: dance music of the Japanese imperial court, characterized by elegant and slow movement.

bunraku 文楽: Japanese puppet theater

chūzao 中棹: medium size *shamisen*

dengaku 田楽: Japanese harvest celebrations consisting mostly of dances performed by villagers during rice planting celebrations either at the New Year or during the planting season in early summer

enbai 塩梅: pitch alterations created by changing the embouchure on the *nōkan*

enka: a genre of melodramatic Japanese popular songs that developed in the postwar years of the Showa period (1926–89).

fusuma 襖: sliding doors made from Japanese paper

futozao 太棹: large *shamisen*

gagaku 雅楽: Japanese imperial court music imported from China during the seventh century

Gidayū 義太夫: a style of chanting accompanied by the *shamisen*, developed by Takemoto Gidayu (1651–1714). Also used to describe the thick-necked *shamisen* used in genres such as *bunraku* puppet theater.

hayashi 囃子: an instrumental ensemble consisting of Japanese drums and tranverse flutes, used in *nō* and *kabuki*.

hichiriki 篳篥: a double-reed instrument that plays the main melody in *gagaku*

hishigi 日吉: an extremely high-pitched dramatic motive of the *nōkan* used for heightening the tension of a scene in *nō* and *kabuki*

hitoyogiri 一節切: a single-node end-blown flute considered to be an early prototype of the *shakuhachi*. See also *tempuku*.

honkyoku 本曲: the repertoire of "original pieces" for the *shakuhachi* that have been transmitted over the past 500 years within the context of Zen Buddhism; sacred pieces that are considered a form of "sonic meditation."

hon-chōshi 本調子: standard tuning

horagai 法螺貝: Eastern version of the Western trumpet shell

hosozao 細棹: small *shamisen*

ippon-buki 一本吹き: monophonic *shō* performance

ji 柱: *koto* bridges

kabuki 歌舞伎: a Japanese theatrical form originating in the Edo period (1603–1868) and popular among the merchant classes. It is known for the elaborate make-up worn by the actors. *Kabuki* plays are often based on historical events.

kagura 神楽: sacred Shinto dances

kagurabue 神楽笛: Japan's transverse flute, dating from before the arrival of *gagaku*. Also known as the *yamatobue*.

kaihō-gen 開放絃: used in Japanese to refer to a condition or state where the left hand is not holding or pressing a position on a string; in other words, open strings.

kan 甲: the higher (or second) octave of the *shakuhachi*

Kansai 関西: the area of Kyoto, Osaka, and the surrounding environs. The western regions.

Kantō 関東: the area of Tokyo and the surrounding environs. The eastern regions.

karakara カラカラ: a trill executed by rapidly tapping down on the first hole of a five-holed *shakuhachi*

kari カリ: derived from the verb *karu*, which means "to raise," *kari* is a technique of Japanese transverse and end-blown flutes that involves adjusting the embouchure and increasing the angle between the lips and the mouthpiece order to raise the pitch.

katarimono 語り物: narrative genres of Japanese music

kokin 口琴: a kind of Jaw's harp made from long, thin bamboo by the Ainu people of Hokkaido

komabue 高麗笛: a Japanese transverse flute used in *gagaku*

komagaku 高麗楽: otherwise known as "music of the right." *Gagaku* music is considered to have originated from Korea. Today, *komagaku* survives only as dance accompaniment.

korokoro コロコロ: a *shakuhachi* trill that uses a special fingering. When executed correctly, the *korokoro* creates the illusion of multiphonics.

koto 琴 or 筝: 13-string Japanese zither. Imported from China as a *gagaku* instrument in the seventh and eighth centuries, the *koto* has become Japan's representative string instrument. The dragon-shaped body is made from paulownia wood. *Koto* also come with seventeen strings (also known as the bass *koto*), twenty-one strings, and, less commonly, twenty-five and thirty strings.

kumeuta 久米歌: An ancient genre closely tied to *gagaku*

ma 間: An unquantifiable metaphysical space (duration) of a dynamically tensed absence of sound, a distinctive element found in many genres of traditional Japanese music.

madake 真竹: timber bamboo, used in the construction of *shakuhachi*.

medake 女竹: *shinichiku* bamboo, used in the construction of *shinobue*.

meri メリ: derived from the verb *meru*, which means "to lower," *meri* is a technique of Japanese transverse and end-blown flutes that involves adjusting the embouchure and decreasing the angle between the lips and the mouthpiece in order to lower the pitch.

miyako-bushi 都節: the representative pentatonic scale of Japan during the Edo period (1603–1868)

muraiki むらいき: a *shakuhachi* technique in which an explosive charge of air is blown violently into the mouthpiece, emphasizing the sound of the performer's breath.

nakakari-chōshi 中カ調子: a *biwa* and *shamisen* tuning based on the neutral sound of the augmented fourth

nagauta 長唄: literally meaning "long song,"; a genre of traditional Japanese music that developed in the *kabuki* theater. It is a lyrical form with poetic and allusive texts, accompanied with the *shamisen, ko-tsuzumi, ō-tsuzumi,* and *shimedaiko.*
ni-agari 二上り: a *shamisen* tuning, literally meaning "raised second string"
netori 音取: literally meaning "to check sounds," *netori* are the short introductions to *gagaku* pieces as a way set the tuning or mode.
nijūgen 二十絃: Literally, 20-string. The Japanese term for the 21-string *koto*.
nō 能: an austere Japanese theatrical form combining elements of dance, music, poetry, and acting from the fourteenth century.
nōkan 能管: Japanese transverse flute used in *nō* theater. All *nōkan* have seven holes, but due to its physical structure, the pitches of the *nōkan* are extremely variable (there is no mathematical concordance between the fundamental and what is supposed to be its octave equivalent). The trademark sound of the *Nōkan* is referred to as *hishigi*, which is generated with a particularly strong force of breath. It is an extremely high-pitched dramatic motive used to heighten the tension of a scene and accompany the presence of ghosts.
nōteki 能笛: original name for the *nōkan*
ōteki 横笛: an instrument imported from T'ang-dynasty China in the Nara period (710–94) or immediately beforehand, and regarded as the prototype of the *ryūteki*.
otsu 乙: the lower octave of the *shakuhachi*
pipa 琵琶: Chinese four-string plucked lute, closely related to the Japanese *biwa*.
rōei 朗詠: a genre of accompanied vocal music originating at the Heian court of the ninth to twelfth centuries CE. See also *saibara*.
Ryūkyū 琉球: also known as Nansei Islands, *Ryūkyū* is the Japanese name for a chain of islands in the western Pacific Ocean at the eastern limit of the East China Sea. Known in the West as Okinawa.
ryūteki 竜笛: Japanese transverse flute used in *gagaku*
saibara 催馬楽: a genre of accompanied vocal music originating at the Heian court of the ninth to twelfth centuries CE. See also *rōei*.
sangen 三絃: original from of the *shamisen*, which can be traced back to China, Tibet, and the Middle East.
sankyoku 三曲: chamber music of the Edo period (1603–1868), consisting of *shamisen, koto,* and *shakuhachi*, also referred to as *gaikyoku* among *shakuhachi* players.
san-sagari 三下り: a *shamisen* tuning, literally meaning "lowered third string."
sawari さわり: the characteristic buzz-like timbre of the *biwa* and *shamisen*
shakuhachi 尺八: Japan's representative end-blown bamboo flute. Originally imported from T'ang China along with *gagaku* in the eighth century CE, it later functioned as a tool for meditation in the daily lives of wandering Buddhist monks.
shamisen 三味線: originally imported from the Ryūkyū islands to Sakai port in Osaka in the form of an Okinawan *sanshin* in the mid-to-late sixteenth century. *Shamisen*, also called *sangen*, come in a variety of ranges and sizes but they all have three strings. The *shamisen* became the center of musical culture from the Edo period (1603–1868) through the Meiji period (1868–1912). Today, the *shamisen* can be heard and seen in *bunraku* (puppet theater) and the off-stage music of the *kabuki* theater.
sheng 笙: Chinese version of the *shō*

shinobue 篠笛: the representative Japanese transverse Japanese flute. Used in *nagauta* and festival music.

shirabeo 調緒: a hemp cord used to fasten the membranes of *tsuzumi* and other drums to the body

shō 笙: Japanese mouth organ used in *gagaku*

shōga 唱歌: mnemonic syllables which are sung and used as a memory aid in many genres of traditional Japanese music

sōkyoku 箏曲: *koto* music

taiko 太鼓: Japanese drums

takebora 竹ぼら: an instrument cut from one node of naturally thick bamboo and hollowed out to create one drone-like pitch

tatami 畳: traditional Japanese flooring made from woven straw

tempuku 天吹: a one-node end-blown flute considered to be an early prototype of the *shakuhachi*. See also *hitoyogiri*.

te-utsuri 手移り: the gradual shift of fingering positions between *aitake* chords on the *shō*

tōgaku 唐楽: otherwise known as music "music of the left." *Gagaku* music considered to be of T'ang Chinese origin.

tsutsuguchi 筒口: end piece of Japanese transverse flutes

urushi 漆: Japanese lacquer

utaimono 歌い物: song genres of Japanese music

utaguchi 歌口: mouthpiece of Japanese transverse flutes

wabi-sabi 詫び寂び: A Japanese aesthetic concept that suggests qualities such as impermanence, humility, simplicity, asymmetry, and rusticity, among others.

yamatobue 大和笛: Japan's first transverse flute, dating even before the arrival of *gagaku*. Also known as the *kagurabue*.

yuri ユリ: vibrato

Index

aitake chords, 66–68
arpeggio, 85, 100, 102, 111, 142
Awa odori (dance), 148, 194, 247 n10

bamboo, 3, 6, 7, 8, 25, 35, 36, 54, 55, 64, 74, 90, 91, 129, 156, 182, 183, 189
blind (musicians), 100, 247
blowing techniques, 43, 56–57, 59
breathing, breath, 4, 11, 18, 20, 26–27, 43–45, 56–57, 59, 66–68, 158, 244 n17. See also tonguing
Buddhism, Buddhist, 4, 7, 35, 71, 181, 186, 187, 190–91, 198, 200, 248 n25
bunraku (theater), 88, 104, 105, 110, 244 n9. See also kabuki; nō

China, 1, 16, 35, 63, 68, 71, 88, 113, 125, 126, 152, 156–57, 171, 187, 190, 191, 196, 197, 198
communication, instruments as a means of, 171
contrabass bow, various uses of a, 147, 192, 196

derived pitches, 8–9, 12, 17, 35, 37, 56. See also half-holing; meri
diatonic scale, 8, 133, 134, 152, 243 n3
downstroke, 84–85, 104. See also upstroke
dynamics, 12, 19–20, 27, 43, 59, 67, 111, 122, 167, 185

Edo Period (1603–1868), 2, 87, 88, 91, 103, 116, 185, 247 n9
enka, 2, 51
equal temperament, 79, 115
erhu, 116, 117, 120
expression, 12, 19, 27, 42–43, 66, 78, 85, 87, 100, 105, 121, 122, 173, 178

festivals, 4, 9, 171, 177, 180, 194
finger ornaments, 15, 16
fingerings, 3, 244 n13; for the biwa, 78–79; for the hichiriki, 55–56, 59, 61; for the koto, 125; for the nōkan, 25–26, 32; for the ryūteki, 17, 18; for the shakuhachi, 35, 36–38; for the shinobue, 8–9; for the shō, 65, 69
flutter-tonguing, 12, 20, 28, 44, 59, 67
fundamental pitch(es), 8–10, 15, 18, 26–27, 37, 42, 43, 66, 243 n8. See also nuclear pitch

gagaku, 1, 2, 3, 5, 6, 243 n1, 244 n19, 245 n2; and hichiriki, 54, 56, 69; and koto, 125, 126, 148, 149; and percussion instruments, 157, 167, 168, 169, 171, 174, 184, 192; and shakuhachi, 35; and ryūteki, 16, 18, 19, 20; and shō, 63, 66, 68
gagaku: excerts from (Etenraku), 19, 58, 68; modes used in, hyōjōchō shi, 58; modes used in, ichikotsu-chō, 68
Gidayu shamisen, classical repertoire of the: Hidakagawa, 107; Inori, 108; Kitsunebi, 108; Nozakimura, 107; Sonae, 106; Yūrei, 107
glissando, 12, 21, 28, 49, 82–83, 96–97, 106, 110, 121, 137, 145, 146, 159, 160, 174, 246 n6. See also pitch inflection(s), microtonal; portamento; slide
graphic (notation), 18, 12, 19, 26, 31, 44, 82, 85, 96, 121, 137, 138, 139, 158

half-holing, 8, 12, 18, 37, 43. See also derived pitches; meri

harmonics, 4, 99, 122, 133, 136, 140. See also overtones (for wind instruments)
hayashi, 8, 15, 24, 156, 157, 159, 176, 177, 181, 186, 194, 243 n5, 247 n6, 248 n8. See also nagauta
hayashi, classical repertoire of the: *Chūno Mai*, 31, 161–62; *Kandamaru*, 15; *Kyūno Mai*, 161; *Ranbyōshi*, 160
Heian Period (794–1185), 54, 68, 182, 244 n10, 247 n4, 248 n11
Hokkaido, 7, 247 n10
honkyoku, 42, 244 n18; kokyū, 118; shakuhachi, 42, 51, 52

Ifukube, Akira, 248 n1
Ikuta school, 126, 129, 132, 146. See also Yamada school
in scale, 2, 245–46 n2
India, 7, 71, 74, 81, 116, 156, 168, 190, 198
Indonesia, 152, 156
intonation, 7, 43, 45, 46, 53, 57, 59, 61, 75, 81, 92, 94, 95, 96, 106
Irino, Yoshiro, *Music for Two Kotos*, 134
ivory, 35, 75, 90, 91, 92, 101, 129

jiuta, 88, 91, 95, 99, 100, 148, 247 n3

kabuki (theater), 8, 27, 31, 101, 157, 171, 172, 173, 176, 180, 185–86, 189, 190, 194, 198, 199, 243 n5, 247 n6, 248 n18. See also *bunraku; nō*
kakegoe (rallying shouts and cries of performers), 156, 247 n7
Kansai, 10, 105, 185, 244 n4, 247 n9. See also Kantō
Kantō, 10, 105, 185. See also Kansai
kari, 8, 9, 27, 27, 38, 39, 43
kokyū, classical repertoire of the: *Mushi no ne*, 123; *Tsuru no Sugomori*, 123; *Yachio-jishi*, 120
komagaku, 54, 167, 244 n18
Korea, 1, 54, 88, 147, 152, 190, 244 n19

lacquer (*urushi*), 6, 16, 25, 36, 54, 129, 177
left-hand techniques: for the *biwa*, 78–83; for the *kane*, 195–96; for the *koto*, 136–41; for the *shamisen*, 94–99. See also right-hand techniques

Meiji Period (1868–1912), 2, 110, 116, 199

meri, 2, 8, 9, 27, 39, 42, 43. See also derived pitches; half-holing
Minoru, Miki, works of:
Ada, 133
Ame-zanzan ("A Squall"), 140
Autumn Fantasy, 53, 153
Aya II, 134
"*Berodashi-chonma*"— Karak in one act, 135
Cassiopeia 21, 154–55
Danses Concértantes I, "Four Seasons," 16
Hanayagi ("The Greening"), 152, 153
Honjū, 102–103
Hote, 124, 151
Iki, 20
Jōruri, 109
Kagai, 150
Kokyō, 44
Kuse, 87, 109
Kyū no Kyoku ("Symphony for Two Worlds"), 178–80
Mebae ("A Young Sprout"), 153
Paraphrase after Ancient Japanese Music, 141; second movement, *Sōmon*, 34, 109
Ruika, 53
Sao no Kyoku ("The Venus in Spring"), 135
Sonnet I, 51
Tan no Mai, 102
Tatsuta no Kyoku ("The Venus in Autumn"), 135, 143–44, 145, 151
Tennyō, 135, 147
Tō, 187
Totsu, 175
Utayomizaru ("The Monkey Poet"), 183
Wa, 151
Wakahime, 183
Yui I, 69–70
Miyagi, Michio, 116–17, 126, 136
miyako-bushi scale, 2
Miyashita, Shūretsu, 126
Miyawaki, Keiko, 200
mnemonics (*shōga*), 3; for the *koto*, 141; for the *ko-tsuzumi*, 158; for the *nōkan*, 26; for the *ryūteki*, 20; for the *shamisen*, 103–4; for the *shinobue*, 15
modulation, 2
Moteki, Kiyoko, 244 n9
multiphonics: for the *nōkan*, 21, 34; for the *shakuhachi*, 49 (*koro-koro*), 53–54; for the *shinobue*, 16

multiple stops: for the *biwa*, 81–82; for the *kokyū*, 120; for the *koto* (*awasezume*), 141–42; for the *shamisen*, 93, 96, 102
Muromachi Period (1333–1573), 88

Nagao, Takeshi, 200
nagauta, 8, 15, 88, 91, 92, 100, 105, 111, 177, 243 n5. *See also hayashi*
Nakashima, Utashito, 130
Nara Period (710–794), 16, 88, 244 n14
nature: imitation of natural phenomena, 173–74; Japanese music and its relationship to, 4–5
New Japanese music movement (*shin-nippon ongaku undō*), 116
Nishikawa, Hiromitsu, 181
nō (theater), 24, 27, 31, 157, 176, 177, 186, 247 n6. *See also bunraku; kabuki*
Nosaka, Keiko, 126, 152
nuclear pitch, 36, 37, 244–45 n9. *See also* fundamental pitch(es)

Okinawa, 2, 88, 89, 92, 114, 116, 117, 131, 189
Otsuka, Haiko, 115
overtones, 7, 12, 16, 34 42, 43, 56, 62, 85, 99, 122, 141, 200, 244 n16. *See also* harmonics

paper, various uses of, 89, 129, 158, 165–66, 243 n4, 247 n5, 248 n10
paulownia, 3, 73, 84, 127
pentatonic (scales), 2, 8, 131, 152, 84, 100, 106, 111, 147
percussive (elements and sound qualities of Japanese instruments), 4, 81, 110, 156
pitch inflection(s), microtonal, 2, 4, 28, 56, 74. *See also* glissando; portamento; slide
pizzicato, 246; for the *biwa*, 83, 85; for the *koto*, 130, 140, 141, 145, 147, 150; for the *kokyū*, 121, 122; for the *shamisen*, 97, 100, 104, 110
portamento, 12, 28, 50, 82–83, 96–97, 98–99, 106, 110, 121. *See also* glissando; pitch inflection(s), microtonal; slide
Pro Musica Nipponia (*Nihon Ongaku Shūdan*), 1, 116, 171, 181, 186

resonance, 78, 96, 113, 133, 139, 191, 192, 195, 201, 246 n7. *See also* reverberation

reverberation, 82, 130, 178, 246. *See also* resonance
right-hand techniques: for the *biwa*, 83–87; for the *kane*, 195–96; for the *koto*, 141–48, 149; for the *shamisen*, 99–103. *See also* left-hand techniques
ritsu scale, 2
Ryūkyū, 2, 88, 92, 116

saibara, excerpts from various: *Koromogae*, 19; *Sekida*, 19
sanshin, classical repertoire of the: *Akatsukibushi*, 115; *Kagiyate-kazebushi*, 115; *Shimodashi-jakaibushi*, 115
sawari: of the *biwa*, 74–75, 84, 87; of the *kokyū*, 118; of the *sanshin*, 114; of the *shamisen*, 90, 96
shakuhachi, classical repertoire of the *Shika no Tonne* ("*Cry of the Ancient Deer*"), 52
signals, various kinds of musical, 185–86, 191
silk, 75, 86, 89, 90, 91, 128, 246 n8
slide, 95, 96, 97, 98, 121. *See also* glissando; pitch inflection(s), microtonal; portamento
sōkyoku, 116
Southeast Asia, 63, 196
staccato, 44, 67, 99, 139

tablature (notation), 26, 77, 93, 132, 158, 167, 178, 185
Taki, Rentaro, works of: *Moon over the Ruined Castle*, 15
Tamura, Takuo, 171
Tanabe, Hisao, 116, 126, 131
Tanaka, Yukio, 130, 244–45 n9
tonguing, 11, 12, 15, 18, 27, 43, 44, 67. *See also* breathing, breath
tōgaku, 16, 54, 71, 168, 252
tremolo: for the *biwa*, 84, 85, 86; for the *hichiriki*, 59–61; for the *kokyū*, 122; for the *koto*, 129, 146; for the *nōkan*, 28–30; for percussion instruments, 187, 199; for the *ryūteki*, 21–24; for the *shakuhachi*, 46–49; for the *shamisen*, 99–100, 106, 111; for the *shinobue*, 12–14
Tosha, Naritosha, works arranged by: *Shin-Yachiojishi*, 162–65
Tsugaru shamisen, classical repertoire of the: *Chūbushi*, 112; *Shinbushi*, 113; *Tsugaru-jongaribushi*, 112

tuning(s): for the *biwa*, 75–78; for the *kokyū*, 118–19, 120; for the *koto*, 125, 130–36, 156; for the *shamisen*, 92–94

upstroke, 83, 84, 99, 104, 110, 111, 143. *See also* downstroke

vibrato, 11, 18, 33, 43, 44, 50, 59, 69, 82, 96, 121, 138, 244n16. See also *yuri*
Vietnam, 152

vocal music, 3, 244n9
voix céleste, 141

wabi-sabi, 4, 243n5
Western staff notation, 26, 68, 93, 112, 114, 132, 135, 152, 159, 178

Yamada school, 88, 126, 129, 132, 146. See also *Ikuta* school
yo scale, 2
yuri, 45, 50, 59, 82, 96, 121, 138. *See also* vibrato

Eastman Studies in Music

The Poetic Debussy: A Collection of His Song Texts and Selected Letters (Revised Second Edition)
Edited by Margaret G. Cobb

Concert Music, Rock, and Jazz since 1945: Essays and Analytical Studies
Edited by Elizabeth West Marvin and Richard Hermann

Music and the Occult: French Musical Philosophies, 1750–1950
Joscelyn Godwin

"Wanderjahre of a Revolutionist" and Other Essays on American Music
Arthur Farwell,
edited by Thomas Stoner

French Organ Music from the Revolution to Franck and Widor
Edited by Lawrence Archbold and William J. Peterson

Musical Creativity in Twentieth-Century China: Abing, His Music, and Its Changing Meanings (includes CD)
Jonathan P. J. Stock

Elliott Carter: Collected Essays and Lectures, 1937–1995
Edited by Jonathan W. Bernard

Music Theory in Concept and Practice
Edited by James M. Baker, David W. Beach, and Jonathan W. Bernard

Music and Musicians in the Escorial Liturgy under the Habsburgs, 1563–1700
Michael J. Noone

Analyzing Wagner's Operas: Alfred Lorenz and German Nationalist Ideology
Stephen McClatchie

The Gardano Music Printing Firms, 1569–1611
Richard J. Agee

"The Broadway Sound": The Autobiography and Selected Essays of Robert Russell Bennett
Edited by George J. Ferencz

Theories of Fugue from the Age of Josquin to the Age of Bach
Paul Mark Walker

The Chansons of Orlando di Lasso and Their Protestant Listeners: Music, Piety, and Print in Sixteenth-Century France
Richard Freedman

Berlioz's Semi-Operas: Roméo et Juliette *and* La damnation de Faust
Daniel Albright

The Gamelan Digul and the Prison-Camp Musician Who Built It: An Australian Link with the Indonesian Revolution
Margaret J. Kartomi

*"The Music of American Folk Song"
and Selected Other Writings on
American Folk Music*
Ruth Crawford Seeger, edited by
Larry Polansky and Judith Tick

Portrait of Percy Grainger
Edited by Malcolm Gillies
and David Pear

Berlioz: Past, Present, Future
Edited by Peter Bloom

*The Musical Madhouse
(Les Grotesques de la musique)*
Hector Berlioz
Translated and edited by
Alastair Bruce
Introduction by Hugh Macdonald

The Music of Luigi Dallapiccola
Raymond Fearn

*Music's Modern Muse: A Life of
Winnaretta Singer, Princesse de Polignac*
Sylvia Kahan

The Sea on Fire: Jean Barraqué
Paul Griffiths

*"Claude Debussy As I Knew Him" and
Other Writings of Arthur Hartmann*
Edited by Samuel Hsu,
Sidney Grolnic, and Mark Peters
Foreword by David Grayson

*Schumann's Piano Cycles and the
Novels of Jean Paul*
Erika Reiman

*Bach and the Pedal Clavichord:
An Organist's Guide*
Joel Speerstra

*Historical Musicology: Sources,
Methods, Interpretations*
Edited by Stephen A. Crist and
Roberta Montemorra Marvin

*The Pleasure of Modernist Music:
Listening, Meaning, Intention, Ideology*
Edited by Arved Ashby

*Debussy's Letters to Inghelbrecht:
The Story of a Musical Friendship*
Annotated by Margaret G. Cobb

*Explaining Tonality:
Schenkerian Theory and Beyond*
Matthew Brown

*The Substance of Things Heard:
Writings about Music*
Paul Griffiths

*Musical Encounters at the
1889 Paris World's Fair*
Annegret Fauser

*Aspects of Unity in J. S. Bach's
Partitas and Suites: An Analytical Study*
David W. Beach

Letters I Never Mailed: Clues to a Life
Alec Wilder
Annotated by David Demsey
Foreword by Marian McPartland

*Wagner and Wagnerism in Nineteenth-
Century Sweden, Finland, and
the Baltic Provinces:
Reception, Enthusiasm, Cult*
Hannu Salmi

*Bach's Changing World:
Voices in the Community*
Edited by Carol K. Baron

CageTalk: Dialogues with and about John Cage
Edited by Peter Dickinson

European Music and Musicians in New York City, 1840–1900
Edited by John Graziano

Schubert in the European Imagination, Volume 1: The Romantic and Victorian Eras
Scott Messing

Opera and Ideology in Prague: Polemics and Practice at the National Theater, 1900–1938
Brian S. Locke

Ruth Crawford Seeger's Worlds: Innovation and Tradition in Twentieth-Century American Music
Edited by Ray Allen and Ellie M. Hisama

Schubert in the European Imagination, Volume 2: Fin-de-Siècle Vienna
Scott Messing

Mendelssohn, Goethe, and the Walpurgis Night: The Heathen Muse in European Culture, 1700–1850
John Michael Cooper

Dieterich Buxtehude: Organist in Lübeck
Kerala J. Snyder

Musicking Shakespeare: A Conflict of Theatres
Daniel Albright

Pentatonicism from the Eighteenth Century to Debussy
Jeremy Day-O'Connell

Maurice Duruflé: The Man and His Music
James E. Frazier

Representing Non-Western Music in Nineteenth-Century Britain
Bennett Zon

The Music of the Moravian Church in America
Edited by Nola Reed Knouse

Music Theory and Mathematics: Chords, Collections, and Transformations
Edited by Jack Douthett, Martha M. Hyde, and Charles J. Smith

The Rosary Cantoral: Ritual and Social Design in a Chantbook from Early Renaissance Toledo
Lorenzo Candelaria

Berlioz: Scenes from the Life and Work
Edited by Peter Bloom

Beyond The Art of Finger Dexterity: *Reassessing Carl Czerny*
Edited by David Gramit

French Music, Culture, and National Identity, 1870–1939
Edited by Barbara L. Kelly

The Art of Musical Phrasing in the Eighteenth Century: Punctuating the Classical "Period"
Stephanie D. Vial

Beethoven's Century: Essays on Composers and Themes
Hugh Macdonald

Composing for Japanese Instruments
(includes CD)
Minoru Miki
Translated by Marty Regan
Edited by Philip Flavin

The unique sounds of the *biwa, shamisen*, and other traditional instruments from Japan are heard more and more often in works for the concert hall and opera house. *Composing for Japanese Instruments* is a practical orchestration/ instrumentation manual with contextual and relevant historical information for composers who wish to learn how to compose for traditional Japanese instruments. Widely regarded as the authoritative text on the subject in Japan and China, it contains hundreds of musical examples, diagrams, photographs, and fingering charts, and comes complete with two accompanying compact discs of musical examples. Its author, Minoru Miki, is a composer of international renown and is recognized in Japan as a pioneer in writing for Japanese traditional instruments. The book contains valuable appendices, one of works Miki himself has composed using Japanese traditional instruments, and one of works by other composers—including Toru Takemitsu and Henry Cowell—using Japanese traditional instruments.

Marty Regan is assistant professor of music at Texas A&M University; Philip Flavin is a research fellow in the School of Languages, Cultures and Linguistics at Monash University, Australia.

"An invaluable resource for all composers, scholars, and performers who are interested in Japanese instruments. The aptly chosen examples from both traditional repertoire and Miki's own contemporary pieces, clear charts for ranges and fingerings, and in-depth discussion of idiomatic performance techniques go a long way to help demystify these beautiful instruments. I wish I had this book many, many years ago."

—Ken Ueno, Rome Prize-winning composer and professor at the University of Massachusetts-Dartmouth

"This is the book I've always wished to have. It is not only complete in teaching about Japanese instruments but also challenging and inspiring for those of us who have an interest in new sounds and ways of making music."

—Hyo-shin Na, composer

"*Composing for Japanese Instruments* is a well-organized and systematic manual on how to approach, listen to, and compose for traditional Japanese instruments. When Minoru Miki first published it in 1996, he brought alive the arcane world of traditional Japanese instruments and music for a new generation of Japanese composers. Now, with the English edition, composers and scholars from around the world will have the same opportunity to discover and utilize the rich musical possibilities inherent in these beautiful instruments."

—Christopher Yohmei Blasdel, Shakuhachi performer, Artistic Director, The International House of Japan, Inc.

www.ingramcontent.com/pod-product-compliance
Lightning Source LLC
Chambersburg PA
CBHW021656230426
43668CB00008B/638